The Struggle and the Tools

The Struggle and the Tools

Oral and Literate Strategies in an Inner City Community

Ellen Cushman

STATE UNIVERSITY OF NEW YORK PRESS

Production by Ruth Fisher
Marketing by Patrick Durocher

Published by State University of New York Press, Albany

For information, address the State University of New York Press,
State University Plaza, Albany, NY 12246

Library of Congress Cataloging-in-Publication Data

Cushman, Ellen, 1967–
    The struggle and the tools : oral and literate strategies in an
inner city community / Ellen Cushman.
        p.   cm.
    Includes bibliographical references and index.
    ISBN 0-7914-3981-X (alk. paper). — ISBN 0-7914-3982-8 (pbk. :
alk. paper)
    1. Sociolinguistics—United States.   2. Afro-Americans—Languages.
3. Urban dialects—United States.   I. Title.
P40.45.U5C87   1998
306.44'0973—dc21   98-13321
                                                                CIP

10 9 8 7 6 5 4 3 2 1

The Indians often used the laws, practices, and representations that were imposed on them by force or by fascination to ends other than those of their conquerors; they made something else out of them; they subverted them from within. They metaphorized the dominant order: they made it function in another register. They diverted it without leaving it.

—Michel de Certeau, *The Practice of Everyday Life*

Everyday forms of resistance make no headlines. But just as millions of anthozoan polyps create, willy nilly, a coral reef, so do the multiple acts of insubordination and evasion create political and economic barrier reefs of their own. And whenever, to pursue the simile, the ship of state runs aground on such reefs, attention is usually directed to the shipwreck itself and not to the vast aggregation of petty actions that made it possible.

—James Scott, *Weapons of the Weak*

Those of us who remember living in the midst of racial apartheid know that the separate spaces, the times apart from whiteness, were for sanctuary, for reimagining and re-membering ourselves. In the past separate space meant down time, time for recovery and renewal. It was the time to dream resistance, time to theorize, plan, create strategies and go forward. The time to speak a counter hegemonic race talk that is filled with the passion of remembrance and resistance is now.

—bell hooks, *Killing Rage: Ending Racism*

Contents

Preface

This work began the day I drove through the inner city of Quayville with my California plates, the promise of funded graduate study, and a history dotted with evictions, long stints of unemployment, educational underachievement, hard work, and considerable luck. I soon noticed two things about the relation I would have to the place: first, the private university to which I had been accepted sat on a hill overlooking the inner city; and, second, I identified more with the individuals sitting on their front stoops in the inner city than I did with "my peers" at the university. The schism I felt between gown and town deepened in courses where I was told "my writing really shows my class background," and where I heard implied over and over again that people are to blame for their positions. I would go to a local diner for breakfast where I heard Quayville residents talk about "those students," the "higher-ups." Between classes, literally and socially, I would sometimes call home, and my mother would remind me never to forget where I came from, that, in essence, blood means more than books. It seems so obvious to me now, even though it didn't just then, that this book had to be about class and race—about what people know, how they get by, and how our critical theories don't do them justice.

Three months into my graduate work, I became a literacy volunteer at a local community center. As I gradually began getting to know individuals in this inner city area, the traditional model of participant observation proved troublesome. It required more observation than participation, so the research relationship soon became unbalanced. Individuals would ask me to help them with their literate and educational goals because they knew I taught at the local university, but I would hedge, muttering some excuse about "losing my objectivity"

ix

that did not sit well with my own community ethics, let alone theirs. Using postmodern critiques of ethnographic research as well as selected notions of emancipatory education, though, I cobbled together an activist methodology. These methods of data collection, analysis, and write-up allowed participants and me to make knowledge together, to engage in mutually rewarding reciprocal relations, and to appease our shared ethics of giving in equal measure to what we take.

As I became immersed in the social and cultural symbolic systems of area residents, I eventually recognized their oppositional ideologies imbued in the subtle language strategies they developed through their interactions with institutional agents. After a number of months of observing their daily communications with case workers, police, social workers, and landlords, a pattern of linguistic behaviors emerged where residents would reflect on their "struggle" and "tools." The struggle described their perceptions of the common ways institutional representatives hindered community members' efforts to act for themselves; the tools described the numerous ways individuals linguistically strategized in their everyday strivings for resources and respect.

Some readers will be tempted to take the struggle and tools as little more than coping devices that make minimal gains when viewed across the sweep of systematic oppression. In some ways, their claims can be justified by the examples in this book. Individuals appear to profit little from their energetic strivings. Yet the goal of this book is to present the oral, literate, and analytical strategies inner city residents develop in light of their oppositional ideologies. The greatest strength of this work, then, rests in the variety of stories, accounts, vignettes, and case analyses gathered from the perspective of inner city residents. The goal of this book does not include, however, an accounting of macro-scale changes in institutional ideology, nor can it exemplify social change resulting from micro-interactions with institutional gatekeepers. Because I did not immerse myself in the institutions residents dealt with daily, I cannot be sure how community members' linguistic endeavors actually impacted their receivers. But a focus on the outcomes diverts our attention away from the process of struggle and the sophistication of the tools; in our push to see significant structural change, we trample over the texture of everyday political life.

This book explores, then, the deep games of power inner city residents played with their language and critical consciousness.

With the permission and consultation of community members, I selected illustrations of their linguistic abilities and political insights from hours of tapes, numerous literacy artifacts, and pages of field notes generated during three and a half years of ethnographic fieldwork. Certainly, these examples stem from only a small section of the entire African-American population, and an even smaller slice of their repertoire of rhetorical skills. Further, for some readers, the political endeavors presented here may seem all too familiar. Take for example, the term "tools." This word alone has a long history in African-American vernacular as part of the aphorism "use the master's tools to tear down his own house." And the term "Whiter society," a play on the words "wider society," can be found in scholarship by Black sociologist, Andrew Billingsly, who wrote in the late 1960s. The everyday strivings and the rhetorical tactics presented in these pages represent up-to-date versions of well-precedented political action taking place among the larger population of African Americans. For the women and children in this inner city area, in particular, the illustrations presented here represent a significant pattern of their day-to-day efforts to obtain food, shelter, resources, and respect from wider society's institutions. And, to date, too few ethnographies explore their perspective.

Women and children have been foregrounded in this study for a number of reasons. First, my own gender made it easier for me to interact with the females in the study. Beyond this, though, there just weren't many adult males in this area and my access to the them was limited. Three men lived with their partners for extended periods. One worked full-time in a hospital; one worked part-time in food service; and one drove a truck for various companies. Another handful of men passed in and out of women's lives and did what they could to father their children. With limited schooling, few jobs available, and the desire to contribute to a stable home, these men sometimes resorted to work in underground economies, work that had considerable personal risk, and that often landed them somewhere in the penal system. With so few men and their inconsistent contributions to households, adult women became central to the maintenance of families and community networks. Women ran the homes, contributed to the area's safety, and gathered together around kitchen tables, at the local store, or on front stoops to exchange information and food. Since the women had to provide stable homes, they usually interacted with public service institutions more than any other group in the community. To a considerable degree, the women held the power and status in this community, positions that made them the cultural brokers of knowledge needed to negotiate public service institutions. Their central place in this ethnography, then, mirrors their prominence in this community.

To their mothers, children represented hope and possibility. The ways children construct gatekeepers and learn the language necessary to work (with) institutions figure significantly in this book. Children include both genders and range in age from seven to sixteen. Those between the ages of sixteen and twenty-one comprise the group of young adults in this study who also move into the foreground in numerous chapters. Perhaps not surprisingly, young adults grappled with the formation of their own border-crossing identities: How to maintain a measure of loyalty to Black cultural beliefs, but also work within the predominately White worlds of employment, higher education, and public service organizations? Often their emerging value systems created conflict within families. On the one hand, young adults sometimes challenged their mothers for apparently giving over too easily to Whites; on the other hand, the adult women, who provided their children with a warm home, food, and clothes through their interactions with public servants, would perceive their children's separatist positions as uninformed and idealistic. These conflicts between generational value systems indicate the multifaceted community perspectives on the relations between resistance and identity.

In portraying the complex oppositional perspectives that residents used in their daily living, I hope to show how they conceptualize the power relations that emerge in everyday interactions. Basing their judgments on their own antihegemonic values, residents assessed the utility of specific rhetorical practices needed to negotiate their exchanges with public servants. Yet, even with these forms of critical awareness and linguistic agency, community members' victories were small, few, and hard won. This work honors their daily lived experiences without giving over to a naive glorification of their individual agency apart from the social structures that both enable and constrain their action. We see, then, an up-close account of the tight connection between agency and social structure as individuals maneuver through asymmetrical power relations.

Inner city residents' political sophistication manifests itself in their oral and literate discourses. I use the term institutional language to encapsulate the orality and literacy that often co-occurred in community members' daily negotiations of institutions. Institutional language developed in a cyclic process, a process where residents learned vernacular skills in their neighborhood, deployed them in gatekeeping encounters, then evaluated their language back at home. Individuals learned to work with institutions by listening to the stories of other area residents who had returned from their interactions with wider society's public servants, such as police, caseworkers, social workers, and judges, to name a few. They became socialized into institutional language through direct instruction, observation, and practice. When the time came, residents were well prepared to gather, select, and deploy their community-based language abilities and transfer these to their interactions with gatekeepers. Linguistic transfer sometimes allowed residents to work with gatekeepers; it allowed them to blend together institutional structures and their own agency to gather resources and respect from institutional agents. Other times, gatekeepers remained rigid and unyielding to residents, sometimes insulting, demeaning, and dismissing them. When gatekeeping interactions failed to go as hoped, residents returned home and evaluated the language used by people on both sides of the gatekeeping encounter. This metacommunicative commentary brought out into the open residents' tacitly held assumptions about language and politics. Once in the open, individuals questioned, assessed, honed, and celebrated, their linguistic tactics. Institutional language skills involved residents in critical and strategic negotiations of the everyday political workings of institutions.

During this cyclic process of language development, literacy and orality interwove in such a manner that facilitated meta-analysis. At times, verbal collaboration augmented the ways residents interacted with literacy artifacts from public service organizations. Other times, literate artifacts, such as letters, applications, and forms, became the backdrop and starting point for extended discussions. The context and nature of the interaction influenced the ways in which literacy and orality moved back and forth between the foreground or the background of activities.

Such patterns of behaviors have implications for our studies of literacy and orality. Traditionally, scholars have tended to assign import to one linguistic activity over the other. One (usually literacy) shows more cognitive and rhetorical sophistication, while the other (usually orality) remains linked to its immediate contexts of use and to shared knowledge, and, thus, limits reasoning and cognitive abilities. Yet, when we separate these linguistic actions, we do damage to those we research. We strip away the analytical and political complexity of these linguistic operations as we impose binaries that have little social reality.

However, when we view orality and literacy as mutually informing, we begin to depict the ways inner city residents manipulate the symbolic representations of institutions. When residents faced a troubling letter, form, or other literacy artifact from an institution, the combination of oral and literate discourses offered them ways to name and critique the prevailing institutional assumptions, as well as to weigh the utility of certain oppositional linguistic tactics needed to circumvent their influence. That is, orality and literacy, when brought together, provided the means necessary for sustained metacommunicative analysis of texts. In this meta-analysis, neighborhood residents made apparent, characterized, and weighed, their hidden, antihegemonic values and specific strategies for resistance.

This book explores the underside of power relations where language imbued with antihegemonic ideologies unfolds in gatekeeping encounters. In so doing, I extend Foucault's questions about how power is exercised:

> "How," not in the sense of "How does it manifest itself?" but "By what means is it exercised?" and "What happens when individuals exert (as they say) power over others?" (1983, 217, emphasis in original)

Many critical theorists have explored how power is exercised by institutions *over* others, but this book explores how others construct, manipulate, and negotiate the influences that institutions attempt to exercise on them. What linguistic strategies do they acquire, transfer, and evaluate in their daily power relations with institutions? How are these strategies infused with their oppositional ideologies? What does all of this tell us about hegemony and false consciousness?

To address these questions, the book takes its organizational cue from the community members' institutional language development. The first chapter sets forth the argument in an overview of the developmental process of learning, transferring, and evaluating. I analyze a single exchange where Lucy Cadens, an important figure in the community, turns in paperwork to a caseworker. This brief interplay represents the types and kinds of gatekeeping encounters residents face, but also represents the subtle language tools used to both comply with and undermine gatekeepers.

The second chapter discusses how the activist methods in this study permitted the participants and me to make knowledge together in mutually rewarding relationships. Along the way, I show the limitations and possibilities of activist intervention in order to lay out the boundaries of this methodology. This chapter brings to light ways in which we might begin to close some of the social distance between researchers and participants through reciprocity, dialogue, and collaboration. With activist methods, we begin to see how researchers can facilitate residents' literate goals, at the same time as residents teach us how politics and language emerge in their day-to-day encounters with wider society.

Chapter 3 sketches the historical and community context of this study. I show how a long history of agency extends from travels on the underground railroad in search of freedom, to migrations in search of work, to forced evictions and current searches for housing and steady employment. I introduce a number of residents, key to the rest of the book, and show the values they attach to language varieties. This chapter offers the historical context for residents' present-day material and ideological struggles. It also contextualizes the oppositional value systems residents' attach to linguistic tools. The history of struggle shapes the many current forms of rhetorical strategies needed to interact with the power structures of modern institutions.

The next chapter surveys the cyclic process by which language skills develop in this community—skills that never fully reproduce or resist systematic forms of oppression. I tell the stories of two families (the Cadenses and the Washingtons) as they spend many months looking for housing after they received eviction notices. Their stories illustrate the threefold process of institutional language development discussed in chapter 1 by showing how this process unfolds over time (a year and three months in the Cadenses' case, and five months for the Washingtons' case), and across institutional contexts (i.e., rental organizations, the Department of Social Services, and philanthropic agencies). Their institutional language skills include oral and literate events that are political in nature, and through them children and young adults learn to assert their agency in the face of material and ideological struggles.

Chapters 5 and 6 examine the first phase of linguistic development in which residents become socialized into the linguistic abilities needed to gain resources and respect from institutional representatives. Chapter 5 profiles the socialization of young residents into institutional language strategies. First, I offer two vignettes where a child and a young adult both set and police boundaries of influence with a social worker. Both examples suggest ways community residents learn to head off social workers' unwanted influences. Next come two more vignettes of older residents who discuss the complexities of working with NAACP. The older generation modeled institutional critique for the younger generation playing nearby. I then show how four children, ages 9 to 11, make meaning from a parking ticket I received, how they collectively constructed it as a problematic, and how they looked for ways out of and around its constraining language. Finally, I examine a teen's doodle written on the back of a diner placemat. In this combination of words and sketches scattered across the placemat, this teen explored the power structure of her community using the metaphor of a popular card game in her neighborhood, Spades. Taken together, these examples demonstrate how these individuals learn to construct the power relations between themselves and wider society's organizations, and how through these constructions they develop politically strategic plans to both accommodate and resist.

Chapter 6, "Racism Always on the Front of My Mind," suggests the effects that learning institutional language has on individuals' self-perceptions. The chapter details the ways in which Afriganzia learns how to linguistically navigate her position as a community member employed by the philanthropic agency that operated the neighborhood center. During the summer of 1993, social workers hired Afriganzia to co-direct with me a twelve-week-long youth literacy program. I analyze a handful of interactions between herself and social workers, as well as an entry from Afriganzia's notebook where she compiled the minutes from a meeting between social workers, myself, and herself. She both adopts and adapts institutional language as she moves between her community values and the center's values. We learn through her experience the complex ways residents mask their identities with linguistic devices, and we learn how this White mask, to residents' minds, must remain both separate and separable from their own self-identifications. Inner city residents do not simply internalize the categories that institutions label them with, but manipulate the institutions' symbolic systems to the best advantage possible.

Chapters 7 and 8 reveal how community members transfer their community-based language skills to their encounters with institutional agents. Chapter 7 surveys many ways in which residents deploy language that undermines—at the same time as it enacts—the structuring ideology of various institutional representatives. The chapter begins with a summary of the development of institutional perspectives on the poor and reveals how these dismissive assumptions manifest themselves in a "Behavioral Contract" drafted by social workers in the community center. Through a close look at multiple exchanges and literacy artifacts, the remainder of the chapter discloses some of the ways in which individuals deploy language skills to counter the demeaning ideologies they often find present in gatekeeping encounters. I argue that the institutional language skills residents deploy in gatekeeping interactions manifest the tension between structure and agency, between the structuring ideology of institutional representatives and the linguistic savvy of community members: the duels in the dualities.

Chapter 8 balances a positive gatekeeping exchange with the last chapter's negative ones by showing language skills and beneficial assumptions needed to facilitate the educational opportunities of community residents. I consider the oral and literate strategies Raejone deployed when she tried to gain admission to a local university. I describe how, over a period of several months, she systematically navigated this academic labyrinth by transferring many of the language strategies I point out in the previous chapters. In addition, I analyze the language used by an Education Opportunity Program (EOP) counselor at the university where Raejone applied to show how he deftly handles his role as a gatekeeper. These findings exemplify the rhetorical strategies that people on *both sides* of gatekeeping interactions can employ to make seemingly rigid institutional structures more flexible.

Chapters 9 and 10 show the final phase in the process of institutional language development: evaluating. In this phase, residents use metacommunicative commentary to objectify the unseen ways institutional gatekeepers maintain status quo. In "It's an Everyday Fight to Get Simple Respect," chapter 9, I overview the variety of metadiscursive skills residents used after gatekeeping interactions go poorly. In this chapter, I offer up front a half dozen vignettes showing instances of metadiscursive evaluations of language skills. These interactions point to the forms of talk and literacy residents used to evaluate language using their cultural symbolic systems of resistance. Their evaluations bring into the open the tacitly held beliefs of wider society members who unduly constrain them. Their meta-analyses offer residents a discourse with which to articulate and refine their own oppositional ideologies.

Chapter 10 focuses on an extended gatekeeping interaction between two teenage males (Disco and Chaos), their mother (Lucy), and a judge to show how community members assess an open defiance of authority. Although the judge was fully prepared to release Disco at the outset of the hearing, he ended up throwing Disco in jail for two weeks because, as the judge told Lucy, Disco refused to "address the court with respect." After the encounter, Chaos and Lucy metadiscursively assessed the language and power structure at work during the hearing. They considered: (1) when and how to resist a gatekeeper who is being unduly harsh or dismissive; (2) which language styles they should have used given who was present and their authority; and (3) when and how to intervene in those gatekeeping situations that go poorly. Thus, interactions that may initially appear to only uphold systematic forms of oppression actually admit and manifest multiple forms of linguistic agency.

Institutional language does indeed include both resistance and accommodation, and, as a result, community residents' language neither entirely subverts nor wholly reproduces the structuring ideology of institutions. In this study, then, we see how language cyclically develops in nuanced everyday politics. We see, too, the fallout from these linguistic political struggles, such as: residents' ever shifting social positionings in relation to wider society (we can no longer blanketly term community members the "disenfranchised"); their competing linguistic emic systems across gender and generation (we can no longer homogenize their value systems as a culture of poverty); their daily reliance on sophisticated literacy skills (we can no longer degrade their literate skills as merely functional, basic, or rudimentary).

These findings have important implications for the ways critical scholars go about studying hegemony. When critical scholars describe inner city residents, their daily lives, and their language use, they too often demean, overlook, and underrate the commonplace tactics individuals use to name and challenge their sources of trouble. "They" indicates critical scholars who trace their academic lineages to theorists of hegemony who rely on notions of ideological domination, of false consciousness (i.e., Hegel, Marx, and Gramsci, to name a few). I say, "they," even though I owe an intellectual debt to critical theorists whose work I complicate and extend: Giddens, Bourdieu, and, to a lesser extent, Foucault. I see myself as a critical scholar, but of a different sort. The scholarly work I set forth here pushes beyond critical theory's dependence on the notion of false consciousness, and moves on to describe how individuals perceive and critique hegemony from their own critical vantage points using their own vernacular.

Most critical scholars rely on a notion of false consciousness to describe why individuals seem to consent to value systems and attitudes that least serve their interests. In a nutshell, false consciousness characterizes individuals who presumably hold as truth the prevailing norms that disadvantage them. Because lay people understand their lived conditions to be preordained, taken-for-granted, natural, a matter of fate, or justly deserved, the falsely conscious consent to the ideologies of those who dominate—their consent makes them suffer under ideological domination. When individuals have false consciousness, they evidently lack critical consciousness, or the ability to name, critique, and act in ways that subvert status quo power relations. When social theorists subscribe to a notion of false consciousness, though, they underestimate the day-to-day political insights and strategies that individuals deploy to construct and obviate unequal political situations.

Using the idea of false consciousness, critical scholars fix individuals' political positions on society's hierarchy, calling them: the "disenfranchised," the "marginalized," the "disempowered," the "less powerful," the "underclass," the "subaltern," the "oppressed," the "dominated," the "subjugated," and the "subordinate." They describe their literate abilities with more categories: "the preliterate," the "illiterate," "primarily oral cultures," at best, "the functionally literate." They define individuals by what they do not have, do not do, do not measure up to. Then, as critical scholars and teachers, they claim to have the theories to liberate them; to have the skills individuals need to produce change and organize together against their oppressors. Critical theories become the measuring rods for what counts as social action and agency, and too often, individuals fail to measure up.

Any theory of hegemony that subscribes to the now orthodox notion of false consciousness sets itself up for limited and limiting studies of language and politics. If we assume that individuals unwittingly comply with oppressive ideologies, we will be less likely to gain access to and honor the ways in which they daily, linguistically challenge these prevailing belief systems. Said another way, if critical scholars think urban community members lack critical consciousness, they design their research in self-fulfilling ways; they seek public activities where blatant uses of power manifest themselves, and rarely do they move beyond these behaviors to understand what happens behind the scenes where oppositional ideologies manifest themselves. In *Weapons of the Weak*, an ethnography of Malaysian rice farmers, political scientist James Scott suggests similar shortcomings in the research on hegemony. Because critical theorists often assume "that the transcript from power-laden situations is the full transcript," (1985, 287) they neglect "the extent to which most subordinate classes are able, on the basis of their daily material experience, to penetrate and demystify the prevailing ideology" (1985, 317). As a result, they miss, or dismiss, critical awareness when it does occur in what appear to be taken-for-granted, pedestrian linguistic activities.

Critical theories have too narrowly defined what counts as critical consciousness. Because many scholars believe that critical awareness leads to unified social movements, sweeping structural changes, or radical shifts in consciousness, they disregard other forms of social and linguistic agency found at the point where power is applied in the daily. Here, I take the liberty of responding directly to an anonymous reviewer of an earlier version of this manuscript who suggests that "critical consciousness signifies an awareness of the structural nature of oppression which leads to collective action to challenge the status quo." This definition of critical consciousness represents precisely the one most critical theorists will want to bring to bear upon this book. If critical consciousness leads to *collective action*, the instances presented in this book simply will not live up to this standard. But the problem here isn't with the community members' lack of political awareness and savvy—the problem is with this definition. This readers' definition, a commonly held one, fails to reflect social realities where critical consciousness does not always lead to collective action nor to unified class struggle.

If, however, we alter one wording in this reviewer's demarcation of critical consciousness, then we open up the possibility of seeing and appreciating the nuances of daily political struggles. Delete the qualifier "collective," and the definition would now read: "critical consciousness signifies an awareness of the structural nature of oppression which leads to action[s that] challenge the status quo." Actions can now include even those subtle ones where, at first blush, people appear to obey in the face of an assertion of power. What we have, then, is a definition of critical consciousness that includes every interaction, vignette, story, literacy event, and case study presented in this book.

With this more inclusive definition, we begin to appreciate how individuals can both accommodate and undermine, both placate and rebuff, both obey and challenge while they negotiate constraining social structures. At the place where structure and agency intermingle, we're also able to understand how people construct, question, and analyze the ways institutions influence them. Our theory of hegemony, then, can begin to do justice to the knowledge, language abilities, and political perceptions of those we hope our theory serves.

In the end, this book challenges the validity of the notion of false consciousness by grounding a discussion of hegemony in the daily political and rhetorical tactics of inner city residents.

Acknowledgments

To write with heart, I have to be angry, on edge, and hungry. Any heart this work may have, I owe first and foremost to the community residents in Quayville's inner city, in particular Lucy Cadens. Although I can not name them more directly, they know who they are and will see their influences throughout these pages. Their lives fuel my rage against pernicious and insidious attitudes pervasive in wider society.

When my anger peppered my prose with cheap shots, clouded conclusions, and unfair characterizations, three colleagues pushed me to infuse rage with intellectual rigor. Sociolinguist Tamar Gordon patiently read and honed the crudest versions of this work and helped to shape the overall direction it took. Mike Rose's careful readings kept me honest and reminded me of generosity. And through his continued engagement with me, James Porter helped me untangle the sometimes snarled organizations of initial chapters.

Numerous other colleagues kept me on edge with their insightful responses to particular chapters, papers, and presentations. I thank (deep breath): Arnetha Ball, Elizabeth Britt, Randi Browning, Chris Boese, Michael Carter, Gregory Clark, Yuet-Sim Chiang, Kathleen Dixon, Kathryn Flannery, Jeff Grabill, Janice Gould, Tom Fox, Michael Halloran, Mary Ellen Halloran, Adam Haridopolis, Patricia Harkin, Joe Harris, Shirley Brice Heath, Glynda Hull, Joyce Rain Latora, Scott Lyons, Jabari Mahiri, Terese Quinsatao Monberg, Malea Powell, Elaine Richardson, Tara Rosenberger, Jacqueline Jones Royster, Elizabeth Shea, and Elizabethada Wright. I thank them all for their queries, suggestions, and challenges that helped to shape the present work. I appreciate all the unidentified reviewers and academic audiences who tempered my fury with their blood letting, encouragement, and comments. Special thanks goes to James Collins, Cheryl Geisler, Teresa Harrison, and Lee Odell for wading through my most formative drafts in order to foster my thinking with their sound advice and recommendations for further reading. My appreciation also goes to William Cushman, my father, who generously agreed to proof the manuscript in its final stages of production.

All the editors at SUNY Press have my gratitude. Ruth Fisher has sped the project though with a careful attention to details. And Priscilla Ross has supported this work with her persistent kindness and keen patience.

Finally, I am most grateful to my mother, Virginia Lee Drew Cushman, who taught me to hunger. Her voice, recorded on my computer, reminds me everyday: "Mary Ellen, you better by God do good work."

Notational Devices

. .	speech pause
. . .	long speech pause
[	conversational overlap
acc	accelerated tempo
dec	decelerated tempo
⎯⎯⋀＿＿	moderate, rising, falling pitch
⎯⎯／＿＿	low, rising, evening off pitch
⎯⎯⋀⎯⎯	even tone with one or two words emphasized
/	clause break
//	idea break

1 The Struggle and the Tools

Lucy Cadens didn't even give me a chance to sit down that day I walked into her house: "I need to get this to DSS [Department of Social Services] today." She waved a stack of papers in my direction and headed for the door. Her second youngest child was nineteen and pregnant, and her eldest daughter (age twenty-four) was too old to be living with her, so Lucy was anxious to get them on their own. To do this, she had offered to help with the paperwork involved in getting her daughters into their own households. The following excerpt of a conversation between a DSS representative, Lucy, and myself is taken from my ethnographic field notes written shortly after we left that office. The caseworker began:

> *"So you're looking to get your daughters their own social assistance?"*
>
> *Lucy agreed. "I came in last week and got a list of all the papers I need to fill out." Lucy handed over the stack of the papers to the woman. The assistant accepted them and compared what Lucy turned in to the checklist that Lucy obtained the week before.*
>
> *"Do you have your daughter's birth certificate?"*
>
> *Lucy put her hand on her cheek and leaned against the partition. "It was right there on the table too. I was just so busy this morning." The social worker smirked. Lucy continued: "I been having her on my case though."*
>
> *"We only have this file here. The bigger one is on the other side of the building."*
>
> *There was a pause and Lucy looked at me and said quietly: "get me every time."*

1

The social worker spoke again. "That's all you're missing too."
Lucy looked at her. Another pause and the social worker continued,
"you'll have to bring it in next time. Just a photocopy and then
you're all set." Lucy said she would and we got up to leave. Once out
the door, Lucy vented: "What would it have taken that lazy fu——in'
bitch to get off her sorry white ass and get my other file?"

This exchange is typical—it represents just one of many encounters where inner city residents struggle for resources and respect using
their vernacular language tools. When this interaction took place, Lucy,
a forty-two year-old African-American[1] woman with six kids, was living in an inner city community in Quayville, a medium-sized town in
the Northeast. I spent three and a half years in Quayville observing
and participating in community members' family and social networks.
During my ethnographic research, I studied the oral and literate skills
these individuals need in order to negotiate the many institutional
influences that enter into their lives. I open with this interaction because it represents precisely the place where many critical theorists
would stop their analysis. Here, we see what looks to be yet another
example of domination and quiescence—the caseworker sends Lucy
back home to get a document that already exists on file; and even
though Lucy knows the caseworker is asking for too much, Lucy agrees
with the caseworker's unnecessary demand and leaves. Many social
and cultural theorists would point to this exchange as convincing
evidence of systematic oppression in inner cities, and would paint
Lucy in the dull colors of someone who blindly reproduces the social
structures that may not be in her best interest. Here, their arguments
would leave off—without asking what happened before or after this
public interaction, without seeking the hidden ideologies informing
Lucy's statements, without acknowledging the subtle ways in which
Lucy bends her language to be both accommodating and challenging.
And their convincing discussions leave us with not only an inaccurate
portrayal of the overly determined politics of day-to-day life, but worse,
a shallow and reduced characterization of Lucy as "disempowered"
and unreflective in the face of these politics.

Residents in this inner city have agency—they're savvy negotia-
tors of highly nuanced, everyday interactions with wider society's
institutional representatives. Community members have critical consciousness that manifests itself in various linguistic events and artifacts that scholars often overlook, or simply dismiss as rudimentary

(responding with silence, reading newspapers, doodling, talking with judges, completing applications). Their resistance and agency in the face of asymmetrical power relations rests in the very places one would least expect to find such agency and political awareness.

Within the context of day-to-day inner city life, individuals continually develop linguistic skills, skills imbued with oppositional ideologies. Their language tools, as well as their values attendant upon these tools, complicate the notion that overarching power structures are simply reproduced, carbon copy, over and over again. Social structures, we learn, are not bloodless, unyielding, monolithic forces of oppression and domination, but are instead continually remade, fissured, and manipulated in everyday interactions. This book reveals the daily linguistic means by which residents make social structures more humane, subvert, and co-opt them for their own ends. Systematic oppression—"the struggle" as community members say—isn't the totalizing and erasing experience scholars assume it to be for the "disenfranchised." Rather, the struggle always works simultaneously with "the tools," the linguistic forms of agency residents use in their daily living.

In the final analysis, this work complicates our dichotomous ways of describing daily politics: micro/macro; agency/structure; power to/power over; confrontation/domination; resistance/oppression. Everyday language always already indicates both agency and structure; both power to and power over; both confrontation and domination; both resistance and oppression. Language use fluidly circulates betwixt and between social forces that are "oppositional and interdependent" (Huspek 1993); "constraining and enabling" (Giddens 1984); "durable and transposable" (Bourdieu 1990).

This book centers discussion around the cyclic process by which language develops in this inner city. Specifically, I exemplify ways the residents learn, deploy, and retool their linguistic strategies as they move across many institutional contexts. In comparing opinions of their encounters with institutional representatives, community residents often spoke of not only their material struggles to obtain housing, food, clothing, and resources, but they also spoke of their ideological struggles to gain respect, to complicate insidious stereotypes, and to challenge belittling attitudes. Because public institutions influenced so much of their daily lives, neighborhood members continually honed their language skills. Thus, the most salient example of their agency rests in their cyclic development of linguistic strategies used to push at, resist, and obviate, the structuring ideology of institutional workers.

I want to elucidate a critical theory that moves beyond the dismissive assumption of false consciousness and the facile discussions of reproduced power structures. I'll analyze many forms of strategic consciousness present in community members' daily language development employed to enact their subversive ideologies when dealing with institutional representatives. In everyday experiences with wider society, how do individuals linguistically negotiate a balance between both the constraints and opportunities institutions present them?

To address this question, I use critical discourse analysis to explore a wide variety of language strategies used by members of Quayville's inner city community as they interacted in politically keen ways with wider society's institutional representatives. My intention is to honor what individuals in this community call the "struggle" and the "tools." During face-to-face interactions with institutional agents, their struggle is both material and ideological. The tools are the linguistic strategies that these individuals use to navigate institutions in wider society and negotiate the struggles. To best portray the struggle and the tools, I create a threefold analytical framework: I examine how language strategies were taught and learned in this community; I then characterize the ways in which community residents deployed their linguistic skills in their daily interactions with institutional representatives; finally, I analyze how individuals metacommunicatively assessed and revamped their language strategies after these interactions. We need to study both the struggle and the tools in tandem if we hope to move away from a critical theory that demeans the ones it attempts to uplift, if we hope to characterize the multifaceted ways language carries with it both dissent and compliance in everyday practices.

Silencing the Subordinate

Social theories that characterize systematic forms of oppression too often mute the subordinate. Because critical theory can mistake accommodation for quiescence, placation for false consciousness, silence for submission, subtlety for passivity, it overlooks resistance in the most common language practices and thus silences those it most hopes to liberate. We need a theory of hegemony that makes room for subversive ideologies where we least expect to find them, a theory that allows for the many forms of critical consciousness and action sustained therein. Such a theory moves well beyond the structuralist determinism of Marx and Gramsci, and begins at the places where Bourdieu and Giddens leave off—the places where James Scott picks up.

To their credit, Bourdieu and Giddens advanced critical theories that moved structuralist thought away from the staunch determinism of Marx and Gramsci. Using different terms, Bourdieu and Giddens to some greater or lesser extent rescue the agent, characterize the flexible nature of social structures, and develop notions of power that reveal the cumulative and structuring effects of everyday lived experiences. How they do this merits discussion.

Pierre Bourdieu begins his critical theory with the individual's habitus, a "system of durable, transposable dispositions" (1990, 53) to act in particular ways within "infinite, yet strictly limited generative capacities" (55). The agent, although restricted by social constraints, emerges from the bleakness of structural determinism to find "a relation to what is possible . . . , a relation to power" (64). To Bourdieu's mind, these social structures are more flexible; they "make possible the free production of all thoughts, perceptions, and actions inherent in the particular conditions of productions—and only those" (55). Structures yield to many forms of individuals' strategies. In light of the habitus, Bourdieu's sense of power stems from daily dispositions of giving and receiving:

> A man possesses in order to give. But he also possesses by giving. A gift that is not returned can become a debt, a lasting obligation; and the only recognized power—recognition, personal loyalty or prestige—is the one obtained by giving. (126)

Power is reciprocal, in other words, flowing in a "process of circular circulation" (125) between durable and transposable dispositions to give and receive. In all, Bourdieu's descriptive power resides in the acumen with which he represents agents, structures and power. Agents strategically act within constraints and contribute to the malleability of social structures through dialogic, daily interactions of reciprocity.

With similar descriptive force, Anthony Giddens defines a theory of hegemony that rescues the agent from notions of overly restraining social structures. Giddens's agent "has reasons for his or her activities and is able, if asked, to elaborate discursively upon those reasons" (1984, 3). Individuals reflexively monitor their actions and the actions of others, and this monitoring is fundamental to the maintenance of a continuous flow of day-to-day activities (1984, 9). The daily activities of agents coalesce over time and space, and thus become organized, regularized social practices, or systems. The patterning of behavior in systems of daily routines eventually congeal together to form sets of rules for legitimate behavior, or structures. Agents, their repeated actions, and the rules for those actions, combine in the slow move of history and thus produce the "duality of structure":

> According to the notion of the duality of structure, the structural properties of social systems are both medium and outcome of the practices they recursively organize. . . . Structure is not to be equated with constraint, but is always both enabling and constraining. (1979, 25).

Giddens's theory, then, is predicated upon the recursive ways in which knowing individuals routinely (re)enact flexible structures, structures that allow for possibilities and opportunities in the daily circulation of power relations.

In three crucial ways Bourdieu and Giddens forward an understanding of hegemony: (1) They shift critical attention to the agent while remaining aware of structuring conditions; (2) they characterize the pliancy of structuring conditions; and (3) they account for the fluid ways power circulates in and through and from everyday interactions. Thus, they refresh critical theory that had previously focused on the top down flow of power in rigid structures, and as a result, downplayed individual agency.

As with many critical theorists, though, Bourdieu's and Giddens's frameworks rest on the seriously flawed notion of false consciousness. When subordinate people have false consciousness, they view their daily lives as the result of a natural social order. They accept their living conditions because they see no alternatives; they suffer because they believe the prevailing ideology that says they deserve their low positions on the hierarchy; the subordinate acquiesce to their lot in life. False consciousness holds that the most people are victims of ideological domination—they subscribe to the belief system and cultures that perpetuate their own disempowerment. "Briefly put, the argument is that a system of social domination often appears to be inevitable. Once it is considered inevitable, the logic goes, it is apt to be considered natural even by those who are disadvantaged by it" (Scott, 1985, 331). The less powerful blindly reproduce their domination by taking for granted the terms of their social positions—or so the idea of false consciousness leads one to believe.

However, social scientist James Scott critiques the notion of false consciousness and hegemony. He shows how theories of hegemony rest on the assumption of false consciousness, or ideological domination. Ideological domination

> define[s] for subordinant groups what is realistic and what is not realistic and drive[s] certain aspirations and grievances into the realm of the impossible. . . . By persuading under-classes that their positions . . . are unalterable and inevitable, such a limited hegemony can produce the behavioral results of consent without necessarily changing people's values. (1990, 74)

Ideological domination suggests that the less powerful view social order as destined, taken-for-granted. With the argument of ideological domination, individuals can be said to contribute to their own domination because they reify their lived conditions as natural and just. This view of hegemony compellingly accounts for the "situation of subordinant groups throughout their history [that] has seemed an unmovable 'given,' and realistically so" (75). When hegemony is viewed as natural, the agency of people in their daily experiences is reduced to silent and mere reproduction—agents' intervention in the production of events is read summarily as false consciousness. From the remove of high critical theory, ideological domination, as a concept, seems to have the descriptive power to show why, in the face of continually harsh living conditions, people consent to the structuring actions of elites.

Even in those theories that resurrect notions of individual will and intelligence, we see hegemony discussed in terms of a naturalized form of domination. For Bourdieu,

> the practical world that is constituted in the relationship with the habitus, acting as a system of cognitive and motivating structures, is a world of already realized ends—procedures to follow, paths to take. . . . This is because the regularities inherent in an arbitrary condition . . . tend to appear as necessary, even natural, since they are the basis of the schemes of perception and appreciation through which they are apprehended. (1990, 53–54)

Despite severe living conditions, people consistently act as they do because the relentless repetition of their everyday lives contains the only set of options and possibilities from which they can conceive a better life. In other words, the framework of habitus assumes the idea of ideological domination where people unconsciously, unstrategically, consistently make choices that perpetuate their own living conditions. "The habitus [as] a spontaneity without consciousness or will" (66) makes precious little room for subversive ideologies and for individuals' linguistic strategies attendant upon these hidden ideologies.

Giddens, like Bourdieu, supports a conception of hegemony where people suffer under their own false consciousness. In Giddens's duality of structure, "the reification of social relations, or the discursive 'naturalization' of the historically contingent circumstances and products of human action, is one of the main dimensions of ideology in social life" (1984, 26). Even though people have the ability to reflexively monitor their actions, they unwittingly naturalize their living conditions at the ideological level. And because they believe their daily life is part of the natural order, Giddens's argument goes, people reproduce the oppressive structures of status quo: "Forms of signification which 'naturalize' the existing state of affairs, inhibit recognition of the mutable, historical character of human society thus act to sustain such interests" (1979, 195). Ideological domination leads people to reify existing social practices—to believe they are unflinching. In the end, both Bourdieu and Giddens compromise their notions of agency when they adopt a notion of false consciousness.

When critical theorists support an idea of false consciousness, as many do, they stop looking for ways hidden ideologies can flourish (especially) in the worst living conditions—they silence the subordinate in a tight argument that basically blames the victim. When judged through the lens of false consciousness, hegemony seems to be sustained by acquiescing dupes who themselves are responsible for reproducing their own domination in their taken-for-granted daily activities. Under the banner of false consciousness, theorists sell out their dialogic notions of power to the notion of socially determined actions by uncritical actors. But I've found agency is more than mere blind obedience to the inevitable.

At the local level of politics, agency includes careful assessment of power situations, conscious and continual crafting of language strategies, and a firm, but not naive, belief in the opportunities and possibilities to be found in institutional structures. In the minute interactions taking place in contexts of highly asymmetrical power relations, individuals will both accommodate and resist, both reproduce and undermine, both enact and challenge. If we are to complicate notions of false consciousness and hegemony, we can no longer assume that ideological domination explains the seeming quiescent actions of those who are most influenced by disparities of resources and opportunity. We must assume, instead, that individuals cultivate counterhegemonic ideologies in and from their everyday lives. Working from this assumption, we can better distinguish the nuances of strategic actions individuals employ in their daily strivings to gain resources and respect. If we hope to move away from a critical theory that obscures the politics of daily practices, we must ask: What are the subversive actions and attitudes that individuals craft when challenged with institutional practices and beliefs that least represent their interests?

As they deploy their evolving linguistic skills, Quayville's inner city residents often work from the presumption that opportunity exists in gatekeeping encounters, particularly when gatekeepers linguistically enact institutional structures in more enabling and less constraining ways. My data show that both community residents *and* gatekeepers can actually communicate effectively, mutually indexing the shared task of providing and accessing resources. I point out that the tension between residents' linguistic agency and institutional structures can be fruitful and as such allows us to reconcile political binaries. Institutional language does indeed include both resistance and accommodation, and as a result, community residents' language neither entirely subverts nor wholly reproduces the structuring ideology of institutions. All of these results call into question the validity of "hegemonic" processes described by so many cultural critics.

Within a year from the start of this study, I began to notice how residents crafted linguistic tactics in response to their grapplings for resources and respect. When seen across time and contexts, a cyclic pattern of language development emerged from their interactions with gatekeepers, a pattern where residents first learned, then deployed, then evaluated language skills. By virtue of its existence, this process indicated the oppositional ideology residents' tacitly held. They continually practiced strategies to counter the undue intervention and belittling attitudes of institutional representatives. The remainder of this work examines this threefold process of language learning, deployment, and retooling and locates this process in community members' antihegemonic symbolic systems.

Learning the Tools

Community residents in Quayville's inner city gained institutional language abilities through acquisition and learning. Institutional language includes the reading, writing, and speaking skills continually developed in their daily struggles to obtain resources and respect from institutional representatives. James Gee defines language acquisition as "a process of acquiring something subconsciously by exposure to models, a process of trial and error, and practice within social groups, without formal teaching" (1990, 146): language acquisition and language socialization are one in the same process where, *without formal direction*, someone picks up patterns of language uses through immersion in a speech community. On the other hand, language learning is "a process that involves conscious knowledge gained through teaching . . . or through certain life experiences that trigger conscious reflection" (146). When people consciously add new linguistic features to their repertoires *with formal instruction*, they learn language. Acquiring language, then, is an unconscious activity requiring no instruction; but learning language is a conscious activity requiring instruction. Acquisition and learning are lifelong processes: adults acquire and learn language from their interactions in community, institutional, and formal settings, and pass these on to their kids through both example and direct teaching.

In the vignette that opens this chapter, although it may be easily overlooked, Lucy satisfied the most difficult part of the DSS application process, namely filling out these forms. When Lucy sat down with the social worker, she handed over a stack of papers, a description that glosses the complexity of the linguistic resources needed to fill out these forms in the first place. I mentioned that Lucy offered to help her daughters complete the applications necessary in order to get them their own cases with DSS. A few weeks after Lucy's encounter with the caseworker, I found out why she had to help her daughters. Lucy and I had just come from shopping and, during our trip, she expressed her concern that Afriganzia wasn't doing enough to find herself a new place and get out on her own. When we returned to Lucy's apartment, I went to Lucy's room and sat at the end of her bed where Afriganzia reclined watching TV. We chatted some and our conversation turned to her getting her own case with DSS.

> *"I don't know how to do this shit like Ma. She know what to say and what papers to fill out. If she can get me through it this time,*

I can do it on my own." Afriganzia continued: *"I mean, yeah, I know what the forms look like and all, but filling them out on my own? Unh-unh, no way."*

"You could do that. I know how good you read and write" (she and I had been co-directing a summer literacy program and had been writing a journal back and forth together). *She smiled.*

"Yeah, but that's different. You seen how long those forms be? You answer one question wrong, and you ain't getting shit. I can't risk that. So I ask Ma for help."

Lucy appeared in the doorway to her bedroom. She looked sternly at her daughter as though she had heard what Afriganzia had been saying: "You need to get your WIC [Women, Infants, Children] appointment scheduled." Afriganzia nodded to Lucy and looked back at the TV. "You also need to tell them at welfare that you're in a crisis situation. You got nowhere to live come the end of this month [Lucy knew she would be moving soon]. They'll give you money up front for moving and the security."

"To me or the landlord?"

"The landlord, but you got to get them to agree to it ahead." Lucy put her hands on her hips.

"Do I got to give them anything else?"

"They'll give you the papers once you ask."

"Should I bring them home?"

"I told you what to say. Just gonna take longer to bring them home."

Even when the actual literacy artifacts of a welfare application are not present, as in this example, individuals can be socialized into and learn about the language tools needed to negotiate them. Afriganzia had already acquired some skills needed to complete welfare application materials. After all, she knew the importance of every blank on the application ("You answer one question wrong, and you ain't getting shit"). She acquired her knowledge of these forms from her exposure to and observation of family members completing these forms time and again. She had seen their trial-and-error processes with these forms enough to know the "risk" she would take as she filled in each blank. Afriganzia expanded upon this already acquired knowledge through her mother's direct instructions: "You need to get your WIC appointment scheduled"; and "You also need to tell them at welfare that you're in a crisis situation." Lucy knew about the welfare guidelines and taught her daughter about the literacy and orality needed to obtain and complete these forms.

Community residents use careful linguistic choices to complete a welfare application—the amount and type of resources they receive depends upon the rhetorical selections they make when completing these forms. Afriganzia asked if she could bring these forms home because she wanted to receive input from Lucy about ways to answer the questions on these applications. Her mother assured her that she already gave her the best linguistic strategy ("I told you what to say"). As we'll see in later chapters, community members often brought home forms from agencies and institutions in order to complete them collaboratively and in privacy. This short exchange suggests how individuals can add to their linguistic repertoire just by talking about the oral and literate strategies needed to work within an institution. With this brief illustration of language learning in mind, we're more likely to assume that thought went into what appears to be the simplest of language activities—filling in the blank. This conversation between Lucy and her daughter offers a glance at the language tools community members use to complete the stack of forms like the one Lucy handed over to the caseworker. With this, we are in a better position to appreciate how she negotiated the face-to-face encounter with the social worker.

Deploying the Tools in a Struggle

The transfer of language reveals how community-based language practices are brought to bear in gatekeeping situations in both adopting and adapting ways. To transfer language in gatekeeping encounters, people gather, select, and deploy their rhetorical skills according to the social particulars of the situational context. Here, I assume that language and cultural assumptions are mutually informative and inseparable. That is, our linguistic choices represent our cultural values and our cultural values influence our linguistic choices. In the situational context of most institutional exchanges, the onus to adapt to the rhetorical skills and cultural assumptions of gatekeepers has historically been placed squarely on the shoulders of those seeking services. Many times, the situational context of institutions implies a melting-pot ideology—to receive services or resources, those needing the services and resources must adapt to predominant language norms and cultural values, or at least appear to. However, the social particulars of gatekeeping interactions also allow for, and at times manifest, the pliancy of structuring ideologies that make room for possibility and opportunity where multiple language codes are valued.

The ways in which organizational structures can potentially be enabling or constraining depend greatly upon the actions of institutional agents. In important ways, institutional representatives act as gatekeepers of society's material and ideological resources; their decisions and actions affect community members' opportunities, liberty, intellectual growth, and pursuit of daily necessities. Gatekeepers, particularly those in public institutions (education, criminal justice, health, and welfare) deeply and widely contribute to social (in)equalities in daily language activities. An "institutional gatekeeper . . . has the responsibility to make decisions about the social mobility" of others within the institution and wider society as well (Erickson and Shultz 1982, 4). A social service gatekeeper's position is difficult and often thankless with large caseloads, stark working conditions, and low pay and job status. On top of this, the person in the "gatekeeping interview is supposed to be entirely universalistic in his/her higher gatekeeping judgments, yet s/he cannot be, given the practical circumstances of face-to-face interactions by which the gatekeeping decisions must be made and communicated" (40). The gatekeeper is both "judge" and "advocate" then, and disadvantaged people must transfer their linguistic strategies from their community to the gatekeeping encounters.

Language transfer is a socially complicated process that can best be understood when examined in a back-and-forth fashion between community and institutional contexts. For example, we have identified the rhetorical features of dialect which people carry over or change in gatekeeping encounters. Gumperz examined passages of speech where people alternate between two different sets of grammatical rules; he calls this alternation between dialects "code switching" (Gumperz 1983a, 59), and this alternation generally influences the meaning inferred from the statements. Given research on the features of Black English (Smitherman 1977; Labov 1969), we can easily identify the transfer of it to situations where White English is the prestige dialect. A wide analytical framework for linguistic transfer allows us to consider the variations of language used as people tack back and forth between community and institutional contexts as well as the political and ideological implications of doing so. Turning to the exchange that opened this chapter, let me characterize the ways Lucy transferred language practices and the ways in which this transfer couched a struggle, even as it appears to reproduce the structuring ideology that colors the caseworker's language.

Lucy used both Black and White talk in this exchange. Gumperz would call this a diglossic phenomenon, where "distinct [linguistic] varieties are employed in certain settings" (1983a, 60). This diglossic exchange is historically linked to the "social pattern in early Black America where status—and even survival as a freeman—depended to a great extent on competence in White English. White America has insisted on White English as the price of admission into its economic and social mainstream" (Smitherman 1977, 12–3). The features of Black English and White English differ enough on a structural level to make their use easily identifiable. Lucy started the interaction by selecting and deploying White talk, "I came in last week and got a list of all the papers I need to fill out." (Note that Lucy had gathered beforehand the written linguistic tools, the applications, she would need to transfer language in this oral gatekeeping encounter.) And when the case-worker asked for the birth certificate, Lucy continued, "it was right there on the table too. I was just so busy this morning." Lucy spoke White English by including a tense indicator in her verb "came," where in Black English she would "rely on the context of the immediate sentence to indicate time" (Smitherman 1977, 26). She spoke White English in the second sentence by using a form of "to be"—in Black English, she would drop the verb altogether, or use "I's." Lucy code-switched to White English, perhaps to make a favorable impression, or because she hoped to be more persuasive to the gatekeeper. She deployed her rhetorical skills in White English up until the point where the caseworker smirked.

Lucy then code-switched to Black English with "I been having her on my case though." Here, Lucy challenged the caseworker by index-ing common knowledge they both shared: Lucy had a large file and a long history with DSS. The challenge was subtle, but the caseworker knew what Lucy is after. "Been having," in Black semantics suggest a habitual behavior taking place over a period of time (Smitherman 1977, 22). Lucy was asking the caseworker to refer to the copy DSS already possessed. The worker's reply, "We only have this file here. The bigger one is on the other side of the building," indexed an un-derstanding they both shared. The worker was under no obligation to get the certificate, even though she knew the certificate was on file. While Lucy's transfer of language was understood, it appears not to have potency, because after all, the worker made Lucy return home again in the snow. At least, an initial analysis of the rhetorical features of transfer leads us to this conclusion.

But our analysis of transfer must include an assessment of the ideological undercurrents in Lucy's statement "get me every time." On one level, Lucy cleverly placated a caseworker with this statement, and on another level, Lucy warded off this worker's exertion of influence. Sociolinguists have characterized the logic of the verb structure of Black English in which both the third person singular and plural forms of conjugated verbs drop the "s" (Labov 1969; Mitchell-Kernan 1972). Thus, the verb "get" in Lucy's statement had an ambiguous subject that could be *she, it* or *they*. From the transcript, the caseworker's response to Lucy's statement ("that's all you're missing too") indicates that the worker apparently understood the subject was "it," referring to Lucy's own forgetfulness.

But when Lucy said "get me every time," she also transferred one of the most important vernacular strategies of her cultural ideology: signification. Signifying is one of many complex rhetorical (Gates 1988) and linguistic tools of Blacks (Smitherman 1977; Mitchell-Kernan 1971; Kochman 1970; Abrahams 1974; Baugh 1983), where the speaker says something that has at least two meanings. One meaning is taken literally by people who stand outside Black cultural ideology; the other meaning typically includes a value judgment or political critique and is directed to any hearer familiar with Black culture. Thus, to me, the pronoun "they" was the subject of the sentence "get me every time;" and this pronoun referred to gatekeepers (Erickson and Shultz 1982; Shoemaker 1992). Lucy signified to me that she was in the process of yet another gatekeeper's rigid application of a social structure; at the same time, to the caseworker, Lucy seemed to be accepting responsibility for the missing document. Signifying, then, is one rhetorical skill that allows a person to simultaneously consent to an assertion of power and signal a counterhegemonic assumption as well. We begin to amass more evidence that "the public representations of claims by subordinate groups, *even in situations of conflict*, nearly always have a strategic or ideological dimension that influences the forms they take" (Scott 1990, 92). Thus, transfer includes both the rhetorical skills and cultural assumptions individuals gather, select, and deploy, given the social particulars of an encounter.

Lucy's linguistic transfer paints in broad relief the gatekeeper's behaviors as being much more constraining than necessary. The caseworker's gestures and language show us how even the smallest of our contextualization cues (a smirk) and utterances can be interpreted as unnecessarily dismissive, harsh, and finally unyielding. In encounters like this, we see a caseworker, perhaps unintentionally, undermining the democratic philosophy inherent in her position—she is a public servant, a social worker, after all. Even with this characterization of community-based language abilities and cultural assumptions transferred in interactions, we must still examine the efficacy of these tools and struggles from the perspective of those in the community. If we don't, we risk underestimating the effects of institutional influences on the daily living and language of these inner city residents.

Evaluating the Tools

When individuals assess their language skills after their interactions with institutional representatives, they display politically savvy metacommunicative interpretations of language used in gatekeeping encounters. Metacommunication, or "statements that report, describe, interpret, and evaluate communicative acts and processes," index many types of social knowledge (Briggs 1986, 2). Briggs, a sociolinguist who studied a Mexicano community in New Mexico, describes how children in this community acquire and learn "a set of metacommunicative skills relating to the transference/transformation of speech in a manner that will be deemed appropriate in a broad range of social settings" (76). These Mexicanos' metacommunicative skills differ from those skills interviewers typically bring with them from their culture, which means that adjustments in linguistic techniques have to be made by both the interviewer and the respondent. In order to facilitate the anthropological interview, Briggs and the participants together honed their language skills in meta-analyses of communicative acts appropriate for their respective cultures.

In another anthropological study that features metacommunication, Keith Basso reveals the metalinguistic knowledge indexed by Apache caricatures of the mannerisms and language of Whites; on a metacommunicative level, these jokes reveal "an ongoing process of change in which the conceptions of 'the Whiteman' . . . are being assessed and reassessed, formulated and reformulated, modified and modified again" (80). Rather than simply mocking the Whiteman's culture and language use, these jokes serve as social commentary and cultural critique of Whiteman's ways.

Alongside Briggs and Basso, I'm interested in providing another location for the study of metacommunication. Inner city residents develop an intricate and continually evolving metacommunicative knowledge regarding the language strategies they use to negotiate, subvert, and question what they see as oppressive behavior. This metacommunication often centered on the paradoxes involved in linguistic integration. Du Bois describes one such paradox, the double consciousness of Blacks:

> Born with a veil and gifted with second-sight in this American world,—a world which yields him no true self consciousness, but only lets him see himself through the revelation of the other world, . . . one ever feels his two-ness—an American, a Negro; two souls, two thoughts, two unreconciled strivings; two warring ideals. (1990, 8)

Integration into the language and social norms of wider society during interactions affects the ways in which these community members construct their possibilities, their struggle, their tools and their identities. "Language is always spoken (and written for that matter) out of a particular *social identity* (or *social role*), an identity that is a composite of words, actions, and (implied) beliefs, values, and attitudes" (Cook-Gumperz 1993, 140). Unless we view integration from the perspective of those pressured to adapt, we risk underestimating the linguistic means and metacommunicative knowledge they use to resist, navigate, and challenge what they view to be onerous behavior by institutional agents.

For instance, some may still question the point of Lucy's resistance and the extent to which it reduced this caseworker's stonewalling. Clearly, Lucy's opposition did not make the worker refer to the form that would have facilitated Lucy's application process; again, the caseworker unflinchingly applied an overarching bureaucratic structure in the face of Lucy's needs. However, if our level of inquiry stops here, we will miss what happened during that interaction and then back at her home that evening. We'll hand over our assumption of agency and counterhegemonic ideology to what at first glance does indeed seem to be an example of Lucy's overly determined situation. If we want to measure the ground gained by a challenge like Lucy's, we need to do so from her point of view saturated in her own community-based hidden ideology. From Lucy's perspective, when the representative smirks, her expression revealed a disrespectful assumption. Lucy read this paralinguistic gesture as a sign of the caseworker's apathy to the difficulties of Lucy's life. Lucy made an overt challenge to the woman by pointing out that the document could be found in her main file. Then she signified to me. Taken together, these all mitigate to some extent the indignity of the caseworker's indifference. Simply stated, by signifying to me and resisting the caseworker, Lucy saved face in front of us (Goffman 1967, 1981). She lessens the disparagement of the caseworker's disrespect by maintaining her own self-respect and my respect for her.

When Lucy went home, she described her encounter to a kitchen full of siblings. Over the course of the fifteen-minute conversation that ensued, Lucy's niece, daughter, and sister volunteered alternate language strategies that Lucy could have used.

> Her 16 year-old niece said, "I would have got all over her . . . ooh, she would have heard from me."
> "You do that and you ain't never gonna get no help from none of them. They'll see you coming, know you gonna get in their face, and say, 'Sorry, none for you,' " Lucy's thirty-fiive year-old sister rejoined. " 'Sides, that just makes you look like you think the system owes you. You want them to think that about you?"
> "I don't care what they think."
> "Well you will care when your ass got kids to feed." She looked at Lucy, "I would have talked to her superior. You know, asked her real nice 'May I speak to your superior.' "
> Lucy curled her lip at her sister: "I ain't gonna be their 'uppity nigger.' " Her sister shrugged to admit Lucy's point. Finally, Lucy's eldest daughter suggested that Lucy could have told the caseworker a hard-luck story. Lucy's sister added, "They got so many people telling them their mother died, or their baby sick, or the buses weren't running. They ain't hearing it anymore."

In the end, Lucy maintained that all that effort wasn't worth the trouble, that her daughter would have to bring in her own birth certificate. As they listed and critiqued these linguistic strategies, they displayed metacommunicative knowledge that was politically strategic. They weighed each strategy to determine the extent to which it might actually, on the one hand, motivate the caseworker to act more as a facilitator and less as a bureaucrat, and, on the other hand, obviate the possible negative stereotypes caseworkers may hold. The struggle here is both material and ideological, then, and is matched with language tools that assess the political factors contributing to the gatekeeping encounter. Note too, the competing subversive ideologies between generations. The older generation held that language is most useful and valuable when its subtlety persuades bureaucrats to open up opportunity and cut them some slack; but at the same time, the language strategy would lose both its efficacy and value if it ended up supporting caseworkers' stereotypes ("I ain't gonna' be their 'uppity nigger.' "). For the younger generation, though, the subversive ideology borders more on separatism than negotiation ("I don't care what they think"). These competing, counterhegemonic ideologies between generation and gender we will see exemplified further in later chapters.

Still, some will describe Lucy's signifying and code-switching as nothing more than coping mechanisms. Choosing to see this interaction in isolation, they will say resistance only counts when it is framed in overt, sweeping political terms and social upheavals. However, James Scott reminds us that thousands of such " 'petty' acts of resistance have dramatic economical and political effects" (1985, 192). Many times interactions like the one that opened this chapter were recounted in kitchens, in living rooms, and on front stoops. Here, people clarified, agreed with, suggested other, sympathized with, even, at times, applauded the vernacular methods of striving used with gatekeepers. From these micro-interactions, we see just where "counterhegemonic discourse is elaborated," and where "infrapolitics may be thought of as the . . . foundational form of politics" (Scott 1990, 201). These minute political struggles taking place daily in the language between these individuals and institutional workers, as well as the discussions they generate "in the 'hood," are the building blocks for the more "elaborate institutionalized political action that could not exist without [them]" (201). Lucy, by preserving her own dignity in light of this worker's disrespect, walked away from the welfare office with some of her own status intact, and this struggle, then, became grist for the resistance and meta-analysis mill at home—another example of the type of language tools to be used in the struggle. We must remind ourselves that grand-scale political struggles take root in these hidden language strategies.

The ways in which community residents reflect on their talk and interactions, and inscribe ideological import to specific linguistic and paralinguistic features, can be terribly instructive for gatekeepers. We can see how our actions become constructed in ways we may not have intended. We understand how we all too often appear onerous and oppressive to the people whom we strive to serve in our positions as institutional representatives. In other words, their metacommunicative tools reflect our social and political actions back to us, and with these in mind, we can begin to reflect on our own language strategies. These inner city residents have a lot to teach us about using language to undermine stereotypes and open up the promise always present in public institutions.

Conclusion

This three-pronged analysis, which considers language learned, deployed, and revamped, builds on previous studies pertaining to African Americans' literacy and discourse. This study elaborates on African-American communicative competence and adaptive strategies in the face of long-standing social deterrents to their advancement. Researchers in anthropology, education, and sociolinguistics challenged ethnocentric deficit theories: Hannerz (1970) and Stack (1977) described the logic and complexity of African Americans' social and cultural practices; Labov (1969) and Smitherman (1977) revealed the internal coherence and sophistication of Black English; and Heath (1983) challenged the artificial dichotomy between "oral" and "literate" cultural practices with her comprehensive ethnography *Ways with Words*. The work of Labov, Smitherman, and Heath has proven especially informative for any analysis of the "communicative competence" of Blacks. Hymes defined communicative competence as the acquisition of the abilities to "produce, understand, and discriminate any and all of the grammatical sentences of a language," as well as to discern when and with whom to use this grammatical knowledge (1974, 75). Expanding our view of the linguistic and literate competencies of African Americans, I relate these individuals' language tools across contexts to their daily burdens of working with the legal system, finding better housing, gaining entrance into college, and getting off welfare.

In other words, I reveal the political significance of African Americans' everyday communicative competence. In doing so, we can understand how their communicative competence gives voice to the material and ideological struggles taking place in daily interactions with the wider society. The counterhegemonic principles imbued in ever-developing communicative aptitudes provide a cornerstone for critical theory: we can begin to appreciate the strategies and attitudes of individuals who neither wholly comply, nor wholly resist, in their daily dialogic power relations with institutional agents. In the remaining chapters, I strive to detail a theory of hegemony that honors the critical consciousness of individuals in this community as well as depicts the multifaceted means by which they both enact and challenge structuring ideologies.

2   Activist Methodology

The Bororos of Brazil sink slowly into their collective death, and Lévi-Strauss takes his seat in the French Academy. Even if this injustice disturbs him, the facts remain unchanged. This story is ours as much as his. In this one respect, . . . the intellectuals are still borne on the backs of the common people.

—Michel de Certeau, *The Practice of Everyday Life*

But the question remains: What gives [the ethnographer] the right to speak for another, to tell another's story? If this "what" is the academy itself, or knowledge itself, or research itself, then isn't the story she tells merely another chapter in the West's master narrative?

—Patricia Sullivan, "Ethnography and the Problem of the 'Other' "

However monological, dialogical, or polyphonic their form, [ethnographies] are hierarchical arrangements of discourse.

—James Clifford, *Learning How to Ask*

The subaltern cannot speak.

—Gayatri Spivak, "Can the Subaltern Speak?"

This stems from my sense of politics, a sense that presumes (1) all political endeavors take place in the daily; (2) individuals cultivate and deploy language skills with great cunning; and (3) language skills aim for the glimmer of possibility found in even the darkest instances of insidious politics. With these presumptions as a basis, I set pen to paper in the hope I could do some small justice to community members' struggles and tools. Rather than trying to write myself out of the unavoidable hierarchy of discourse in any ethnography, I strove to compose a piece that community residents authorized through our

21

dialogue and reciprocity. If the subaltern cannot speak, it is only because the scholar cannot listen and hear. The methodology presented in this chapter exemplifies possible ways for de Certeau's intellectuals and common people to share the burden of representation, with the hope that the ethnographic exercise is one that fulfills our civic duties. The representation before you arrives from a dialogic flow of meaning exchanged through mutually beneficial relations where participants and I listened to and heard each other speak.

Any authority I may have to represent residents in Quayville's inner city has been sanctioned in large part by those who appear in this work. I copied and discussed all my conference papers and early publications with the individuals who appeared in each piece. When it came time to write the dissertation (on which the present book is based), I called community members, read them passages, and asked if I had it right by them. I copied and distributed the dissertation and asked for comments. With comments in hand, I revised accordingly. Most often they extended my analysis, provided caveats, or confirmed my observations. Often they said, "Yeah, but you got to consider," or "That's part of it, but it's also, . . . " or "It ain't so much [this], but more [that]." As they explained other considerations to me, I wrote furiously and reread the changes to them. In the end, their collaboration in this piece presents itself in nuances of the interpretation.

On the whole, their reactions to reading the first draft of this book seemed positive. Some said they were honored; some said it was "all right." But one comment took me by surprise, even though it probably shouldn't have: "You didn't say nothing bad about us. I thought you were going to criticize what we do. Or how we talk." On the one hand, I was dismayed because I thought this person knew me better; but on the other hand, I saw his perspective. He knew I was doing research and research can center on fault-finding. Such research smacks of a top-down perspective, where the researcher judges actions against a pet theory and often finds participants lacking knowledge or skills or cognitive abilities. Labov shows how sociolinguists mistook the resistance of African-American youths as an indication of their oral abilities. He quotes at length a taped interaction between a White researcher in a lab behind a large table and a young African-American child. In the asymmetrical interaction, the child understandably shows "monosyllabic behavior" that unfortunately was used as "evidence of the child's total verbal capacity" (207). Labov smartly points out, "if one takes this interview as a measure of the verbal capacity of the child, it must be as his capacity to defend himself in hostile and threatening situation" (207). If we approach research with a set of questions and theoretical presumptions that are based on notions of deficit, or for that matter, false consciousness, we will be hard pressed to adequately represent participants in honoring and respectful ways. As a rule of thumb, activist research demands we show how people can and do act instead of how they cannot and do not act.

Because other chapters in this book typically include at least one example where my intervention, or lack thereof, moves to the surface of the exchange, here I will background some of the practical and theoretical considerations involved in activist research that fostered these exchanges. I consider the ideas of empowerment and positionality elsewhere and recognize these also play central roles in activist research (Cushman 1996; Cushman and Guinsatao Monberg, forthcoming). Briefly, empowerment and positionality are sustained and negotiated in mutually beneficial relationships between researchers and those with whom we hope to create knowledge. Researchers and participants empower each other when they: (1) enable each other to achieve goals, (2) facilitate each other's actions, and (3) lend to each other their respective social statuses (Cushman 1996). This definition of empowerment assumes that both the researchers and participants occupy multidimensional social positions, or highly interpolated subjectivities. For example, area residents invited me to attend the mosque with them (this group of Muslims happened to be particularly private and only allowed Whites to attend if invited by a member). With their invitation, I was granted entry into a religious arena that I would have been hard pressed to enter otherwise. In other words, they lent me the status of their positions as African Americans. In like fashion, I invited residents to use the computer facilities of the private university I attended. Because this institute was private, residents would have been hard pressed to use the computers without my invitation. I transferred to them the status of my position as graduate student. With attention to empowerment and positionality, then, researchers and participants fluidly negotiate power relations together as they try to facilitate each other's goals. Such a statement presumes that participants have the critical reflexivity necessary in order to openly and carefully negotiate the terms of the ethnographic relation.

Premises of Activist Research

This work examines the dialogic place of power in the everyday. When seen in the dim light of false consciousness, hegemony appears either as an unyielding top–down force, or hegemony appears to be unwittingly reproduced by individuals who see their day-to-day situations as natural, and therefore indomitable. Instead of assuming that individuals lack language strategies because they believe in the terms of their oppression, then, this work began with the assumption that individuals have many complex forms of linguistic agency nurtured in subversive ideologies.

To start with, critical theories work from presumptions about human capabilities. Take for example the set of premises about individuals that Brian Fay's *Critical Social Science* offers: "Humans are broadly intelligent, curious, reflective, and willful beings who, as a consequence, are at least potentially able to transform themselves and their societies within certain wide limits on the basis of their own reflection" (1987, 57). Fay develops this framework after a careful survey of primary works in sociology and political theory, and his list represents one of the best set of ontological beliefs I've seen. To his list, though, we still need to add the belief that humans are creatively strategic: even if they appear to consent to the terms of their existence set forth in prevailing ideologies, we can count on individuals to work from dissident beliefs using refined language skills.

Even with his noteworthy suppositions about human capability, Fay's notion of critical social science unfortunately suffers from a theory of ideological domination that erodes the ground of his position. "The suffering of people occurs in part because they have had inculcated into them an erroneous self-understanding, one embodied in and supporting a form of life which thwarts them. The aim of critical social science is to stimulate these people to subject their lives and their social arrangements to rational scrutiny" (66). Yet we have evidence enough that shows how individuals already subject their lives to rational scrutiny (Huspek 1992; Scott 1985, 1990; Dirks 1994). When doing critical social science research, we need to assume that human beings not only know that they are implicated in cultural reproduction, but that they also craft ways to use these positions to their own advantage. With such a premise, we are much more likely to accurately account for the subtle ways in which people resist the terms of their living conditions, even as they seem to reproduce these terms.

How can we account for this methodological gap between what critical theories believe people are capable of and what individuals actually do and believe? Because they assume subversive ideologies do not exist, critical theorists, like Fay, gain too little access to human beings' subversive self-understandings. Looking at cultural reproduction from a distance, they can only see apparently complacent behaviors and "erroneous" self-perceptions in the public transcript of daily life.

In daily public activities, subordinant groups rarely have the luxury or even the need to pierce through the dominant ideology present in public interactions.

> In ordinary circumstances subordinates have a vested interest in avoiding any *explicit* display of insubordination. They also, of course always have a practical interest in resistance. . . . The reconciliation of these two objectives . . . is typically achieved by pursuing precisely those forms of resistance that avoid any open confrontation with the structures of authority being resisted. (Scott, 1990, 86)

Because resistance takes place behind the public transpiring of events, most critical theorist haven't inroads to the forums in which urban and minority groups develop counter hegemonic attitudes and craft language skills. When we research daily politics from the social distance high theory provides, we often rely on the public record to support our claims, and at this level "a reading of the social evidence will almost always represent a confirmation of the status quo in hegemonic terms" (Scott, 1990, 90). Without access to hidden ideologies, we cannot depict the political ways in which language used in public transactions will show both conformity and conflict. In the example that opens this book, Lucy did not have the luxury to directly challenge what she saw as the caseworker's disrespectful stonewalling. Through signification she both placated and resisted, complied and challenged, reproduced and subverted.

Without immersion in the community, I would not have had access to the private ideologies that inform residents' cunning language use. Their values about language and the ways they interpret the outcomes of gatekeeping interactions could only be captured through ethnographic fieldwork, which entails in the broadest sense immersion in their social and symbolic systems. My participant-observer role in this community gave me access to the interactive processes by which residents are socialized into and learn the value systems they use to judge the utility of language skills and to comprehend the ways in which they construct their interactions with institutional gatekeepers. Gradually, community members revealed to me the process by which they hone and refine their oral and literate language skills. I began to understand the baselines for their judgments about the success or failure of these interactions. In short, participant observation was the best way for me to study how their daily language use was imbued with the social and cultural complexities of their lives.

But the traditional method of participant observation soon proved problematic for this project. Since I was a composition teacher at a well known local university, community members recognized the value of my position and often asked for assistance in their literate attempts to achieve. Believing structural power relations can be negotiated in everyday activities by skillful agents, I needed a methodology that provided room for reflexively communicating the give-and-take terms of the relations community members and I developed. I needed a methodology that aligned the politics set forth in the first chapter with the politics of doing participant observation and writing ethnography. I wanted to insure that (1) community members and myself would dialogically arrange mutually beneficial relationships; (2) the goals and analysis of this research would center around social issues salient to their daily struggles; and (3) we would author(ize) together the final written representations of their lives.

I reinterpreted the strict anthropological method of participant observation by creating a reciprocal relationship with individuals in this neighborhood. This increased my rapport with them and their confidence in my research agenda. As a result, I at times became privy to their hidden forms of oral and literate events where they candidly discussed and considered wider society and its language. I also was invited to view their oral and literate interactions taking place in many institutional contexts, such as doctor's and welfare offices, philanthropic agencies and universities. They let me record a number of their inter-actions with gatekeepers, and usually let me quote them directly on a notepad I carried with me. They also permitted me to copy or keep many of the literate artifacts generated during their daily routines.

With the permission and suggestions of area residents, I chose a number of specific oral and literate interactions from hours of taped conversations, numerous literacy artifacts, and three and a half years of observations. I analyzed this data using the frameworks sociolinguists developed to describe the social construction of literacy (Cook-Gumperz 1993; Street 1984; Gee 1990), interethnic communication (Gumperz 1983a and b; Erickson and Shultz 1982) as well as language, power, and ideology (Kress and Hodge 1979; Fairclough 1989; Roberts et al. 1992). Critical discourse analysis situates texts and utterances in the immediate and larger political contexts of their use. As such, it offers a method for systematically categorizing data in order to uncover the cultural and political influences shaping the language skills deployed in a given situational context. I used critical discourse analysis because, with it, I was able to examine, first, the minute characteristics of user's grammar and semantics; second, the social context in which the language use unfolds; and third, the larger political and ideological assumptions informing each particular language use. As an analytical tool, then, discourse analysis describes the process by which the social exchange of meaning and the social construction of the context unfold in a historical moment. These premises and analytical frameworks provided the necessary theoretical backdrop for the actual day-to-day interactions in fieldwork.

Reciprocal Relations

From January 1993 to June 1996, I conducted ethnographic fieldwork in what people in Quayville call "the ghetto." I originally met parents and children while I was serving as a literacy volunteer in a neighborhood center, but soon realized I needed to position myself differently in the community. As a volunteer in the community center, the social workers wanted me to inform them about the households in ways that would have compromised the ethic of confidentiality central to ethnographic methods. Since I was unable to "be a team player," as the social workers said, they asked me to discontinue my volunteer work. So I broke ties with the community center and soon became closer to a number of families on the block. African-American women and youths allowed me to observe their reading and writing activities and make copies of the pieces central to their everyday practices. In some cases, I facilitated their reading and writing activities with tutorials, trips to libraries, and access to university computing facilities. I tape-recorded personal histories, conversations, and interviews with adults in the community, at local universities, and in numerous social service agencies. I also tape-recorded and noted the interactions between community members and social service gatekeepers; and I copied most of the literacy artifacts generated during these exchanges. Finally, I was privy to the ways in which community residents perceive their relations to outside institutions and the literacy practices peculiar to them.

I began this research with the fundamental belief that participant observation can positively influence the local politics of individuals— a process where the researcher and participants interact in a variety of reciprocal, mutually beneficial exchanges. Under the banner of reciprocity, I've united theories of praxis together with notions of emancipatory pedagogy in an effort to create a theoretical framework for activism. Scholars who advocate praxis research find the traditional anthropological method of participant observation unsatisfactory because it has the potential to reproduce an oppressive relationship between the researcher and those studied (Oakley 1981; Lather 1986; Bleich 1993; Porter and Sullivan 1997). That is, instead of emphasizing the observation side of research, research as praxis demands that we actively participate in the community under study (Johannsen 1992). Originally developed by Aristotle, the term *praxis* resembles "phronesis, [that is,] action adhering to certain ideal standards of good (ethical) or effective (political) behavior" (Warry, 1992, 157). Marx embellished this political agenda for participation in his "Eleventh Thesis," and some applied anthropologists have since adopted praxis as a term describing, loosely, ethical action in the research paradigm to facilitate social change. While expanding the participant side of social science research is necessary in order to achieve praxis, many researchers have suggested this only in theory. Even though applied anthropology provides theoretical models for how praxis enters into the research paradigm, many scholars still need to do the work of intervention, particularly at the community level.

Praxis research can take emancipatory pedagogy as its model for methods of intervention when conducting research. Notions of emancipatory pedagogy work with the same types of theoretical underpinnings that praxis research employs. Paulo Freire's *Pedagogy of the Oppressed* exemplifies the pragmatic concerns of politically involved teaching aimed at emancipating students. His work, centered in Latin America, has been adapted to American educational needs in schooling institutions (Apple and Weis 1983; Giroux 1981; Luke and Gore 1992; Lankshear and McLaren 1993). Emancipatory teaching can only go so far in instantiating activist research, though, because teachers often only apply liberating teaching in the classroom. Here, we're hard pressed to create solidarity and dialogue within the institutionalized social structure of American schools. In order to implement Freire's pedagogy in the United States, we must also practice it outside the academy where we can often more easily create solidarity. In a conversation with Donaldo Macedo, Freire says: "it is impossible to export pedagogical practices without re-inventing them. Please, tell your fellow American educators not to import me. Ask them to recreate and rewrite my ideas" (Macedo 1994, xiv). Our revisions of his pedagogy can be more fully expanded if we move it out of the institutionalized setting of classrooms and into our communities. In this way, liberatory teaching can be brought together with praxis research to form activist research.

Activist relations with participants reformulate how researchers can facilitate community literacy events in reciprocal and mutually beneficial ways. In return for the letters, applications, notes, diaries, books, handouts, and so on, and valuable critiques these men and women offered me, I contributed my time, resources, and knowledge to their linguistic strivings, when—and only when—they asked. Intervention without invitation slips into paternalistic imposition: missionary activism. Because activist research eschews a notion of false consciousness in favor of more respectful ideas of individual agency and intelligence, we can safely assume that community residents know what's best for them and will be quick to let researchers know when and how to help.

An example: Mirena was served an eviction notice and asked me to help her "sound right" to the prospective landlords she needed to call. She told me to act like I was looking for the apartment so she could hear how I would say it. We began to role play a mock conversation of a landlord and Mirena. As we went through the conversation, she wrote my responses on the back of a Chinese take-out menu that happened to be handy. Then she imitated herself speaking to the landlord, reading and improvising from what she'd written on her menu. "Should I tell them I rent from RIP [Rehabilitation and Improvement Program]?" she asked. I thought that might put her in an awkward position since they were evicting her and weren't going to give her a sound recommendation. We decided that she should tell them all the reasons why she wanted to move from the neighborhood (the stray bullets through her front windows would be a convincing starting place). She created a position statement that offered prospective landlords convincing reasons for her to move, reasons that drew attention away from her pending eviction. She eventually found an apartment and thanked me for what she saw as my contribution. And, in return, I received valuable information not only about the ways she best acquires and learns the ability to code-switch, but also about how she troubleshoots and redefines her linguistic strategies necessary in order to get ahead.

Some may question my easy affirmation of Mirena's adoption of White talk with landlords. Some will say I paternalistically fostered the means of her oppression. But such criticisms would overlook the very real constraints Mirena faced as well as the very real rhetorical tactics present in her linguistic choices. Mirena knew all too well the status of my linguistic code, and she knew how landlords hold in low esteem her own linguistic code. Although she and other community members regard Black talk highly (as we'll see in the next chapter), adult females also know the utility of code-switching when talking with landlords and other institutional representatives. She conceptualized the competing value systems present when meeting landlords, and she shopped in wider society's linguistic market for skills to help her reach her practical goals. The point here is not so much that she adopts the linguistic coin of the landlords' market, but that she artfully masks her own linguistic values though her adoption in order to (seemingly) comply with landlords' values. Therefore, we should not view her adoption of White as an *unwitting* compliance to the rules governing wider society's values of linguistic competency. Knowing she would have to deal with landlords on their terms or she would be homeless, she shrewdly manipulated dominant belief systems to open up opportunities for herself.

Our collusion marks my status in this community as simultaneously both insider and outsider, a position we continually negotiated. Mirena recognized—and employed to her own advantage—my linguistic code as an outsider to her community, an insider in Whiter society. She saw me as an institutional representative who not only knew how to speak White, but was also getting a degree in English to become a broker of the linguistic code she now needed. One might think my outsider position as an academic might preclude me from ever being seen as an insider by residents of this neighborhood, but Mirena and most other residents came to know my history of eviction (four times in my life, once homeless for two months). She knew I was no stranger to the strategies needed to convince landlords, that despite previous evictions, one could still be a good tenant.[2] In short, Mirena invited me to join her chicanery as an insider who had been through evictions before, and as an outsider who trucked in the language strategies of wider society. I knowingly engaged in her trickery because I assumed her assessment of the political situation was accurate, and because I assumed that researchers should contribute to the everyday struggles of individuals we hope our studies serve. This brief illustration suggests the types of give-and-take possible when scholars and participants work together to achieve goals.

Making Knowledge Together

If reciprocity requires that both the researcher and participants know and agree on what to give and what to take in the relationship, dialogue, in the Frierian sense of the word, insured the research relationship is mutually beneficial to everyone involved. Remember the interaction between Lucy and the social worker that opened chapter 1? I needed to confirm my hunch about why she was so angry when we left the office: "What would it have taken that lazy f——king bitch to get off her sorry white ass and get my other file?" Soon after that exchange, I told Lucy I thought she held her own during it. "What do you mean?" she asked.

"Well," I said, "the way you told me they 'get you every time.' But she thought you were talking about something else. Your own forgetfulness. She didn't even see what you were saying." Lucy smiled: "Oh you got that, did ya? I figured if I looked right at you, you would listen close." Dialogue comes into activist research because it reduces the "objective distance" between ourselves and the people from and with whom we make knowledge. As I began thinking about what made Lucy so mad, I would ask her if my interpretations did right by hers. Of course, ethnographers are supposed to triangulate their findings to insure the validity of their results. But when dialogue is incorporated into this process of triangulation, the traditional roles between researcher and participants evolve into something more, something Freire might call researcher-as-participant, and participant-as-researcher, where we make knowledge *together*. Just after I asked Lucy about her exchange with the caseworker, she said: "I'm so glad that someone takes the time to listen and hear." She looked at me as she said this. We were sitting in my car outside the buffet where we had just gorged ourselves, and taking advantage of the greenhouse effect, we relaxed. And as soon as she said: "I'm so glad that someone takes the time to listen and hear," I knew what research is supposed to do: listen and hear social issues that participants deem important so that we can begin to make knowledge together, as opposed to the researcher "being borne on the backs of the common people" (de Certeau 1984, 25).

I finally began hearing the many stories participants had been telling me about unresponsive caseworkers, landlords, doctors, policemen, and social workers, to name a few. Because so many men and women described these encounters in terms of a struggle, I realized I was looking at a larger social problem—an urgent problem that maybe we could address with this research. In addition, I came to see a cyclic process of language development, a process they agreed was important and used in their lives. As one participant said when I explained my interpretation to her: "We got to keep striving, you know? No matter what comes our way, we turn it around and make it into something we can use." The residents' persistent development of rhetorically sophisticated language revealed to me some of the ways they grappled with institutional representatives, even when and especially when their chances for success seemed most bleak. Once I identified issues and patterns of action important to them, I created an analytical framework that enabled me to detail how this cyclic process of linguistic advancement becomes useful and valuable in their daily struggles.

Community-based language strategies prepared these individuals for gatekeeping encounters with institutional representatives. Learning and acquisition are lifelong processes: the adults acquire and learn language from their interactions in community, institutional, and formal settings, and pass these on to their kids through example and direct teaching. To understand the ways residents learned language, then, I kept many questions in mind as I analyzed exchanges and literacy artifacts: What models of language use were these men and women exposed to in their daily activities? How did these community members use these models in a process of trial and error? How did they practice these models with each other? And since my initial analysis revealed that area residents learn language practices through a critical demystification of texts, I asked: How did these men and women "read the world in the word?" (Freire 1977; Freire and Macedo 1987). Once answered, these questions helped develop an understanding of the ways in which community members learned and acquired language in this community, useful knowledge if we hope to learn more from inner city residents about ways their daily language use maneuvers through the structuring ideology of institutional representatives.

Within the situational context of any interaction, the transfer of language strategies manifests itself in both the grammatical features of language (i.e., semantics and syntax), and the ideology these features index (i.e., cultural value assumptions and social statuses placed on particular language uses). Critical discourse analysis offers a theory and method for the close study of the ways language marks a trail to the value systems and beliefs people bring to their exchanges. Community residents' face-to-face interactions with gatekeepers were analyzed using devices developed by both John Gumperz (1982 a and b) during his research on interethnic communication, and by British scholars who developed a critical discourse analysis for texts and utterances (Fairclough 1989; Kress and Hodge 1979). Beginning "with the hypothesis that the text [or interaction] has some specific signification in social structure," my analysis of transfer then worked on three levels (Kress and Hodge 1979).

In the first level of analysis, I looked for the salient features of language used in the exchange or text in order to describe the social functions that a particular linguistic choice represented. I analyzed the semantics and grammar (i.e., syntax, verb conjugation) to see what was said, by whom, and with what meanings. These linguistic choices serve a social function, assuming that language is performative (Austin 1962; Searle 1979; Gumperz 1982a, 75–80). For instance, an imperative sentence structure has the function of commanding someone to do something. The lexical choice of the speaker may also show a person's inclusion or exclusion from a speech community, as Gumperz (1982a) found in his analyses of code-switching. Here, I asked two fairly straightforward questions: What are the rhetorical features of this text? and What social functions do they perform? An examination of the features of language takes initial steps toward a portrayal of the larger social issues involved in these gatekeeping exchanges. People enact their agency with the linguistic choices they make because these choices have social functions.

This agency can only go so far within the context of gatekeeping exchanges. This noted, in the second level of analysis of transfer, I tried to portray the situational context in which the utterance and text unfolded (Fairclough 1989). This situational context depicts the reciprocal relations of the actors in an exchange. Fairclough finds that "when it comes to the question of relations, we look at subject positions more dynamically, in terms of what relationships of power, social distance, and so forth are set up and enacted in the situation" (148). To uncover these dynamic relations of people during verbal exchanges, I noted the contextualization cues that accompanied the language uses of each person. In addition to the semantic content of messages, all face-to-face interactions contain contextualization cues. Contextualization cues include "code; dialect and style switching processes; . . . prosodic phenomenon; . . . choice among lexical and syntactical options; formulaic expressions, conversational openings, closings and sequencings" (Gumperz 1982a, 131). Analysis of the contextualization cues in these exchanges often indicates the ways in which the people in the interaction collaborate in the social construction of their relation to each other as subjects. Similarly, the situational context of a literacy event manifests itself in the ways people interact together when reading and writing texts. Specifically, I analyzed how social relations are defined or refined when texts are present. For every exchange, then, I asked: How are situations mutually constructed or subverted through cueing? What relations and subject positions are promoted through the creation of this context? In what ways is the literate artifact contributing to these social constructions? With these questions, I characterized the immediate context in which the social relationships unfolded, and I began to uncover how encounters in these institutional interchanges often presented a struggle for the African Americans involved in them.

In the third level of analysis, I considered the text or exchange in terms of the ideological assumptions underpinning the participants' language use. Here, my goal was to locate the interaction and text within larger institutional and social struggles. Fairclough believes that "we can [either] see discourses as parts of social struggles, and contextualize them in terms of these broader struggles . . . , [or], we can show what power relationships determine discourses. . . . This puts the emphasis on the social determination of discourse" (163). I disagree with his dichotomy between how discourses *either* work to challenge onerous behavior and power structures *or* discourses are predetermined and thus simply reproduce power structures. My initial analysis of data led me to believe that what may initially appear as a simple reproduction of a social structure could be, in fact, both a clever way to placate *and* undermine someone's oppressive actions. To my mind, the larger social implications of language use in interactions and literacy events must be decided on a case-by-case basis with two questions in mind: How do the features of the language used, together with the situational context, reveal the ideologies of the participants? That is, how are the values present in the language and literacy of these encounters part of larger institutional and social value systems? And is there an overt or covert conflict between these ideologies? When answered, these two questions help locate every interaction and literacy event I examined in the broadest types of social structures. Taken together, these three levels of analyses were used to uncover the ways in which the people in this community gathered, selected and deployed their linguistic strategies and cultural assumptions in face-to-face and textual interactions with people in wider society's institutions. However, I still needed to account for the ways in which community members used language to discuss the utterances and texts present in gatekeeping interactions.

To do this, I employed a theory of metacommunication to examine how people assess and revamp their language skills. As Stubbs (1983) finds: "utterances with a metacommunicative function do a particular kind of work; namely, smooth out periods of talk, guide messages, and generally prop up . . . the metacommunication process" (63). For Stubbs, metacommunicative utterances have the function of maintaining the direction and quality of communication channels. So, the question "Can you hear me OK?" is metacommunicative, according to Stubbs's definition. Duranti and Goodwin, like Stubbs, find that metacommunication is necessary for the maintenance of the flow of conversation in a context (1992, 34). Yet, these definitions assume language can be extricated from the political context of its use. In the end, I found Briggs's definition of metacommunicative knowledge most useful. Briggs's definition includes those statements that individuals use when they want to analyze the political ramifications of their own and other's language use in particular situations (Briggs 1986, 2). This definition provides a way to characterize the metacommunicative assessments of language taking place when community residents considered the social consequences of their communication with gatekeepers.

Often, after interactions with gatekeepers, neighborhood residents returned home and evaluated the outcomes; in these discussions they assessed and refined their language strategies and metacommunicative constructs. Within these exchanges, identifying metacommunicative tools was relatively simple using the three tiered framework and set of questions I described earlier. Again, I examined the lexical and semantic structures of the statements and identified their salient functions as interpretations, evaluations, or descriptions of users' own communicative strategies. I asked what social function do these metacommunicative statements have and how do the features of the utterance show this? Next, I depicted the situational context, paying particular attention to contextualization cues that marked these individuals' relations to each other. These cues often indicated the places where residents were of divided mind on the extent to which a Black person must integrate his/her language use in order to achieve social mobility. Here, I asked: To what extent do these men and women relate to each other as Black people given this situational context? How does their metacommunication reference hidden ideologies that might subvert or reproduce long standing racial struggles? At this level, I wondered how the features of the language used, along with the situational context, revealed the ideologies of participants. With this examination, I depicted the types and extents of linguistic and political knowledge drawn upon and revamped when area residents returned from dealings with public institutions.

Overall, activist research sets for itself the goal of portraying participants in respectful ways while also conveying the texture and complexities of participants' lived conditions. In any ethnography, participants' actions and language uses must be contextualized in the social and symbolic emic systems of community residents, even, or especially, when these actions and language uses run contrary to prevailing notions. At the same time as participants must be respected, activist research resists creating representations drawn from the perspective of liberal idealism. Liberal idealism might lead to Pollyannish representations or naive glorifications of individuals' acts of agency. Because activist research demands we describe the tension filled place where individuals' acts wrangle with larger structural constraints, some of the representations in this work will strike readers as unflattering, perhaps problematic. In short, the individuals presented here may not live up to readers' own standards for proper speech, conduct, and ethics. Instead of this being a reflection on the participants in this study, though, their "shortcomings" should be perceived as stemming from readers' own biases. Certainly, activist researchers have their own values and biases; however, activist researchers use self-reflexivity, dialogue, and reciprocity to bring out into the open values and biases and to negotiate through these with participants.

Dialogue and reciprocity have not ended with the dissertation and book drafts. Most recently, some community members wondered about royalties from the sale of this book. Some wanted the book contract to assign royalties to them. Others wanted a share of royalties, but under the table. Others said it was my book, I spent all that time writing it, I should have all the royalties. Although the rules of DSS and the IRS prevent me from detailing the specific terms of our final arrangement, here's where I stood: In real ways, I've already profited from their stories. My current stability, I owe in no small measure to the generosity of Quayville's inner city residents; so of the royalties I receive, 60 percent will go to them.

In all, activist methodology advances our thinking about what counts as socially responsible research. David Bleich points out that research in composition must move past traditional forms of ethnographic inquiry where "the standard of objective, detached observation is invoked to conceal problematic social disparities between researcher and researched" (1993, 179). Instead, he believes that "socially generous research [is] an initiative that contributes to the empowerment of the subject's community" (178). He takes this stand alongside Porter and Sullivan. *Opening Spaces* presents a timely and useful theoretical framework for the "resituating of methodology as a rhetorical, political, and ethical action that has as its goal the improvement of researchers and research participants" (Porter and Sullivan 1997, 122). In order to improve the relations of those involved in research, we need a notion of power that accounts for daily give-and-take relations between researchers and participants. Open and careful negotiation of mutually rewarding relationships between the researcher and participants must be in place if we ever hope to do research that mirrors critical theory. Activist research shows how knowledge can be made with those we hope our critical theory serves—the social and political particulars of everyday living become the basis of a well-grounded theory of hegemony.

3 African Americans and Quayville

Policies and institutions that appear oppressive today are built in significant measure of human agency and choice.

—Michael Katz, *Improving Poor People*

Before we can understand the developmental process of language in inner city Quayville, we need to consider the historical forces that contributed to the cultural, architectural, and linguistic landscape in this area of the United States. If, as Katz says, individuals' day-to-day agency and choices uphold institutions, then we need to ask: What values pervade these choices, and how do these attitudes compete with the cultural perspectives of those whom public institutions serve? This chapter answers these questions by providing background on, first, the influences contributing to African Americans coming to live in this section of town, and, second, introductions to the individuals and their belief systems central to this study. In the first half of the chapter, I show how a long history of self-determination extends from travels on the underground railroad in search of freedom, to migrations in search of work, to forced evictions and current searches for housing and steady employment. These historical acts of self-help contribute to many current forms of agency needed to negotiate linguistically the power structures of modern institutions. The second half of the chapter shows how residents value various vernacular means they use to critique and skillfully manage their relations with bureaucracies. I tease out the sites of competition between the predominant attitudes of institutions and the beliefs of community members, as well as the sites of competition within community residents' own emic system that attaches differing levels of value to particular oral and literate uses.

A History of Struggle

Located on a major river, Quayville's waterway proved central to state-wide transportation of farm products, coal, and manufactured goods. In 1823, final construction of a dam upriver from Quayville meant that the town would become a hub for the increased trade that the Industrial Revolution brought to many Northeastern cities. Because of Quayville's ideal location, it quickly grew into an industrial leader in the manufacturing of clothing, textiles, iron, sewing machines, horseshoes, and bricks. Between 1829 and 1850, African Americans held various jobs: in the shipping industry they worked as cooks, boatmen, and laborers; in the service industries as barbers, steamer waiters, musicians, beer peddlers, and saloon keepers; in the mills as scourers and tenders of grain machines; and in the skilled labor sector as shoemakers, tanners, and carpenters. Black men and women also worked in households as coachmen, washers, waiters, and cooks. (Before 1857, the City Directory of Quayville italicized the listings of African Americans' names, addresses and occupations.)

Up until 1850, the economy of Quayville was relatively hospitable to the African-American population living here and emigrating from the South. By 1850 the types of jobs the men held diversified and included: a tanner, carpenters, a fruit peddler, two musicians, a shoemaker, tailors, a beer peddler, grocers, a confectioner, two barbers, one of whom operated his own shop, a physician, and reverends (City Directory 1850). Women were listed in the directory if they were married or widowed and usually worked as washers or cooks in the households. Of the 108 individuals listed in the directory in 1850, 11 men were whitewashers, 16 men were waiters, and 22 men were "laborers." The work for both men and women, but especially women, however, still remained largely in the realm of service to White middle-class business owners and professionals.

The latter half of the nineteenth century and the early twentieth century brought substantial economic growth to this area that attracted many more emancipated African Americans from the South. The population of African Americans in the state grew steadily, from 49,005 in 1850 to 70,092 in 1890 (Dodd, 1993). By 1895, Quayville saw the apex of its economic growth. The 1895 business directory lists no less than 591 grocers, 216 meat markets, and 683 saloons. And for the repentant, Quayville provided a choice from over 70 churches. Quayville was home to 42 milliners, 92 painters, 10 paper box makers, and 7 pork packers. The 1895 City Directory also listed five railroad lines. Despite the availability of jobs for men and women throughout the North, work was still exploitive and unstable. For women in domestic jobs, the work paid "low wages, required long hours, and provided little independence in work routines" (Trotter 1993, 60). And "wherever the work was heavy, hot, dirty, and low paying, Black men could usually be found" (60). In the face of these immense odds and with the modicum of economic stability their jobs supplied, Black cultural life advanced in this area as a result of long-standing beliefs in the value of self-help. Postemancipation efforts on the part of Blacks to forward themselves and their communities have been carefully chronicled by Jacqueline Jones:

> After the Civil War, a flurry of institution building among the freepeople, who started their own churches, burial societies, neighborhood and mutual aid associations, workers' groups, and fraternal orders, testified to their determination to provide for themselves. . . . These groups reveal a tradition of group resourcefulness, a corporate ethos that originated in slave quarters, persisted in the postbellum south, and found a new, if similarly harsh home in the urban North. (1993, 38)

As we'll see, the principle of self-help contributes to the types of linguistic strategies still present in Quayville's inner city. At its best, the economic foothold African Americans held in Quayville and the industrial Northeast was slim and slippery.

The First World War provided jobs in the northeastern industrial cities and factored into what historians call the First Great Migration of Blacks from the South to the North in search of jobs. The population of African Americans in the state shows the effects of the First Great Migration: in 1900, roughly 22,000 more Blacks entered the state, a 41.6 percent increase in their population (Dodd 1993). By 1920, two years after the end of the war, 498,483 African Americans lived in the state, over 400,000 more than in 1900. In 1920, the newly emigrated to Quayville likely worked on one of the nine railroads, that number up from the five in 1895. Paper mills, iron foundries, and clothing manufacturing positions likely employed the newly emigrated citizens as well. The promise of work in these factories—even with its long hours and low pay—could have been attractive to Southern Blacks who faced Southern racism, Jim Crow laws, as well as unsteady and unrewarding migrant farming conditions. Nevertheless, because immigrants from other countries vied for the same jobs as African Americans, Quayville Blacks likely experienced discriminatory hiring practices by Northern Whites who preferred to hire Irish and Italian immigrants instead (Jones 1993, 28). In addition, certain types of class and regional prejudices among "the old elite Black families who had been in the Northeast and the newly migrated Blacks from the South" had to be overcome (63). In effect, the move North for many Blacks became a choice between Southern forms of overt racism and prejudice, or Northern forms of insidious racism and prejudice.

If African Americans in the Northeast held jobs during the economic boon before 1920, they were usually the first to be fired when the Great Depression hit. "In 1932 when the nation's unemployment rate peaked between 25 and 30 percent, urban unemployment was higher, and Black unemployment in Northern cities was even higher: well over 40 percent in Harlem, Philadelphia, Chicago, and Detroit. . . . Blacks remained tied to work on New Deal public emergency projects" (Trotter 1993, 72). After the Great Depression, the racist employment practices that favored immigrants over African Americans led to Blacks' increasing reliance on social assistance programs. Of the 606 African Americans residing in Quayville in 1930, a small number held jobs at the iron foundry, or in the steel industry. But the majority of males and females were employed in wholesale, retail and domestic service (U.S. Census 1930). Of the 612 Blacks in Quayville in 1940, 318 were in the labor force, and 237 were employed. Males were most likely to work as clerks, salesmen, laborers, and service workers. Women likely worked in textiles and in retail (U.S. Census 1940). Forty-seven of the 612 African Americans in Quayville were seeking work, and another 34 were on "public emergency work" through the WPA programs Roosevelt designed to bring the country out of the Depression (U.S. Census 1940).

This doesn't mean, however, that those receiving social assistance were "merely passive recipients of aid from the Black middle class and its White allies" (Trotter 1993, 78). Not surprisingly, "the Black poor took a hand in devising ways of surviving poverty . . . [and] supported regular social welfare efforts within the Black community" (78). These survival strategies included fund raising activities for charities and storefront churches. Those men and women who earned a living in the underground economies of gambling, pimping, and prostitution also supported their communities (78–80). Lucy Cadens (44) recalled that her maternal grandfather, after losing his railroad job, "ran two busy whorehouses near the tracks long before I was even born and right up to my teens. Every Sunday we'd go to the Presbyterian and he'd give his share." When the wellspring of economic opportunity dried up and preferential hiring and firing practices increased, Blacks' reliance on public assistance and on community-based support increased in like fashion. War economies offered some relief though.

The Second World War opened more jobs in the Northeast, a contributing factor in the Second Great Migration of Blacks from the South. In 1950 the African-American population in the state increased 60.7 percent over the 1940 census (Dodd 1993). Quayville's Black population rose to 914. The men were employed as craftsmen, sales managers, and in the metal industries, while women were employed in telecommunications, apparel production, and private households (U.S. Census 1950). Even though there were some jobs for emigrating African Americans, the housing situations in Quayville grew more acute because of the first and second waves of population increases.

The northeastern cities built in the 1800s began to show signs of wear, signs recognized and addressed by the federal government. President Johnson proposed three urban renewal solutions: (1) "provide sites for new residential construction serving a variety of income groups . . . , (2) undertake downtown redevelopment . . . , and (3) upgrade the quality of existing housing" (Weaver 1965, 86). In April 1965, President Johnson drafted the Housing and Urban Development Bill to offer federal subsidies to local programs of urban renewal. "The goals were to reduce the substandard housing; to replace it with better housing; to retain in the central city the middle class white families tempted to move away . . . [and] to strengthen the tax base of the central cities, so that the cities could provide better education and social services" (Weaver 1965, 43). To enact such goals, politicians in the Northeast also had to factor in complicated racial issues. With desegregation and the Civil Rights Act of 1964, social integration of dislocated Blacks into White neighborhoods became a central issue during urban renewal efforts. "Proponents of racial integration in housing opposed slum clearance and, frequently, advocated rehabilitation of existing structures; but rehabilitation tended to perpetuate existing residential racial patterns" (Weaver 1965, 86). Unfortunately, with so many economic questions to face, Quayville's local government often overlooked racial issues in implementing its plan for urban renewal.

The city's master plan for urban renewal lists the urban problems Quayville faced: "problems of blight, congestion, and inadequate living environments" brought about by the "reduction of manufacturing employment" lead to White flight to the suburbs, which decreased the tax base of the city (Weaver 1965, 3). While the general population of Whites in Quayville dropped as they fled to the suburbs, the Black population grew in the heart of the city to 1914 by 1960 (U. S. Census 1960). The first phase of urban renewal centered on the demolition of the housing near the railroad tracks and central city—the housing that many African Americans occupied. Oral histories gathered from three families that moved there during the Second Great Migration from the South revealed that all lived within a five-block radius of the railroad tracks. The apartment flats near the railroads had poor plumbing, roaches, and rats, and were cold in the winter. All of the families were large, so the flats were crowded. For example, Lucy Cadens's father and mother moved to Quayville from Memphis, Tennessee, in 1956 to join Lucy's maternal grandfather, who came to Quayville during the First Great Migration. The father found work in the railroads and the mother worked as a seamstress in a clothing factory. They had eight children and lived in a three-room apartment near the tracks; then, in the late 1960s, both parents lost their jobs.

In accord with the master plan's outline for urban renewal, their housing was demolished in the mid-sixties, sending them further North in Quayville to find other places to live. When White flight left many buildings in the hands of absentee landlords, North Quayville was one of the only places African Americans could find housing. South Quayville was populated with Irish and Italian bluecollar workers. Some years later, Quayville built three units of low-income housing for older people, as well as housing for returning veterans just south of the city's only hotel. At the northernmost edge of this "renewal" site, Quayville built a towering six-lane freeway bridge that in effect bisected the downtown from what is now the "ghetto" in North Quayville. In short, the primary problem with Quayville's urban renewal plan was the dislocation of the African Americans initially removed in order to "renew the neighborhood." With the Second Great Migration, the displacement of Blacks through Urban Removal, the movement of jobs to the suburbs, the Civil Rights Movement, and integration, finding housing and keeping a job became central to the twentieth-century material struggles of African Americans in Quayville.

Along with addressing the housing problems in the Northeast, Johnson also designed federal programs to aid in the expansion of social service institutions. Historian Michael Katz reveals how Johnson's War on Poverty expanded federal spending in important ways: (1) "The number of persons receiving Aid to Families with Dependent Children (AFDC) exploded"; (2) "food stamps became more widely available"; and (3) Medicaid for the poor and Medicare for the elderly provided national health insurance (1993c, 102). All of these programs, with their forms, procedures, applications, and institutional lingua franca, remain significantly influential in community members daily lives.

Besides these federal programs born out of the national War on Poverty, local philanthropic and housing agencies also gained a foothold. Katz finds that the War on Poverty program "linked two major strategies: equal opportunity and community action. . . . Community action required the establishment of local agencies to receive and spend federal funds . . . it deliberately bypassed existing local political structures, empowered new groups and challenged existing institutions" (1993c, 95). Using federal funds from the War on Poverty and affirming the liberal ideology of equal opportunity and community action, a number of Quayville's current philanthropic and housing institutions sprung from the federal War on Poverty. Ironically, much of the modern struggle for many African Americans in Quayville stemmed from the gatekeeping processes involved in the disbursement of these federal funds—particularly HUD, AFDC, food stamps, and Medicaid, as we'll see in later chapters.

To understand how this is so, we turn to a brief consideration of the principles informing public institutions. Katz sums up the predominant ideology informing the views on poverty held by many social service representatives; poverty "results from some attribute, a defect in personality, behavior, or human capital. . . . Poverty in America is profoundly individual" (1993c, 237). Katz deftly traces the historical precedents leading to this blame-the-individual notion of poverty. Before the 1900s when almshouses and churches offered some relief from poverty, many believed that "poverty itself became not the natural result of misfortune, but the willful result of indolence and vice. . . . Before the middle of the 19th century, the unworthy poor had become a fixture in the 'popular mind' " (Katz 1994, 14). Though it would take different forms, this view would remain in the public mind well into the twentieth century, stigmatizing those who sought relief. "Asking for relief became a sign of individual failure; no label carried a greater stigma than pauper" (Katz 1993c, 16). However, in the 1960s, with Oscar Lewis's theory of the culture of poverty, popular attitudes toward the urban poor shifted.

No longer attributed to individual shortcoming, poverty, the popular theory held, could be attributed to the social patterns of behavior poor people developed and passed through generations in response to their meager living conditions. Lewis believed poor people develop and reproduce values, family structures, and patterns of behavior in response to their economic hardhips. In his books *The Children of Sanchez* (1961) and *Five Families* (1959), Lewis relays his culture-of-poverty notion through detailed ethnographic accounts of poor families in Mexico. Lewis found that when immersed in a culture of poverty, people respond apathetically to institutions of the larger society, and therefore perpetuate their communities' fragmentation, violence, and ill will toward institutions (Katz 1993c, 16–20). Katz offers a cogent and detailed critique of the ways Lewis's assumptions informed public policy from Johnson's War on Poverty to conservative attacks on welfare in the 1980s (16–35). Basically, liberals, social scientists, and policymakers adopted Lewis's notion as their platforms. The theory's "emphasis on the development and transmission of adaptive coping strategies preserved some dignity and rationality for the poor even as it deplored the culture that resulted and stressed the importance of intervention by sympathetic elites" (Katz 1993c, 23). Many of the programs and institutions that President Johnson founded in his War on Poverty grew out of the belief that poor people could be acculturated into more productive attitudes toward public institutions. For example, in order to begin poor people's acculturation into public schools, "Operation Headstart . . . sought to counteract the familial and environmental disadvantages of poor children through intensive preschool education" (21). With the Civil Rights Movement, prevailing views on poverty shifted somewhat to become "an urban problem that most seriously affected Blacks" (23). So out of 1960s, popular beliefs about poverty and its causes became intricately linked to Black cultural practices in inner cities.

Black family structure, particularly those families headed by females, was now to blame for poverty and urban blight. Daniel Patrick Moynihan's report "The Negro Family: The Case for National Action," referred to the growing number of female-headed households among many Black families to attribute "a self-perpetuating cycle of poverty" in urban Black communities (Katz 1993c, 24–29). His report profoundly influenced assumptions and beliefs held by politicians, social scientists, and lay people. This ideology views poor people, especially poor Black people, as passive, disorganized, and apathetic.

To this day, the policies of service institutions and the actions of their representatives point to these diminished and diminishing ideological assumptions. Social scientists, politicians, and institutional representatives "collectively seem to sanction an image of poor people that denigrate[s] their culture and personality, belittle[s] their capacity for self-motivation, and reinforce[s] direct or indirect colonial rule" (Katz 1993c, 37). Those who serve often hold such demoralizing assumptions despite the fact that their jobs have been created and maintained under the democratic framing of the Constitution, "to promote the general welfare and, hence, secure the blessings of liberty." Indeed, representatives from various agencies often united together under their collectively held dim view of inner city residents.

For example, in the early 1970s, United Ministry of Quayville began offering programs with the goal of "empowering people who are less fortunate with the tools necessary to live independent and productive lives" (1992). Three sisters from a Catholic church established the program that ran out of a first-floor flat. Today, the ministry has a large and sprawling infrastructure, owning seventeen buildings in the city, employing 150 administrative, clerical, and social workers, and surviving on a modest $7 million budget (mostly federal and state funding). Another agency, founded in 1968, worked with United Ministry. The Rehabilitation and Improvement Program (RIP), funded mostly through HUD, bought, gutted, and remodeled entire blocks of Quayville. In fact, RIP owned all but four of the sixteen buildings where the inner city residents in this study lived. RIP had rejuvenated over 250 rental apartments in an effort to "provide decent, affordable neighborhood housing to low income families" (1992). RIP manages these properties and has, in the three plus years of this study, evicted five of the thirteen African-American families who lived on this block (three families own their homes).

Together, United Ministry and RIP opened the Community Center in Quayville's inner city in 1988. The ministry staffed the center with two to three social workers; RIP owned the building; and Architecture Program (AP) designed the space. Their goal was "to combine human services with housing to make lasting improvements in the physical and social fabric which make up a neighborhood block" (pamphlet 1993). RIP hoped to maintain "a responsible presence in the neighborhoods [they] helped to revitalize" (1991). The White middle-class philanthropists who created this statement assumed that the "social fabric" of the poor is deficient, that people of modest means lack will and capacity, and that without the assistance of benefactors, dependent people would remain mired in their degradation. Born out of urban renewal and the War on Poverty, these public service institutions influenced the daily living of the people in this neighborhood. All three of these local institutions worked side-by-side with other state and federal assistance programs and agencies, such as HUD, the Housing Authority, and the Department of Social Services that provided welfare, Medicaid, and food stamps to many of the people in this area. Besides these public institutions, individuals interacted with business owners, private landlords, and the justice system. The migrations, removals, and wars on poverty profoundly shaped the location, demographics, and literacy practices of these inner city residents.

The Value of Tools

Quayville's inner city area is located between the working class Central North district and the gentrified downtown, or Central South district. The inner city stretched for several blocks bounded, on the west by the river and on the east by Hillcrest Drive. Small convenience stores can be found on every block or two, and up the hill one shopping plaza provided a grocery store, two restaurants, an electronics store, and a beauty supply shop. People in the inner city depend in large part on all of these stores for their everyday purchases. The stores have higher prices, which the residents recognize as exploitive: "They know we can't go nowhere else without a car, so they charge us whatever they want," one woman told me as she held up a can of corn with a $1.09 price tag. Ironically, the plaza was built as part of Quayville's urban renewal plan.

The two 1990 census maps included below reveal the poverty and unemployment of residents. City officials termed census tract 404 the inner city. 35.9% of all the people living in the inner city area had below poverty-line incomes (see figure 3.1); that's 1,146 individuals out of a total of 3,193. Citywide, 17.2% of the entire population of 54,

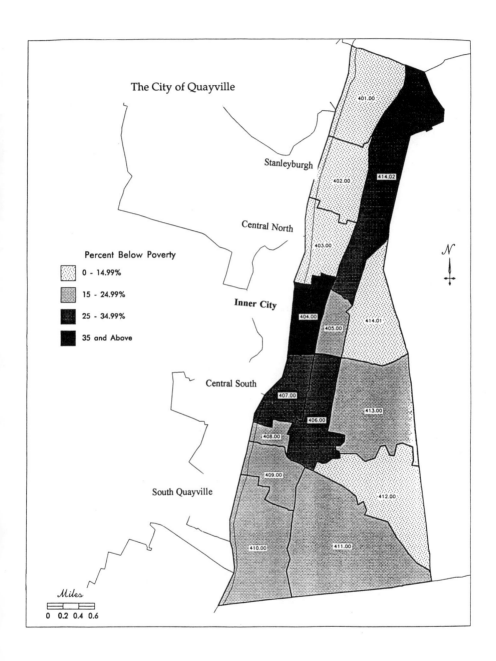

The City of Quayville

Stanleyburgh

Central North

Percent Below Poverty

0 - 14.99%

15 - 24.99%

25 - 34.99%

35 and Above

Inner City

Central South

South Quayville

401.00

414.02

402.00

403.00

404.00

405.00

414.01

407.00

413.00

406.00

408.00

409.00

412.00

410.00

411.00

N

Miles

0   0.2 0.4 0.6

Figure 3.1   Percent Below Poverty

49

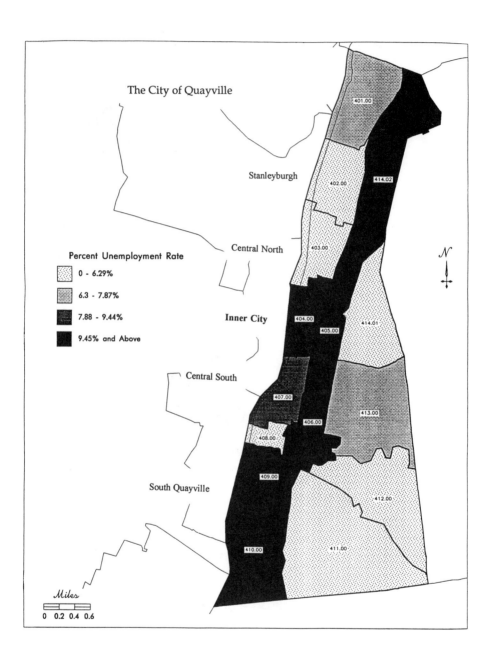

Figure 3.2 Percent Unemployment Rate

50

269 had below-poverty-line incomes. In other words, compared to the rest of the city, more than twice as many inner city residents lived on incomes below the poverty line. Of the households, 21.9% received some form of public assistance, compared to the 9.1% of the households citywide; 13.2% of these inner city residents were unemployed; citywide, 7.8% of the citizens were unemployed (see figure 3.2). Compared to the rest of Quayville, poverty, reliance on the dole, and unemployment are almost twice as bad in the inner city.

With White flight and urban renewal in this area, the rowhouses, which were originally single family homes at the turn of the century, were remodeled and divided into three or four apartments for each building. The four-story brick buildings lined the streets, all built close together, all with front steps connecting the first floor to the sidewalk. The two-block radius around the Neighborhood Center had twelve RIP-owned buildings, all built before 1919, and all renewed during the '70s with HUD funding. While two Vietnamese, and three White families lived near the center, I interacted primarily with adult women and the children in the thirteen African-American families living near the Center. These thirteen families had kin in another eight households in nearby sections of the inner city.

A small number of the women in the area held jobs as nurse's aids, daycare providers, and beauticians. Since they depended on the bus lines or walking, they had to find work close to home. If there were jobs open, they could only apply if all their kids were school-aged, if their health permitted, if they could save enough cash to dress for an interview, if their own parents were looked after, and if the jobs paid enough of a hourly wage to insure they could afford a sitter. The teens and young adults held jobs at gas stations, or restaurants that paid minimum wage (read poverty wage) with no benefits, and offered unsteady hours that fluctuated anywhere between 5 and 25 hours a week. Of the roughly two dozen young adults aged 17–21, four women and three men held high school diplomas. They were too old to be at home, but didn't earn enough to get their own places. A few of these young men ended up somewhere in the justice system, and four teenage women had babies over the three plus years of this study.

Few adult males lived in this neighborhood continuously. One was a janitor in a hospital and was married to a nurse's aid, and one was retired. Another half-dozen adult males passed in and out of women's lives. They found temporary employment in restaurants, shipping, or gas stations: poverty wages, no benefits, few hours. They also found cash in underground economies, gambling and drug dealing mostly. They watched kids, ran errands, and tried to add to the household's income, but always in ways that maintained the *appearance* of a "female-headed household" for DSS officials. Carol Stack, in *All Our Kin*, showed how women would report selected bits of information about their household composition in order to maintain their meager benefits. Katz (1994) also cites the large number of female-headed households in urban areas as one trend in the demographics of inner cities. But it's important to remember that the men had to remain hidden from wider society's view if these women and children were to have enough to eat, even though in actual day-to-day living, men tried to do their share to help raise the children.

The largest group of African Americans socialized together on the front stoops, playing cards, reading newspapers, gossiping, and "catching up." Kids and teens would be sent to Mike's to buy snacks or "loosies," cigarettes sold individually for a quarter each. Mothers braided their daughters' hair into neat rows beaded at the end in black and white or green, yellow, and orange; or they ponytailed their little ones' hair into small round balloons of soft black or red or brown hair clasped at the top with "knock-knocks" (hair-ties with two brightly colored bulbs at the end that knocked together when tied) and at the ends with plastic bowtie barrettes. They shared plates of food, bags of chips, watermelon, and mangos. On these stoops and in their kitchens during inclement weather, adults also shared information about programs and advice.

Summer stoop-sitting provided a public forum for the exchange of knowledge and discussion of issues. Young children sat on their mothers' laps, adolescents played around the stoop, and teens hung out nearby. From an early age these residents learned and were socialized into the language and knowledge necessary to get ahead. Often their discussions centered on questions about the numerous institutions impacting their daily lives. Young mothers would ask older ones about the ins and outs of Medicaid, or getting on waiting lists for Section 8. People talked about the police picking up a friend or relative, or about the newspaper's slanted portrayal of a story that happened on their block. They talked in hushed tones about RIP landlords and the social workers. In all, these stoops and kitchens were schools for, what I call, institutional language: the reading, writing, and speaking skills needed in the daily struggles to obtain and maintain resources and respect from institutional representatives. Institutional language revolved around the modern legacy of material struggles: unemployment, eviction, high costs of living, little cash, cut benefits, drugs up from the city, illness, taking care of children, runaway teens, arrests, shootings, beatings, police harassment, and schools with few resources.

But institutional language also centered on a legacy of ideological conflicts and struggles that these residents encountered in other people's value judgments of them. Sitting on the stoop over two summers, you would hear observations like the following: "In the South, you see the 'Boy,-sit-in-the-back-of-the-bus' racism. Out there for God and everyone to see. Here it be slick. Under cover like. You know, like when a woman hold her purse tighter when you sit next to her on a bus." And on another day: "It's a struggle just to get simple motherf——king respect." And another: "Why they [Whites] cross the street when they see me coming down the sidewalk? Why they always think I'ma hurt them? Just once I wanna see one say 'hello' to me." And another: "Why Megan [the White social worker from the neighborhood center] cross her arms when she talk to us? Never come out the center neither?" One woman replied, "Fool, she afraid of us. We Black. We all dangerous. Didn't you know?" And another, "My caseworker can't even look me in the eyes. Why he disrespect me?" And another, "I walk into the Stanleyburgh clinic and this bitch gonna ask me if I need help filling out my application. Because I'm Black, I can't read or write?" And another, "I apply for Section 8, and she read every line out loud to me. Like I'm a baby getting a bedtime story." Or after a relative, who had a desk job in an insurance company came to visit from a nearby city: in some ways "she made it, but she still got to put up with the same shit. She gotta work twice as hard to prove herself." The modern legacy of insidious ideological struggles.

Although I've had access to and collected data with many families in this inner city neighborhood, I've chosen episodes found in the daily lives of one family in particular, the Cadenses. Because four generations are still living in Quayville, and because the family has 86 immediate members, the Cadenses represent the generational scope and range of experiences typical of other community residents. I refer to the Cadenses and Washingtons throughout chapter 4, though, to offer a more comprehensive overview of these community members' daily strivings to find new housing as well as the cyclic process through which individuals develop, deploy, and hone linguistic tactics. Let me briefly introduce some of the men, women, and children central to this work.

The Cadenses

Lucy (now 44)

Known as the "mother of the community" by her neighbors, Lucy Cadens organized gatherings, cook-outs, and ceramics classes in the Neighborhood Center. Because she grew up in Quayville, she knew many people in the city and often couldn't walk to the store without running into an old acquaintance and having to catch up on their children and partners. When a teen left her baby girl with Afriganzia, Lucy obtained custody of the little girl until "her mother came to her senses." Her voice was soft and throaty, but would rise quickly when talking with her friends. Community residents commented on her beauty and many courted her friendship.

Sasha (26)

Lucy's oldest child was a walking paradox. She cultivated an image of herself as a "ghetto bitch," with her cap pulled down past her eyebrows, Walkman, hooded sweatshirts, baggy jeans, and heavy black leather shoes. She held two part-time jobs, one at a gas station, and one as a care provider to the physically challenged. Her eyes and hair, to her mother's way of thinking, were her best features: jet black and shiny. She kept her hair in tiny braids, three inches long and no wider than a pencil point. A woman of few words, she commanded attention when she spoke in her low round voice.

Raejone (25)

The second oldest in the family, she had two children, one girl and boy. In the neighbors' eyes Raejone was "smart" and "fly" (lovely). Her hair was thick and curled and she often wore it back with a head band. She wore long skirts or dresses that accented her sashay. When migraines or arthritis didn't prevent her, she studied for her GED and looked for a meaningful job that could offer her enough to cover child care. To make ends meet in the meantime, she provided child care out of her home to other AFDC recipients.

Chaos (23)

The middle child, Chaos was the one who Lucy "just don't know what to do with." His features shocked Lucy at first: green eyes, light tan skin, and reddish hair that turns blond at the ends in summer. She owed "his coloring to his Cherokee blood." His sense of humor, savory barbecue, and friendliness made him the favorite among his aunts and uncles. He was baptized into a Baptist church his partner belonged to and wanted to go to college someday. He held part-time jobs in the service industry as a waiter at the country club and a dishwasher/fry cook in a brew pub.

Afriganzia (21)

The youngest daughter, she called herself the baby of the family. A large woman who made her presence known as she walked, she attracted many to her with her incisive, if unflattering, imitations of Whites. Two years after her baby boy was born, she earned her GED, found a part-time job, and enrolled in community college. She also had noted skills in code-switching to White, although she didn't code-switch often for fear of being mistaken as White herself. She had features similar to Chaos's and tried desperately "to darken up in the summer," as she said.

Disco (19)

The youngest in his family, he was the "sweety" of his brothers and sisters. He sometimes carried a boombox as he walked. The music, coupled with his dancing, earned him his street name. He looped himself into and out of street culture over the past years, between part-time jobs. He dropped out of high school, and has since taken classes to prepare him for his GED.

Jolinda Lee (36)

Lucy's sister, the youngest of Lucy's siblings, and still the center of attention, lived with or close to Lucy for many years. She had two children from her marriage, and after her divorce, she had her third child, Zimbabwe, just under two years ago. A striking woman with large eyes, she sized people up quickly. Chaos was her favorite nephew.

The Washingtons

Mirena (36)

A mother of four, people were drawn to her because of her hospitality and warmth. Her laugh rumbled deep inside her. She described herself with a little wink as "a mostly good woman." She arrived in Quayville in the late eighties with her partner, who was in the military, and four children. When she left him, she moved across the street from the center. She worked on and off as a certified nurse's aid, but working the swing and night shifts precluded her from finding reliable child care. With no family in the area to help her, she often felt isolated and burdened.

Upstate (19)

A friend of Disco's, Mirena's oldest was so named for his short sentence in an upstate prison. Mirena often sent him elaborate care packages while he was "away," packages including fruit, cookies, snacks, clothes, and cigarettes—even cash if she could.

Richard (15)

The second eldest had a warm smile and blushed easily. He seemed equally comfortable with a book, fishing pole, or broom in his hands. Mirena spent a few hours a week carefully braiding and beading his hair, which he liked to wear on the longish side. His grades have always been high, and he held a job at a local fast-food place. When the establishment offered him a shift leader position, he dropped out of high school to work full-time.

Samson (13)

The next to youngest, Samson was a "house afire" with energy and enthusiasm. He played rough, laughed loud, and always watched out for his younger sister. His huge appetite was often commented on by neighbors. He would put his hands on his chest and say, "I need to eat. I'm a growin' boy." They would chuckle: "So full of himself."

Kateesha (8)

The youngest and only girl was by all community members' standards something to behold: "She so grown. Look at her bad self. She bad as hell." Kateesha was rock-solid muscular from rough housing with her older brothers. As the only daughter, she was fiercely protected by her brothers and attached to her mother.

These community members, as with all African Americans in Quayville, had a long history of striving for, against, and with: for places to live, for safety from removal, for jobs that offered stability without degradation; against institutional representatives who had offensive assumptions of them, against discrimination in hiring and renting practices, against individuals who believed that Blacks want to be tied to social services; and with other African Americans to establish strong community supports, with some Whites who understood the struggles for and against, and with each other to learn the language skills needed for all their struggles. Striving as an everyday action stemmed from forces intrinsic to all levels of society, such as: the federal level with Johnson's War on Poverty; the state levels with universities; the local levels with landlords (as we'll see in the next chapter); the familial levels with the court system; and the individual levels with personal goals to "be someone," and "do better for myself," as I so often heard. Language, particularly in the literate mode, has historically been involved in every manifestation of these struggles.

Their striving for, against, and with shaped their multifaceted cultural logic about language that included the competing value systems residents held regarding the types and kinds of language to use in wider societal contexts. To begin with, residents recognized the importance of Black English when speaking with peers in the neighborhood or in certain public situations. However, they were more divided by gender and generational perspectives on the utility of White English used with institutions.

Residents valued, to some greater or lesser, extent many forms of language strategies depending upon the context of use as well as their own gender and generation. Generally speaking, African Americans in this area believed talking Black was important to show solidarity. In particular contexts, community members would indicate their shared value of being Black—that is, their shared sense of Otherness in Whiter society.

> *Raejone and I walked in a mall located thirty minutes outside of Quayville on the suburban side of the state capital. As we walked and chatted, an African-American woman with a few bags strolled along toward us. When she was close, Raejone addressed her casually: "How you doin'?"*
>
> *"Alright. Gettin' the shoppin' done."*
>
> *"You know it."*
>
> *I thought I recognized the young woman and asked if she was the daughter of Raejone's aunt.*
>
> *"Who? Her? I never seen her before." I asked why she said hello to her if she didn't know her.*
>
> *"How many other Black people you see here today?" Indeed, not many.*

Raejone greeted her precisely because so few African Americans happened to be shopping that day. Raejone recognized and valued her presence and used Black to show her solidarity with another African American in that situational context. When the woman responded in kind, they together honored their co-presence. Once in a while, though, talking Black to reference shared identity backfired on individuals. Same mall, different day:

> *A well-dressed African-American woman approached a display of some fancy and overpriced gadgets that Lucy and I stood looking at. When Lucy addressed her with an "Ain't these somen'?" the woman replied, "They certainly are," and quickly moved away. Lucy turned to me and grumbled, "Bleached. . . . Can't even say hello."*

The woman's response, constructed with a White form of the verb to be, as well as her rapid departure, indicated to Lucy that she either did not want to be recognized as Black, or that she did not value Black English enough to speak it with Lucy, or that she felt a class difference. But these possibilities were not separable in this context—to speak Black English in that situation would have shown mutual identification; to speak White English only separated. Lucy chastised the woman as someone who sold out her identity because the woman responded in a way that failed to recognize their seemingly shared identity.

Residents' prevailing esteem for Black English had specific limits in particular contexts. In this inner city, the African American who refused to *ever* speak Black English quickly became stigmatized as an "oreo" (Black on the outside, White on the inside), a "sell out," or a "whitewashed nigger" (their terms). On the other hand, the person who radically embraced Black talk in every context quickly made others uncomfortable because s/he was "too Black" or "sweatin' motor oil." One African-American caseworker who briefly held a job in the center managed to alienate the residents and social workers because, as one adult told me, "she so Black, she can't work with no one." Muslims also risked stigmatization because they advocated a Black separatism that all women and some men found immensely impractical and heavy handed. Mirena said of one minister, "He be tellin' us we need to overthrow the White devil, but how can I when I got kids to feed?" With certain limits, talking Black English confirmed positive values of identifying one's self as Black, and therefore residents generally held Black English in high esteem.

Even with the preference of Black English over White English, individuals in this community made room for competing values placed on specific varieties of Black and White English. Tables 3.1 and 3.2 show which types of orality and literacy residents most esteemed given their gender and generation. Both tables show a selection of language uses and values and should not be seen as exhaustive or even nearly complete. Many, but certainly not all, area individuals held these attitudes. The names for forms of Black and White English should be seen as idiosyncratic to this community. For example, "preachin' " (talking down or lecturing to someone) in this neighborhood had little to do with church rhetoric since most families only attended church for funerals and weddings and did not consider themselves to be religious. In other places, "preachin' " may well be linked to the stylistic mannerisms of reverends.

Some interesting points about these tables merit further discussion. For youths, group dynamics shaped the professed literacy values of young kids and teens (youths ranged in age from seven to nineteen). No one in this age range wanted to be seen as standing distinct from their peers. When teens had the option of moving into higher tracks at school, they did so only if their friends were also moving into those tracks because, as Asia once told me, "I don't want my friends thinkin' I'm a higher up. Someone so smart they can't talk to me." Despite these pressures, though, many female teens found ways to obviate these group dynamics. They hid books and writing tablets around their house. They would pull me aside and ask for a book by

TABLE 3.1

Youths' Values of Language Varieties

High Value

Young Males	Young Females
Orality	Orality
Street/Bad	Low Down
Rap	Playin'/Messin'
Trash/Junk/Shit	411 (information/gossip)
Dissin'	Dissin'
With Respect	With Respect
Literacy	Literacy
Rap (composed lyrics)	Letters
Numbers (handling	Journals/Diaries
street business)	Books by Black women
	writers

Moderate Value

Young Males	Young Females
Orality	Orality
Markin'/mockin'	
Preachin'	Book /Fancy
411 (information/gossip)	Trash/Junk/Shit
Playin'/Messin'	Psychin' out/Spoofin'
Psychin' out/Spoofin'	Rap
Literacy	Literacy
Poetry/Love letters	Short stories (read, written)
Applications	Applications
Graffiti	Essays (Du Bois, hooks)

Low Value

Young Males	Young Females
Orality	Orality
White	Strokin' (placating authority)
Book/Fancy	Talkin' Mess (nonsense)
Talkin' Mess (nonsense)	Baby talk
Strokin' (placating authority)	White
Literacy	Literacy
Schooled literacies (worksheets,	Schooled literacies
vocab. lists, textbooks,	
workbooks, notebooks)	

TABLE 3.2

Adults' Values of Language Varieties

High Value

Males	Females
Orality	Orality
Preachin'	Read (judge power relations)
Rappin'	Low Down
With Respect	With Respect
Book	Book
Playin'/Messin'/Fishin'	Playin'/Messin'/Fishin'
White	White
Literacy	Literacy
Newspapers	Journals/Diaries
Race sheets (gambling)	Newspapers
Employment Applications	Bills/Business Letters
Numbers (street business)	Applications (employment,
Schooled	college, AFDC, housing)
	Schooled

Moderate Value

Males	Females
Orality	Orality
Stylin' (older version of rap)	Markin'/mockin'
Playin' the man (placating)	Baby talk
Low down	Playin' the man (placating)
411 (information/gossip)	411 (information/gossip)
Trash/Junk/Shit	Trash/Junk/Shit
Literacy	Literacy
Letters (personal, business)	Procedures/Directions
Procedures/Directions	Brochures (new programs)
Tickets	Articles on health matters
Bills	Coupons/Flyers

61

TABLE 3.2 (CONTINUED)

Adults' Values of Language Varieties

Low Value

Males	Females
Orality	Orality
	Bad/Street
Talkin' Mess (nonsense)	Talkin' Mess (nonsense)
Baby talk	Preachin'
Literacy	Literacy
Applications (AFDC, etc.)	Race sheets

Terry McMillian, bell hooks, or W. E. B. Du Bois. When secretly supplied with these literacy artifacts, the teens would stash them deep into pants pockets or in a secret purse pocket.

Then these books would circulate through a covert network. I once loaned Afriganzia a copy of *Coffee Will Make You Black* by April Sinclair. I hadn't yet finished the book and asked for it back a few days later, only to find out that she had lent the book to Asia. A few more days passed and I asked Asia for the book, but she said her sister was only part way through it, and could she keep it a few more days? I waited and asked Asia's sister for my book, but she had lent it to Raejone. Apparently Afriganzia had told Raejone that Asia's sister had it, and Raejone beat me to the punch. When I got the book back from Sasha, who had borrowed it from Raejone, the well-circulated book fell limp in my hands. The front cover had been bent back from someone's pocket or backpack, the pages were dog-eared, the binding so worn it hardly holds the pages anymore. Someone had underlined all the one liners that appealed to her: next to "Good Black don't crack" (Sinclair 1994, 7) someone wrote "Use this!" If public libraries could only loop into the trade routes taken by teen's smuggled literacy, they would never again want for patronage. These literacies, although openly stigmatized in a group because they were associated with the schooling institution and being schooled, were also highly valued by individuals. Thus, they became smuggled literacies, done on the "low down" (in secret).

Other literacies, such as letter writing and reading, teens practiced in private places because of their personal nature. These literacies I call hidden literacies, not because they were stigmatized, but because they were deeply private; teens maintained relations using hidden literacies, and they therefore valued them dearly. Both young men and women moderately valued creative writing. Although I rarely saw these literacy events, I often saw in passing the results: short stories, raps, notebooks with doodles and letters throughout passed from one teen to another or left on bedroom dressers.

Youths eschewed any form of language one might associate with wider society, which explains their easy and open dismissal of schooled literacies. Black forms of talking, though, teens regarded highly. At times, teens actually chastised adults for appearing to sell out when the adults code-switched with Whites during gatekeeping encounters. For teens, the high value of Black English and being Black often remained inflexible up until that time when they moved into adulthood and had to provide for their children. In other words, teens had a certain amount of luxury to openly despise White forms of talk. Since they did not typically have to provide for themselves, their lives moved in tight social circles. They went to school with the same kids and to the mall with their friends. They walked downtown together; they hung out with each other on front stoops; they flirted and joked (messin' and playin') with each other down on the corner; they visited each other's homes in the winter. While their neighborhood had Whites in it, they principally socialized only with other African-American teens.

The social networks of adults, on the other hand, swept widely across many institutional contexts and demanded continual interaction with wider society. Predictably, their value systems grew and shifted as they got older. Adults valued schooled literacies because they attached to them the promise of social mobility. Code-switching to White became a daily necessity if one wanted to gather resources from institutions or apply for colleges and employment. Adult residents appreciated those who code-switched well, at the same time as they valued many forms of Black talk unique to their generation. Although highly valued by youths, adults devalued "taking all bad," especially when a youth acted "like he bad" with an adult outside of the community. Being bad showed irreverence to authority, the person would act like s/he just didn't care. On the other hand, adults highly valued talking "with respect" because this talk indicated regard for age and social position, particularly for those in the immediate community. Youths, while quick to show respect for adults in their community, didn't value the transfer of this linguistic skill to wider society contexts. In fact, youths typically saw talking with respect to institutional representatives as nothing more than "strokin'" or placating authority. Chapter 10 portrays what happened to Disco when he and his mother went before a judge and Disco refused to speak with respect to the judge. As the social circles of adults necessarily widened, so too widened the breadth of linguistic values.

Between genders though, the types of literacies valued shifted noticeably with age. When young, males and females, on the whole, comparably valued similar language varieties. Even though young men may not have written many letters, they certainly received them, and in return many wrote poetic raps for young women. But as individuals aged, the types of literacies required of men and women cleaved down the middle. Women highly valued the applications of institutions because these applications (i.e., for DSS, Medicaid, and WIC) impacted their daily living. Men, however, often refused to apply for welfare even when steady employment eluded them. In those cases when no jobs came up in a search, they often resorted to underground economies before they "stooped to collecting," or lowered themselves to apply for DSS. Cash always had more value than food stamps, and men would have much rather supplied their loved ones with the former than the later. This brings me to an important caveat: residents could value a type of literacy or orality without liking it at all. Value sometimes meant placing an attendant economic worth on language skills. Thus, for adult females, journals and diaries were both highly valued and well liked although these literacy practices had no obvious economic value; applications for social assistance, while valued, adults never liked. No one enjoyed filling these out over and over again, and few rested easy with the social position indicated by virtue of these forms.

In all, we see the ways in which Black forms of talk remained important to community residents especially because these forms allowed individuals to identify shared conceptions of their struggles. The discourse of mutual identification sustained their antihegemonic ideology and practices. When residents faced material and ideological struggles from gatekeepers, they worked from their vernacular discursive practices to evaluate the gatekeeper's presumptions and name their struggle. With these understandings in mind, they looked for weaknesses, vulnerabilities, soft spots in the gatekeeper's thinking that, if linguistically negotiated carefully, might admit the possibility of opportunity. Black English not only indicated a mutual sense of their marginal positions in relation to wider society's institutions, but also provided the conceptual and linguistic foundations for resistance in interactions where power is applied. Yet, this isn't to imply that Black English and the emic systems imbued in it can be talked about in homogenous ways. While Black English does contain and advance oppositional ideologies, it also contains and advances residents' own competing notions of what counts as resistance. Community members' counterhegemonic perspectives should be seen as dynamic and shifting with age, experience, and gender roles. With a history of their struggles and a sense of residents' value systems, we're in a better position to understand the cyclic process by which they learn, deploy, and refine institutional language skills.

4   The Language of Eviction

The potentially strategic element in appeals to hegemonic values is appar-
ent from almost any setting; it follows from the domination of language.
                                    —J. Scott, *Domination and the Arts of Resistance*

In this chapter, I hope to render a large-scale picture of the cyclic
process by which community members learned language skills, deployed them in gatekeeping interactions with landlords and DSS representatives, and then revamped them according to their metadiscursive
interpretations of the encounters. Residents use institutional language
skills to counter the taken-for-granted nature of their daily material
and ideological struggles with public service agents. Broadly speaking, institutional language includes the oral, literate, and analytical
tactics that community members learn, deploy, and revise over long
periods of time and across numerous institutional contexts. To use
Scott's terms, institutional language describes "the potentially strategic element in appeals to [the] hegemonic values" of institutional representatives. The "domination of language" can emerge in the written
and oral communication gatekeepers use, such as interviews, applications, verification forms, letters, or phone calls. When area residents
engage the language of domination, they insightfully tease out the
underlying values, critique these beliefs, and choose ways to linguistically complicate them. To characterize institutional language skills
and the counterhegemonic beliefs pervading them, I illustrate Mirena
Washington's and Lucy Cadens's searches for housing after they were
evicted.

Mirena's household of six included herself, her four children, and her
boyfriend; Lucy's household of thirteen included herself, her boyfriend,

67

sister, foster child, five children, three grandchildren, and a newborn nephew. Mirena's and Lucy's situations were remarkably similar: evicted by the same landlord, for a number of the same reasons, and within a year and a half of each other. Yet their situations had notable differences too; Mirena drew resources solely from public assistance in the form of welfare and food stamps; Lucy drew resources from social security, Section 8, and the public assistance she received to care for her custodial child, Leanna. Mirena had no kin in the area and had moved from North Carolina in the late 1970s; Lucy had a large extended family that had lived in Quayville for generations. In fact, four generations were living at the time of this study: Lucy's father (age 78), his 9 children (ages 34–53), his 58 grandchildren (ages 13–28), and his 14 great-grandchildren (ages 18 months–5 years old), for a total of 82 immediate members. These demographics, as we'll see, contribute to how Mirena and Lucy's stories develop.

These women use carefully crafted institutional language tools to negotiate gatekeeping interactions in order to provide for others. They use this language with deliberation because they wanted to provide a clean and safe living environment for their children, and because they wanted to be in a position from which they could contribute to their extended family and community. In other words, they used institutional language to work with society's public organizations in order to provide for their kids, kin, and community, in precisely that order of importance to them. As you read, keep in mind that Mirena's and Lucy's stories indicate many ways language strategies continue to develop in contexts of highly asymmetrical relations with wider society. Their stories reveal as well their dogged persistence in finding opportunities where few seem to exist. Residents craft, deploy, and retool language skills so that they appear to conform to "mainstream" values, even as they are critiquing them.

To understand how they do so, we need to characterize the public and hidden transcripts found in the daily politics generated between themselves and institutional gatekeepers. As Scott reminds us:

> The theatrical imperatives that normally prevail in situations of domination produce a public transcript in close conformity with how the dominant group would wish to have things appear. . . . In ideological terms, the public transcript will typically, by its accomodationist tone, provide convincing evidence for the hegemony of dominant values. (1990, 4)

When interacting with gatekeepers, inner city inhabitants often have few choices but to appear to comply fully with prevailing norms, using convincing performances of deference. When referring to the public transcript alone for evidence of hegemony, one will find ample examples to support claims about ideological domination. Indeed, this chapter, when read only in terms of the public transcript, will offer compelling exchanges that could suggest individuals' false consciousness—at least they could if one ignores the many examples showing residents' hidden transcripts. Scott finds that "If subordinate discourse in the presence of the dominant is a public transcript, . . . the term hidden transcript characterize[s] discourse that takes place 'off stage,' beyond direct observation of power holders" (4). The hidden transcript indicates precisely those places where individuals critique dominant values that they seem to uphold publicly. The hidden transcript shows where counterhegemonic ideologies foster the discursive tactics that question, undermine, placate, challenge, and push at predominant values present in the public transcript. In revealing the tension between these transcripts, some readers will want to praise one over the other as indicative of their brand of politics and resistance. Others may read these transcripts as mutually exclusive texts. Both positions would have to overlook the dialogic nature of daily political interactions. The public and hidden transcripts intertwine and coexist in mutual dependency.

Residents in Quayville's inner city rehearse their lines in order to perform the public transcript—even though their hidden transcripts reveal their antihegemonic beliefs. Mirena and Lucy may appear to uncritically conform to landlords' values, but we must realize that they critically shape their language in order to make this appearance. In their cunning attempts to obviate the attitudes they see present in gatekeeping exchanges, they hone their linguistic performances to create the appearance of consent. And while some may say that such subversion only diffuses resistance that should be made more overt, we have to keep in mind the pressing circumstances in which Mirena and Lucy found themselves.

In February of 1993, I first met Mirena in the Neighborhood Center, where I tutored her two sons, Richard and Samson, among other neighborhood children. Richard and I were reading a book together on the couch when she walked in to ask him to run to the store for her when he was done reading with me. She chided Richard for not introducing us, "Didn't I do better than this? Where your manners?" I noticed the roundness of her laugh, how it came from somewhere deep inside her. A welcoming laugh. I told her how smart her kids were; she asked me where I went to school. I said I would be happy to take her to campus sometime. She told me "to stop up when I was through with that one," pointing with her chin to Richard.

Community members called her apartment the "center across from the Center," where the adults gathered around her kitchen table in the evening to drink, smoke, play cards, and listen to music. Mirena's living room was just to the left when you walked in the door, the dining room directly in front of you, the kitchen to the right, and then a long hallway with five doors leading to the four bedrooms and a bathroom. Twelve-foot-high bay windows flooded her catalog-picture-perfect living room with daylight. Only used for special occasions and guests, the living room represented Mirena's expensive rent-to-own endeavor. No one knocked on her door, or if they did it was merely a gesture to announce their presence. Everyone was welcome. The mothers brought their kids to play with Mirena's youngest daughter, Kateesha, and Mirena's two youngest sons. The teens went in the back bedroom and listened to music with Upstate, Mirena's oldest son. Mirena's gatherings brought as many as twenty-eight people into her apartment at a time: laughter often erupted over the din of screaming children and the low thumps of rap with heavy bass. Mostly people talked about their day's activities, ate Mirena's fried chicken and garbage bread (bread dough stuffed with cheese, meat, and vegetables), told stories, gossiped about people in the neighborhood, and sang along with their favorite songs.

Besides Mirena's welcoming attitude, her apartment created a safe space for neighbors to "chill." Although the Neighborhood Center originally provided that space for the adults, most people felt invaded by the social workers' probing questions about their daily lives. "They too nosy over there," I was told time and again. Besides this, Afriganzia, Lucy Cadens's daughter, found the social workers' log book left open one day and read from it to other community members. The social workers had recorded intimate details about the individuals who had used the center's services. When I asked center staff members why they were writing these entries, they said that the logbook served as justification for calling welfare, child protection, police, and landlords; in addition, the logbook proved to United Ministries that the social workers they employed were productively advocating for the people in this neighborhood. As was noted in chapter 3, the Neighborhood Center's mission was "to combine human services with housing to make lasting improvements in the physical and social fabric which make up a neighborhood block" (1993). This may seem like an odd form of advocacy, but RIP hoped to maintain "a responsible presence in the neighborhoods [they] helped to revitalize" (1991). The social workers, then, served in the roles of policing agents who helped maintain the "social fabric" of the block, and, as a result, the adult community members removed themselves from the watchful eyes of the center's staff. To socialize they went to Mirena's for a safe space.

These gatherings caused the social workers a great deal of angst, and they reported them to RIP as unruly parties. The lady above Mirena, a Jehovah's Witness who never attended any of Mirena's get-togethers, also reported Mirena to the landlords. Added to these complaints, Mirena's eldest was under surveillance by the Quayville police, and the police colluded with RIP to use one of the empty apartments across the street from Mirena to watch the "traffic" coming into and out of her house (the social workers told me this, fearing for my safety). Relations between Mirena and RIP strained further when RIP inspected her apartment and found holes in the walls. In early March, RIP told Mirena her lease would not be renewed, but that she could continue to live there under a month-to-month tenancy. Mirena told me "they looking for reasons to get rid of me, and when Upstate brought that damn puppy home for Kateesha, I knew that was all she wrote." The social workers found out about the puppy and told RIP.

I finished tutoring in the center in the early afternoon of May 10, 1993, and it being spring, many community residents gathered together on Lucy Cadens's front stoop. Mirena motioned for me to follow her. We walked across the street to her front steps where her boyfriend, eldest son, and many other men sat. "Get off my goddamn stoop," she surprised them with her roughness and they scattered. She sat on the third step, I sat on the second: "I been put out," she said as she took a folded paper from her front jacket pocket. I read the eviction notice that she had been served earlier that morning by the county marshall. When she went to court three days later on the 13th of May, she found out that she was evicted because of the "traffic" in and out of her house, the young men continually on her front stoop, the neighbors' complaints, and the dog. Since she occupied the apartment on a month-to-month basis, she had thirty short days to find a new place to live.

Lucy Cadens's daughter, Afriganzia, and Lucy's son, Disco, spent quite a bit of time at Mirena's house. Disco and Upstate were "tight" (close), and Afriganzia loved to smoke and drink around the kitchen table with the young mothers in the neighborhood. Lucy had mixed feelings for Mirena, as she told me in June of 1993: "She couldn't control her kid and depended on him like he her husband. Besides she got Afriganzia over there doing God-only-knows what." Not long after Mirena left the community, Lucy signed a new lease with RIP for a year. Community members considered Lucy to be "the mother of the neighborhood" because "she gave to everyone, and never took no shit from no one. No one in their right mind would f——k with her." Neighbors and the social workers respected her temper and discipline.

Lucy's apartment was next door to the center on the third floor. She decorated her pristine living room with dried flower arrangements, ceramics, plants, candles and pictures. One drawing her eldest daughter did in high school, a 3' × 5' of African-American men and women standing together shoulder to shoulder. Her youngest's asthma prevented her from having a carpeted living room, but she mopped her floor religiously, a fact that prompted kids and visitors to leave their shoes on the landing outside the door.

Lucy had been living in that apartment for two years before she and I were introduced through her daughter, Afriganzia. On June 26, 1993, just a month and a half after Mirena had been served an eviction notice, Lucy began having problems with RIP. We sat together around her kitchen table with afternoon sun streaming through the open windows. Her ferns, spider plants, and ivy flourished in this light and threatened to outgrow their coffee-can pots. I touched the leaf of one, and Lucy said apologetically that it needed to be replanted. She held up a pair of peach-colored shorts she was sewing and took stock of her handiness: "for my granddaughter's back to school." Mind you, this was June.

I stomped on a cockroach and Lucy laughed real loud at me: "Killing one ain't gonna make a bit of difference. They everywhere." And they were, large ones, tiny ones, winged ones, red ones, brown ones, black ones—in the family's clothes, behind their pictures, under the rims of their pots, on the ceiling, among their blankets, and in their purses and backpacks, despite the fact that Lucy and her kids tried to keep their apartment fastidiously clean. "RIP come in here to spray in this corner and that corner. It be better for a day, but they always come back worser. You hear that?" I winced at the faint scratching of claws on wood, maybe coming from behind the walls, or maybe the ceiling, "Rats?" "Motherf——ing pigeons. Gary [the apartment manager at RIP] tried to tell me that the ceiling was insulated. Nothing can get in them [the ceilings] and that I must be imagining pigeons inside the apartment. . . . They think they're smarter than us, like they can get away with telling us something and we'll just believe it. Those pigeons get all the way into the bedrooms and everything." The roaches, the pigeons, and the ways her living conditions were too quickly dismissed, comprised only a small part of her daily material struggles, though.

Megan, one of the social workers, "told RIP that Tony be living with me [Lucy]. But he ain't on the lease." I asked how she knew Megan said it. "People around here thought that Mirena gave me up to RIP because she got put out. But Megan told me *she* told them. . . . Sure they're keeping tabs on us over there, but they're giving me something back. Megan offered to get me certified in ceramics so I can teach classes beyond the center. I can take that anywhere. They're giving me something even though they have to tell RIP on me. Don't they get you?"

But Lucy had good reasons to ask Tony to stay with her. Lucy explained that the center staff and landlords didn't "realize I had to ask him to move in. I was afraid of being jumped by the drug dealers I'm fightin' to keep my son away from." Disco along with Upstate had been hanging out on the corner and on Lucy's front stoop since Mirena was gone. Lucy continued, Disco "young so he not into the shit deep. Still getting his ass to school. And plus, he ain't got no money or clothes to speak of." Regardless, the center staff spoke about him in hushed tones and carefully noted his daily activities. Lucy recognized the risk she took in fighting with the drug dealers who were "up from the city so they got no kin" in the area. Despite the problems she was having with RIP, she convinced them that she was doing the best she could to keep her son in line and out of trouble. The story of how she convinced RIP to leave her alone I heard from Lucy herself, from four other women on the block, and from the social workers.

Two weeks before, it seems, someone rushed into Lucy's kitchen and told her "Disco whipping some ass down on the corner." Lucy ran out to the corner and found her son surrounded by other people on the block and the dealers from the city. With a long iron pipe, Disco was beating a White man who huddled on the ground. Lucy grabbed the pipe out of her son's hand, and in a mother's loving rage, beat her youngest with the pipe screaming: "This how it feels to be beat with a pipe." She told him to meet her at home and had words with a few of the people Disco had been hanging around lately. The crowd followed Lucy back to her house and stood on and around her front stoop. Through her open windows they heard her scream at Disco again and again: "This how it feels to be beat with a pipe. You like it?" Afriganzia pleaded with her mom to stop beating her brother. After a short time, Disco ran out of the apartment and stayed gone for three days. Later that week, Disco and Upstate walked into Lucy's kitchen and Disco apologized to Lucy. Upstate, Lucy told me, looked at Disco and said: "She sure must love you to beat you like that," and, thus, Upstate captured the general sentiment of the neighborhood.

The social workers heard the entire story from kids first, then parents, then Lucy herself. They told me Lucy was indeed "cleaning up the block and had the dealers scared to even look at her." For the next year, whenever Lucy appeared at the top of her stoop, the group of young men and women scattered. And when Lucy and I came home from her monthly grocery shopping, the young men and women took her groceries up three flights of stairs for her. These gestures of respect, and the fact that RIP left her alone, cinched her high social status in this neighborhood for the next year.

She continued to be "the mother of the neighborhood," and helped organize cook-outs, a neighborhood watch program, and residential meetings. Of course, her family had the largest claim over her resources and time. She obtained custody of a one-month-old baby girl who was left with Afriganzia but never picked up. Her youngest sister, Jolinda (33), moved into her apartment because she was pregnant, and as Jolinda said: "All her sisters lived with [Lucy] when they had babies. She knows how to take care of newborns better than anyone." In February of 1994, Raejone also moved in along with her two children. Afriganzia announced her pregnancy in the same month; her baby was born in May. So in June of 1994, when Lucy's lease came up for renewal, RIP refused to offer her another lease and put her on a month-to-month tenancy. Besides having an overcrowded apartment, Disco had dropped out of school and completely immersed himself in the street culture. In all, nine adults, two children, and three babies lived in that four-bedroom, one-bath apartment. The teens slept on sofas and a mattress that had been moved into the living room; mothers and their newborns had their own rooms, as did Raejone and her two kids. Foreseeing her eviction, Lucy told everyone to find places of their own. The marshall served Lucy her eviction notice in October 1994.

Once the marshall served them their eviction notices, Mirena and Lucy had to find new housing, which demanded that they relearn language strategies, deploy them in countless gatekeeping interactions, and assess and revamp their linguistic skills. For the rest of the chapter, I show the threefold process by which knowledge of institutional language continually unfolded and increased in this neighborhood around these eviction notices.

Practicing the Tools

Mirena and Lucy both had to brush up on the language necessary to find new housing. They (re)socialized themselves and those around them into the language skills needed to work within numerous institutions; a short list included DSS, HUD, RIP, apartment complexes, courts, and utility companies. Yet Mirena and Lucy both already had extensive knowledge of the language skills needed for negotiating these institutions—Mirena had been evicted at least twice before in this area, and Lucy had been evicted five times before this. In the upcoming sketches of interactions, note how Mirena and Lucy both displayed their linguistic knowledge and built upon it.

Mirena Begins Her Search for Housing

Mirena and I sat at her kitchen table. The morning sun filtered into her living room. Kateesha played with her brothers in their room. Mirena opened the newspaper onto the kitchen table and leaned over it, scanning the "Apartments for Rent" section according to her primary needs: a three- or four-bedroom apartment. "None of these landlords will let me rent when they hear me on the phone. They probably won't even show me the place or tell me where it is."

"Why's that?"

"The way I talk. They'll know I'm Black. You want to help me practice what I'm gonna say on the phone?" I agreed. She said my talking with her would "help [her] sound more respectable, you know, White." She asked me for more information about these apartments,

and as I modeled some lines for her, she wrote down what I said on the back of Chinese take-out menu.

Foreseeing an Eviction Notice, Lucy's Sister Jolinda Gathers Resources

Jolinda, in her early thirties and pregnant, her older sister Lucy, and their eldest sister, Vivian, sat around Vivian's dining room table to fill out Jolinda's applications for welfare together. Jolinda read each line of the form aloud to her older sisters, and they collectively decided what information was needed to fill the blanks. Jolinda read: "They want my name. Should I use Johnson?" [her married name].

Vivian answered: "Well, you don't want them checking on Sam's income, right?" Sam and Jolinda were separated, but Sam still occasionally sent her money for their two kids. Lucy thought it would be best if Jolinda used her maiden name as well. "If you still married, even if you separated, they gonna use his income to decide how much you gonna get." Jolinda agreed and wrote down her maiden name. She came to the line for address. At that time, Jolinda had been living with Lucy, even though Lucy had too many people living with her and risked being evicted because of it. Lucy said: "I don't want them running over to RIP [landlords] and telling them you staying with me. I'm already pushing it with Tony there." Tony, Lucy's boyfriend, lived with her, even though he wasn't on her lease. If Jolinda filled this blank with Lucy's address, the caseworker likely would have told the landlords at RIP that Lucy was breaking her lease. The town was small enough that an extended information network existed between social service agencies, so that they all tried to keep track of who was awarded what kinds of assistance from which agencies. Vivian spoke up: "Just say you live with me. We'll say I'm charging you rent while you look for a place on your own." Lucy added, "You might get more money too." Jolinda wrote Vivian's address.

And so the application process went—each blank filled only after considerable discussion.

In these literacy events we see the use of many kinds of institutional literacy tools. Mirena, Lucy, and Lucy's sisters all asked questions that uncovered the institutional constraints and possibilities indicated in each blank of the application. Their assumption: even the typically taken-for-granted aspects of language use can work for you or against you. Thus, they paid attention to how they chose to speak a phrase or fill in a blank. All of these women selectively read the literate artifacts for information that would help them achieve their goals. They constructed bureaucratic literate artifacts as always containing a material problem to be solved: for Mirena the problem was finding suitable housing; for Jolinda the problem was twofold: contributing resources to Lucy's household and establishing a case for herself in the welfare system. They solved these problems together, collectively, because bureaucratic literacy required extensive knowledge of what institutional agents might assume when reviewing these applications. Lucy and Mirena sought out people who they saw as knowledgeable about language used in these situations: Mirena asked me to help her talk White, and Jolinda asked Lucy and Vivian to help her fill out the application. For Mirena, the experience was educational. As she wrote down her White-sounding responses, she practiced and refined her linguistic skills. For Jolinda, the experience was educational as well because her older sisters had applied before. They contributed their extensive knowledge of strategies for gaining more resources from the Department of Social Services.[3]

Some might view this application as needing only the most rudimentary literacy skills, fill in the blank. However, filling in the blanks of these forms required knowledge of the ways in which social workers assign funds. It requires strategic maneuvering through the options of which information to include and which to eliminate. In other words, Jolinda was being educated through the reading, writing, and the discussion surrounding it, in the ways she could make her application more persuasive to the caseworkers who would be judging the "need" based on these applications. In this community, then, filling out forms is rhetorical: you present only that information that best persuades the caseworker to offer you the maximum allowance possible. In fact, the people who are best able to fill out these forms are sought out, asked for assistance, and are appreciated for their knowledge about which information prompts which responses. They revealed the prevailing beliefs of institutional representatives as they completed each blank, always looking for the path of least resistance through what they saw as gatekeepers' mire of requirements, codes, and insidious attitudes.

Keep in mind that these two interactions were far from isolated events of language socialization. Rather we should see these vignettes as part of intricately connected interactions occurring numerous times in various contexts. These sketches represent the types and kinds of (re)learning of linguistic behaviors necessary for survival when evicted. Over the three and a half years of this study, six households were evicted by RIP and each time adults used similar oral and literate strategies. The language skills Mirena and Jolinda rehearsed and appropriated, then, are part of much larger patterns of linguistic behaviors community members use when looking for housing.

Let me illustrate this point further by describing what both Mirena and Lucy did in order to prepare themselves in the language needed to find housing. Both women collected many resources that listed available housing: the typical ones, such as newspapers and rental guides, but also listings from the Housing Authority, the university's Office of Resident Life, word of mouth, the Urban League, as well as from driving, walking, and biking around the city to look for "For Rent" signs in windows. They had to collect this much information because they knew precisely how limited their housing choices were. Quayville is segregated into college housing (from the central city and up the hill to the university), working-class Irish and Italian neighborhoods (South Quayville), and middle-class homes in North Quayville. Mirena and Lucy lived in Quayville's "ghetto," a stigma indicated as soon as they wrote their inner city addresses on their applications. With such clearly demarcated neighborhoods, very little housing was made available to people trying to cross class and race lines.

In addition, they had to collect a significant number of housing listings because they were being evicted from RIP housing. In Quayville, there are three routes to finding a new place to live: Quayville Housing Authority (QHA), which maintains the projects, Rehabilitation and Improvement Program (RIP), and private landlords. Many of the women in this neighborhood rented from RIP, but when they were evicted from their RIP homes, the stigma usually followed them to QHA because the agencies often ran in tandem. As soon as they received that eviction notice from RIP, Mirena and Lucy had, in effect, burned their bridges to other housing organizations. They also had a difficult time renting with private landlords because they could not get decent references from the people at RIP, and because the landlords often didn't accept public assistance. As a general rule, the landlords set their rental prices too high for public assistance to meet. Mirena wanted to stay in Quayville because she knew the bus routes and her kids were still in school; Lucy wanted to leave Quayville because her kids were out of school and she was tired of the inner city. But for both, the best way to get an apartment was to gather as many listings, leads, and advertisements as possible in order to increase their options.

Along with their research into alternative housing opportunities, Mirena and Lucy also collected information about and applied for as many social services as possible. Mirena went to HUD for Section 8 (Lucy already had Section 8); both went to United Ministries to be put on waiting lists for furniture; both went to DSS to apply for emergency assistance, which included money to rent a moving truck and money for a security deposit; both went to the Housing Authority on the slight chance they might be considered for housing in the projects; and both had to negotiate with the electric and phone companies to establish budgeted payment plans (heating bills could be as high as $600 in the coldest winter months in their electric/gas apartments). Each of these institutions required an application, appropriate identification, and income verifications. All of these language resources had to be in place before they could represent themselves well to their potential landlords.

"Do You Accept Social Assistance?"

During gatekeeping encounters with prospective landlords, the level of discursive formality in the community members' language increased because the situational context left precious little room for them to take risks with their language; even if they understood the situation to be dismissing, they realized that a bold-faced challenge to housing gatekeepers would impede their chances of finding a place. Linguistic transfer in these cases boiled down to a ruthless axiom: use the language tools of the gatekeeping landlords or else risk homelessness. Although some readers might be tempted to dismiss this type of linguistic integration as merely a passive acquiescence to dominant social structures, we have to remember the tremendous influences women faced after an eviction. A mother's social status in this neighborhood rested in large part on her ability to provide a good home for her children. Women rarely lost status when they were served with an eviction notice because evictions were so common. Neighborhood residents did, however, stigmatize those women who went homeless, particularly when small children were involved, as in Mirena's case. If a mother went homeless, she lost face and place in the social hierarchy defined on the stoops, where people would ignore her, and in the kitchens, where people would "talk shit" about her to their neighbors. All of this is to suggest that, in addition to the threats to their own and their children's security, Mirena and Lucy dealt with social pressures from within the community to linguistically integrate into dominant discursive conventions when interacting with landlords. The point is subtle— even though residents understood all too well how odious gatekeepers were, adults pressured each other to *act* like they were "respectable," to *appear* to gatekeepers to uphold prevailing values, to scheme in whatever ways necessary in order to take care of kids, kin, and community. In short, residents pressed each other into playing up to, but not necessarily into, the ideologies of gatekeepers. To do this, they gathered, selected, and deployed a range of rhetorical tools in order to linguistically represent themselves, over the phone, in person, and on paper in ways they believed landlords would deem appropriate. Some examples of their language transfer are shown in figures 4.1, 4.2, and 4.3.

[From Lucy's Housing Application]

Mirena's Search for Housing, Continued

Mirena and I sat together at her kitchen table looking through the classifieds of the local newspaper. We had been practicing talking White, because she thought this might sound "respectable" to landlords. Mirena read to me what she had written on the back of the Chinese menu: "Yes, I'm calling about the apartment?" she read in a low voice, "how that sound?"

"Sounds just like you think you need to sound." She picked up the phone and dialed a number from one of the ads and waited for an answer.

"Yes, I'm calling in regard to the four-bedroom you have listed? Can you tell me where it's located?" She wrote the information next to the ad. "May I make an appointment with you to see the place?. . . . Four will be just fine. Thank you." She hung up the phone and smiled a little at me, "Well, there's one." When she had two more on her itinerary, we left for a quick bite of lunch, then hurried on to view the apartments.

We pulled up to an apartment house on 35th Ave., just two blocks down and one over from where she was being evicted. We got out of the car, and the landlord asked if I was Mirena. Mirena smiled, held out her hand and said, "That would be me. This is my friend, Ellen." The landlord told her about the place as we walked two flights of stairs to see it. We entered into a clean, freshly painted

Social Security Administration
Supplemental Security Income
Notice of Change in Payment

Date: November 28, 1994

Claim Number: DI

I₁₁₁II₁₁I₁I₁₁III₁₁I₁II₁₁₁₁₁II₁I₁I₁II₁₁₁II₁₁₁II₁I₁₁I₁I₁I₁I

We are writing to tell you about changes in your Supplemental Security Income payments. The rest of this letter will tell you more about this change.

Information About Your Payments

- The amount due you beginning January 1995 will be $481.00. This amount includes $23.00 from the State

- The amount due you is being raised because the law provides for an increase in Supplemental Security Income payments in January 1995 if there was an increase in the cost-of-living during the past year.

Things To Remember

You may use this notice when you need proof of your SSI payment amount for other assistance programs such as food stamps, rent subsidies, energy assistance, medical assistance, bank loans, or for other purposes. However, if you get another notice saying your SSI payment is changing again, use that notice instead.

Do You Disagree With The Decision?

If you disagree with the decision, you have the right to appeal. We will review your case and consider any new facts you have.

- You have 60 days to ask for an appeal.

- The 60 days start the day after you get this letter. We assume you got this letter 5 days after the date on it unless you show us that you did not get it within the 5-day period.

- You must have a good reason for waiting more than 60 days to ask for an appeal.

- To appeal, you must fill out a form called "Request for Reconsideration." The form number is SSA-561. To get this form contact one of our offices. We can help you fill out the form.

SSA-L8151-08A-2-014127   See Other Side   P22-0014127 12365

Figure 4.1 Notice of Change in Payment

81

How To Appeal

There are two ways to appeal. You can pick the one you want. If you meet with us in person, it may help us decide your case.

- Case Review. You have a right to review the facts in your file. You can give us more facts to add to your file. Then we'll decide your case again. You won't meet with the person who decides your case. This is the only kind of appeal you can have to appeal a medical decision.

- Informal Conference. You'll meet with the person who decides your case. You can tell that person why you think you're right. You can give us more facts to help prove you're right. You can bring other people to help explain your case.

If You Want Help With Your Appeal

You can have a friend, lawyer or someone else help you. There are groups that can help you find a lawyer or give you free legal services if you qualify. There are also lawyers who do not charge unless you win your appeal. Your local Social Security office has a list of groups that can help you with your appeal

If you get someone to help you, you should let us know. If you hire someone, we must approve the fee before he or she can collect it.

If You Have Any Questions

If you have any questions, you may call us toll-free at 1-800-772-1213, or call your local Social Security office at   . We can answer most questions over the phone. You can also write or visit any Social Security office. The office that serves your area is located at:

DISTRICT OFFICE

If you do call or visit an office, please have this letter with you. It will help us answer your questions. Also, if you plan to visit an office, you may call ahead to make an appointment. This will help us serve you more quickly when you arrive at the office.

Commissioner
of Social Security

SSA-L8151-08A-2-014127   P22-0014127 12365

Figure 4.1 *(continued)*   Notice of Change in Payment

```
        ** PA BUDGET **         VERSION 04                        01/05/95
CASE NAME                     CASE NO.     OFC  UNIT   WORKER  TRAN  CASE SANC

HH CA  DP-HH DP-CA HC FST NR PI SI FP      ********* EARNED INCOME *********
03 01            00                          #    LN  30I   30M  SRC  FRQ  D  CCR
   R         ACTUAL   ALLOW                  1:
      BASIC           7933                   2:
      ENRGY           1000  **** OTHER INCOME ****      0  GROSS              0
      SPMNT            767  LN SRC F AMOUNT EXEMPT       0  TAXES             0
39 E  SHELT    4200   4167                0       0      0  NYS DIS           0
      WATER      0       0                0       0      0  WORK EXP          0
 0    FUEL       0       0                0       0      0  EXEMPT            0
      OTHER      0       0  TOTAL NET              0      0  CH CARE           0
      OTHER      0       0  $$$$ PA GRANT  $$$$$          0  CH CARE           0
      OTHER      0       0  TOTAL NEEDS       13800      0  CH CARE           0
      TOTAL NEEDS    13800  TOTAL INC             0      0  30&1/3-$30        0
********** RECOUPMENT **********  CD / AMT   D  13800      0  TOT DED          0
   BALANCE   %   MO   AMT   REM  RECOUPMENT     1380      0  UNAVAIL          0
 3  377201 10.0  273  1380  461  UTIL/RES          0      0  NET INC          0
         0 00.0      0     0     0  SHELT/RES       1400
         0 00.0      0     0     0  RESTRICTED         0  * EFFECTIVE DATE *
RECALC Y   10.0  273  1380       CASH GRANT     11020     010195 TO 013195
FS CASE NO.                      SEMI    5510   5510   DATE STORED   /  /
```

Figure 4.2 Public Assistance Budget

apartment. *The kitchen was far in the back, a bathroom just off of it, a dining room, and a large front room that overlooked parked cars and the street. "When will the place be available?" she asked the landlord after seeing the entire apartment. He told her two weeks. She asked about the utilities, and verified the amount of rent and security deposit she would need. Then, hesitating, "Here's the question." Mirena took a deep breath and spoke softly: "Do you accept social assistance?"*

"Certainly. I've had very good tenants on public assistance and, besides, I look at it as guaranteed money" She smiled and asked if she could apply for the place.

Lucy Meets a Landlord

Lucy and I parked in front of the rental office of Lakeview, a sprawling apartment complex in the wooded hills of an area suburb. She heard they accepted Section 8, so she set an appointment with the landlords to see the place and pick up an application. As we approached the office, Lucy touched my elbow, "Why don't you start the talking?" I was surprised because she usually seemed so comfortable in these interactions. "They'll understand you. You speak their same language. You sound respectable. I'll do the talking once I'm in, but I want you to help me get in." I agreed and we went in to meet the manager who was much younger than Lucy. I said that we had called earlier that day about the three bedroom. He asked who the apartment would be for, and I looked to Lucy. He asked her name,

Mary Ellen Cushman
PhD Candidate

To whom it may concern: Nov. 15, 1994

Please take this letter of recommendation for Ms.   into consideration
when deciding on her housing application. I've know Ms.   for almost two
years now and have found her to be just the type of conscientious and a diligent
homemaker who landlords seek.

I first met Ms.   through   community center where I was a
literacy volunteer. She was introduced to me as one of the most respected people
in the neighborhood–a pillar of her community. She's lived in this neighborhood
for over four years. In fact, Ms.   is the only community member to have keys
to the neighborhood center. She volunteers many hours to the development of
improvement programs for the center including: craft-making classes, cook outs,
and neighborhood watch to name a few. I'm sure her conscientious community
involvement will be an asset to your area.

I'm also continually impressed by the pride Ms.   takes in the maintenance
and appearance of her home. Her priorities seemingly always center on the
upkeep of her home–I can't count how many times I've seen her with a mop or
broom in her hands. And I've often asked her to make me some of the crafts
which decorate the walls. She's invested in her home much more than people in
my generation (I'm a number of years younger than she). I admire and respect
her abilities to provide a comfortable, clean, safe home for her children.

Unfortunately, her investment in this community and her dedication to her home
has offered only diminishing returns which is why she's moving. I sincerely hope
you will consider her application favorably and that this letter will help you do
so. Please call me if you would like further information. Thank you,

Ellen Cushman

Figure 4.3   Recommendation Letter

*and although she gave her full name, Lucy Cadens, he chose to call her
Ms. Cadens instead of Lucy. From there on, Lucy spoke for herself.*

Some important patterns of linguistic behavior, which I'll sketch in
greater detail in chapter 7, play through these interactions and literacy
artifacts. Both Mirena and Lucy crafted linguistic representations of

themselves in order to sound over the phone and look on paper like the type of person they believed landlords would rent to: Mirena practiced sounding White; Lucy included letters of recommendation in addition to the other forms of verification the landlords requested. Both women said that using White English sounded respectable. However, they weren't conferring a lower status to their vernacular but were revealing their awareness of the common prejudices against Black English. After each interaction, I asked them why White English was valuable to them. Mirena told me that "that's what landlords want to hear. They want to rent to someone they recognize"; Lucy said that "it ain't that *I* think White is more respectable than Black. But I think they gonna think that way." Both women were aware that the high value they placed on their vernacular would likely conflict with the cultural assumptions or biases of landlords. So they selected discursive and literate tools that indexed the cultural assumptions they believed the landlords had in order to present themselves in such a way that strategically catered to landlords' belief systems.

Both women also created a safe space for themselves before they used their language with gatekeepers: Mirena screened potential landlords through the phone; Lucy screened the landlord by placing me between herself and him, if only for a moment. They got their bearings in these gatekeeping interactions by clearing a rhetorical space for themselves to listen and be seen before they said anything. The space they managed to gather for themselves, if only for an instant, allowed them to weigh the dynamics of the situational context, to get their political bearings.

Finally, both Mirena and Lucy knew and addressed what they believed to be their linguistic shortcomings; Mirena practiced her lines by literally reading them off a script she wrote for herself before delivering them in the interaction; and Lucy knew that landlords would need to see other sides to her as a renter, so she asked other people to represent her in letters, and momentarily in person, to the landlords. Housing applications and all of the verifications they required left little room for the applicant to create a status for herself. The verifications certified the type and amount of social service benefit or public assistance they received. And these verifications earmark a class status that often stigmatized the applicant; housing ads in newspapers frequently stated "AFDC [Aid to Families with Dependent Children, or welfare] and Section 8 need not apply." Their rental history, if the landlord checked, usually turned up pasts besmirched with evictions.

Letters of recommendation, though, augmented and offset the other representations of the self that housing applications required. Recommendations serve as a means for legitimizing one's self to prospective landlords. When Lucy asked me to write this letter for her, she said: "Just give them a better idea of who I am and what I do. Tell them *why* I moving. Just so they can't blow me off as a welfare queen." The first two paragraphs of the letter depict Lucy within the context of her daily life by highlighting her community service and the care she takes in homemaking. Lucy asked me to include this information because she wanted landlords to understand better the kind of civic-minded and family-oriented person she is. The letter from Social Security and the printout of Lucy's Public Assistance benefits show that Lucy relies on the public dole as the sole means of her income, a reliance that Lucy understood stigmatized her application for housing. She asks me to talk about the kind of person she is in order to expand upon the message landlords would receive from her other application materials. By including this letter, Lucy manipulates the symbolic order of the application in an effort to assert a more favorable representation of herself.

She also asked me to mention why she's moving. Her emphasis on "why" cued me well—she wanted me to indicate reasons for her move other than her eviction. She asked me, in effect, to create a rhetorical space for her to discuss with landlords the motivations she had for moving beyond the eviction notice she received. The opening line in the last paragraph of the letter sends readers a purposely ambiguous message: "Unfortunately, her investment in this community and her dedication to her home has offered only diminishing returns." Landlords who read this often asked Lucy to explain her reasons for moving, and one even telephoned me to ask if I would expand on that statement. Lucy uses the letter with the aim of drawing her readers' attention away from the stigma of her eviction, "just so they can't blow [her] off as a welfare queen." When deployed, these three literacy artifacts (Figures 4.1, 4.2, and 4.3) would indicate to landlords that Lucy was the kind of person who, although receiving public assistance, also maintained the well-being of her home and neighborhood.

Because these literate artifacts *had to* augment their applications, they're interesting—someone with a different class standing typically fills out one application alone for an apartment. These texts constructed various subjective positions of the applicant. Yet, even with such savvy language skills and well-crafted presentations of the self to gatekeepers, community members' housing applications were often dismissed and sabotaged.

Mirena thought she had two sound opportunities for housing, the one she looked at on 35th Avenue and one in the Housing Authority's projects. It turned out, however, that on 35th Avenue Raejone (Lucy Cadens's daughter) and Thomas, her boyfriend, lived on the second floor of that building. Thomas's mother lived directly across the street from the apartment from which Mirena was being evicted, and his mother was the focus of vicious gossip that he believed Mirena and her friends circulated. Thomas's mother, knowing that Mirena was being evicted, told Thomas why she thought Mirena was being put out. When Thomas found out that Mirena was hoping to move in above them, he called the landlord and warned him away from accepting Mirena's application because of "her drug-dealing kid and the parties." Raejone, who overheard the phone call, told her younger sister Afriganzia, who in turn told Mirena. (Many months later when Raejone and I worked on her college application together, I asked Thomas why he sabotaged Mirena's chances of getting a place. He said he didn't "want [his] kids dealing with coming home to a stoop full of no good niggers.")

Mirena's second hope for finding a place to live rested with the Housing Authority that might give her an apartment in the projects, but she encountered foot dragging. By May 25, she had just a few short days to get a place. When she called the housing authority to check on the progress of her application, the representative told her that she was at the top of their list for an apartment. But Mirena's girlfriend who lived in one of the Housing Authority's projects, told Mirena that her building had vacant apartments. Mirena called the Housing Authority again, and, again, the person told her that she was at the top of their list. Mirena sensed the woman was placating her and asked to speak to the woman's supervisor. The supervisor assured Mirena that they could do little more than they already were and suggested that Mirena check into a drug rehabilitation center for a few months or to the homeless shelter until something became available.

On May 26, I asked Megan, the social worker from the center, to explain to me why Mirena was having problems with the Housing Authority. She told me that "Mirena was in a crisis situation. She's gone from one social service agency to another over the years, and to our mind she hasn't shown any more commitment or follow through on her part." I wrote furiously in my notebook as Megan spoke. The other social worker told me: "She's been running away from her issues and now is in a tough spot with no references from RIP and less than a week to be out. We've decided to let her hit rock bottom. Fall through the cracks. We think this will force her to change." "We?" I asked. "All of us. Mirena's case is known all over the city." Mirena slammed onto rock bottom. On May 31, she received a 72-hour notice to vacate the premises. She went to RIP to ask for an extension. They refused.

Lucy's best language skills met with defeat for different reasons from Mirena's. The apartment in Lakeview was a clean, well-lit, three-bedroom. Rent was $766 a month, and she had to put $100 down, along with $20 for the processing fee. We found out that Lakeview needed more information about the types of income that Lucy had outside of HUD. They believed that their renters should have enough income to meet the payments for the place before they could move in. In other words, they needed assurance that Lucy had enough money to make the rent if her HUD didn't come through for some reason. They said that she must have double the move-in costs, $1523 up front, or she had to prove she had an income of $551 per week.

She had some options at that point. She went to HUD and asked for more money to move in, but they refused, stating that the apartments were overpriced for Section 8. She also met with her father and asked him for $1,523, which he didn't have. Finally, she decided to try to prove she had a $551 per week income. Transferring her SSI from one county to the next, which she would have to do because this complex was in a different county, would give her a cost of living increase. But even with that, she alone could not meet the $551 weekly income. So her hope rested on Disco's getting and keeping a job, an option that never materialized. Disco dropped out school and drifted further into the street culture from which she was trying so desperately to move. In the end, Lucy lost the apartment.

"You Gotta' Be Slick"

These frustrations were all too common for community members who faced eviction. Despite their linguistic efforts to find a place, they often met with unyielding institutional representatives, foot dragging, and prejudice, even from people within the community. The more gatekeeping interactions went awry, the more Mirena and Lucy assessed, weighed, and revamped their language skills. Gatekeeping interactions rarely went as planned, no matter how much thought community members put into their language use. This led them to metadiscursively assess the useful-ness of their strategies and also to assess the larger social and political context that confounded their attempts to get up and out of the ghetto. By way of illustration, let me close this chapter with examples of metacommunicative discussions of gatekeeping encounters.

Mirena Revamps Her Language Tools in Order to Find Housing

Mirena happened into the Neighborhood Center, almost three weeks after she had been evicted from her apartment. Talking to me about her most recent interactions with landlords, she said, "You gotta be slick cause telling them the truth won't get you no place. Sometimes you have to lie to get around shit. . . . "

"So are you still telling them that you wanted to move off of 34th Ave. because of the stray bullet through your window?" Not five weeks before I had stuck my finger in the hole, small, maybe the work of a .22.

"I was for a while. Telling them that and that I wanted to go back to school."

"But there's still a certain amount of truth to that, right? I mean you were talking about going back to school way back in February when everything was still OK."

"But see, it weren't getting me nowhere and I gotta get a place soon. So now I say: 'Hello, I'm in a bind. I'm separated from my family and without a place to live, can you tell what my chances are of getting into your apartment?' "

Mirena Evaluates the Likelihood of Getting Housing

Mirena, Kasha (16), and I were sitting on the front stoop of Kasha's mom's apartment building. Mirena and Kasha had just come from visiting an apartment in South Quayville (the Irish and Italian working class neighborhood).

"That looked pretty good, I thought," Kasha said to Mirena.

"I ain't gonna get that place. And it was nice too."

"Why not?" Kasha furrowed her brow.

"Didn't you see? Them four people sitting on the stoop? Every one, all of them, White?"

"Yeah, but you sounded just as good as them."

"Don't make a bit of difference to them how I sound. I still Black, and they ain't even gonna call me back. You wait. You'll see." Two days later I found out from Mirena that she had called the landlord back and was told he already rented the place.

Lucy Comments on Her Success in Finding Section 8 Housing

Lucy Cadens and I were driving to various apartment complexes looking for one she might be able to move in to. The first two we visited were in a well-groomed neighborhood with flower beds bordering the manicured lawns. Neither one accepted Section 8. We walked back to the car. "I just don't get it. How can they not accept Section 8. Or if they do, set the rent so high that Section 8 can't match it? It's guaranteed money in their pockets."

Lucy said to me as we drove, "I'm gonna ask the woman at Lakeview. It won't be nothing to ask her 'cause she on Section 8 herself. And I know I can't get the place anyway" We went to Lakeview, and Lucy found one of the managers, a middle-aged mother of two on Section 8. Lucy asked why other complexes didn't take Section 8.

"We can afford to wait for the rent. It's guaranteed money, but sometimes it's not on time. When someone's check is late, we're big enough to make ends meet. Just draw the money from someplace else."

Lucy continued: "If you all accept Section 8, then why are the rents so high?" The woman said: "That's their market value. Everyone pays that rent. Everyone here pays the same amount for rent, regardless of the funding source." Lucy still didn't have an apartment, but she had answers.

Lucy Evaluates and Refines Her Vocabulary for Section 8

The entire five-month period that Lucy spent looking for housing, she carried with her all of the important documents she would need to complete applications, all tucked into an accordion file folder that she clutched when we went into rental offices. In this folder, she kept: birth certificates, previous rental agreements, verifications of funding, references, blank forms to be filled out by the new landlords for HUD benefits, her current applications for places, a few "move-in special" coupons from the newspaper, previous utility bills, and budget statements from the utility companies. Anything related to a source of income, housing arrangement, and vital identification documents she kept in her file. This was her literacy tool chest to unlock bureaucracies' doors. "What gets me is that HUD, DSS and all them could fax each other these things instead of making me run around like a damn fool."

She brought her file into one apartment complex's rental office. We sat in front of the manager of the office, who said, "So, you have your application, verification forms, good. References, oh, nice. About your HUD, do you have a voucher or certificate?" Lucy looked at him like a deer frozen in an oncoming car's headlights.

"I have the verification of benefits. Isn't it there? Did I forget it?"

"Well, I'm looking for your voucher or certificate."

"I'm not sure what the difference is. But I'll call HUD and see what I have. I can get that to you in two days."

"Well, I'll hold the place for you." As Lucy and I walked to the car she said, "Couldn't he just pick up the f——ing phone and call over there?"

"We called the HUD office and found out, first, that Lucy had a voucher to receive HUD funding, not a certificate, an important difference. The voucher guarantees that Section 8 will be paid in the county in which the recipient currently resides. The certificate, though, is the E ticket of HUD funding. It allows the recipient to move across county and state lines, and still be guaranteed his/her Section 8 funding. On the phone Lucy asked, "Can I just get you to fax these forms? It's really hard for me to get around without a car." They said they couldn't do this because the place she wanted to move into was outside of their county, so she would have to go to the HUD office in Baxter County and ask them to fax it to the apartment complex, even though her case was still in the Danford County office. Since Lucy only had a voucher for Section 8, she had to live in a new county for one month before she could get a voucher in that county. Lucy explained this all to me after she hung up the phone. "Don't they get you? How I gonna move in the first place? They all got me coming and going."

Mirena and Lucy used their metacommunicative tools to judge the utility of certain language strategies: Mirena understood that her first tries at finding housing were meeting with failure, so she changed her approach; Lucy assessed the ways other people used their language to uphold regulations ("I just don't get it. How can they not accept Section 8. Or if they do, set the rent so high that Section 8 can't match it? It's guaranteed money in their pockets"). Their assessments reveal their understandings of the politics of language—what words can or can't do, how they're valued, by whom, and in what contexts. Mirena said, "Don't make a bit of difference to them how I sound. I still Black, and they ain't even gonna call me back. You wait. You'll see." She recognized the ways certain landlords looked for certain types of tenants— she knew that apartment would go to someone else. And Lucy knew she was caught between the political rock and the hard place: "Don't they get you? . . . They all got me coming and going." Mirena and Lucy both used metacommunicative assessments of the language in gatekeeping interactions to construct their multifaceted understandings of the political aspects of their numerous gatekeeping interactions.

Finally, both Mirena and Lucy used their assessments to intervene on their own behalf when they saw themselves in a perplexing situation. Mirena checked on the progress of her application only to find out that the landlord already rented the place. Lucy couldn't understand why the apartment complex set their rent so high, so she asked someone on the inside of two institutional structures. The woman she asked received Section 8 herself, but also worked as a manager part-time. Mirena and Lucy sought that point where they could enact their agency to try to push at the barriers they encountered.

What can we learn from these vignettes and stories that will help us understand the struggle and the tools? First and foremost, literacy is central to their daily lives, but especially when faced with the hardships of eviction. The applications, letters, and verifications represented these women's agency—their continued fight to work within the public institutions to find opportunity when confronted with constraints. Every turn of phrase, every blank filled in, every letter, represented a thoughtful, carefully weighed, persuasive appeal. Nothing taken for granted. Nothing easy. Residents called these literacy and discursive strategies "tools," after all, which is a word play on the functional and political uses of these literacies.

Their politically savvy literate skills also allowed them to co-opt the constraining language of institutions and make it more enabling. For example, eviction was sometimes constructed as a process that offered possibility; some women would joke about an eviction notice: "I don't move without it." (The joke echoes the commercial for

American-Express cards: "Don't leave home without it.") An eviction notice could be constructed as an invitation, a possibility to get out of the inner city, as Lucy's case shows. If the women happened to be on welfare, an eviction notice meant DSS would often provide her with the cash to move that she wouldn't be able to save otherwise. Besides this, their crisis situation made them eligible for other social services and resources. Ironically, they would have a much more difficult time moving if they *didn't* get an eviction notice. In a cleverly wrenching twist of logic, these woman sometimes constructed a forced removal into something of potential benefit to them.

In this chapter, we also see the cyclic process by which people in this neighborhood learned language skills, deployed them in gate-keeping encounters, and assessed and revamped them. In this cyclic fashion, interactions with gatekeepers built on one another and formed a textbook of cases from which people constructed their linguistic strategies. When looking at this process over time, though, one is struck by the sheer tenacity of the women in this neighborhood to do right by themselves and their kids, even under, or especially because of, the tremendous odds they faced. Mirena was homeless for three months. She and Kateesha stayed in Mirena's boyfriend's studio apartment; Richard and Samson stayed with Mirena's Italian friend, whom she affectionately called Pasta; and Upstate was arrested in late June and went to prison for another year and a half. Lucy spent five months looking for housing once she received her eviction notice (more on their stories in a moment). Still, these women managed to get up in the morning and hit the pavement, called landlords and caseworkers on the phone, waited in line, and talked to people they thought might help them out. They learned daily what to say and write differently in order to find opportunity despite the dismissive ideological presumptions of gatekeepers.

Since I don't want to paint the eviction process as strictly repressive, I need to end with outcomes, where they live and how they're getting by after their evictions. Both women eventually found a place to live using the same types of oral and literate skills illustrated in this chapter. Mirena moved six blocks east and up the hill from her inner city apartment. She's been living there ever since her eviction, going on three years now. Her house is clean, new drapes, small but cozy. When I last visited with her, her son Richard had just come from fishing, and Mirena was cleaning his good catch on her table. Her daughter and two middle sons are her hope: "Richard been working at Popeye's and doing real good in high school." He smiled at me from the living room looking taller and thinner, hair longer and braided, grown. "Samson still crazy, but going to school. And Kateesha in the third grade already. She's even writing in cursive!" Mirena had taped to her refrigerator some of the sentences and paragraphs Kateesha had written. Mirena had plans to return home to the Carolinas where her people were. But so far, she hasn't been able to pull her resources together. She found occasional work as a nurse's aid, but usually lost her job when a crisis hit her family. "My kids got to come first. What can you do? But I'm thinking I can get back home if I get enough back in taxes."

Lucy Cadens moved into a bright, three-bedroom apartment in a suburb of a neighboring city. She traded in the sirens, gunshots, and loud cars, for birds, squirrels, and maples. She fishes in a nearby creek and the river when the fish are running north in the spring. For $2, she can take a bus into the city to shop, file papers, and see doctors. Her child by custody, Leanna, is three years old and is now in preschool. Tony, who had left her for two years, is living with her again. She's wallpapered every room, made drapes and pillowcases, and bought new dishes and lamps through lay-away plans at a nearby K-Mart.

When she decreased her household, her kids and sister all had to find places to live on their own. Afriganzia, her son Xavior who just turned two, and Sasha live together just down the street from their old apartment. They moved across the street from their Aunt Vivian. Sasha works as a daycare provider for neighborhood babies, and also works with her Aunt Vivian taking care of physically challenged adults. Afriganzia will attend classes in the fall of 1996 in the local community college. Jolinda, her son Zimbabwe who will soon turn two, her two daughters, and grandchild, all live in Lucy's same complex in the country. The two households share a car between them. Disco has moved in with his girlfriend, but faces sentencing on drug charges. Chaos will move in with his girlfriend, whom he met while living in Lucy's new place. Chaos was recently baptized in the local church to which his girlfriend belongs.

All of this is to say that eventually, slowly, surely, Mirena and Lucy's daily language activities helped them shape a better life for themselves and others around them. Despite the many bureaucratic obstacles they faced along the way, they were able, in the end, to find better, safer, cleaner places to live—and in Lucy's case, her extended family benefited as well. We've seen the material and ideological struggles these women faced when evicted. The struggles to get a decent place to live, to avoid homelessness, and to get out of the inner city required them to work with many institutions. Even though many of these institutions were founded on liberal principles, these women also encountered institutional representatives who safeguarded the resources through foot-dragging, apathy, disrespect, unyielding adherence to unrealistic rental criteria, and prejudices against public assistance as a form of payment. We've seen, too, how these women continually developed and refined strategic language tools to obviate these struggles and eventually succeed using these strategies to find better places to live outside the inner city. All of these gatekeeping encounters and the trans-institutional literacy skills used before, during, and after them shape the cultural logic the community members used daily to gain a measure of the social and political equality these institutions were originally established to foster. This cultural logic was contingent upon these individuals' tacitly held hierarchy of civic duties to support their children, kin, and community.

Pulling back a bit further, we learn that we can no longer rely on the public transpiring of events as our sole indicator of the workings of hegemony. In public displays of deference, we see evidence of the types of consent that lead us to believe ideological domination is alive and well. The idea that consent is central to ideological domination figures heavily in Antonio Gramsci's thinking. Rhetorician Victor Villanueva summarizes Gramsci this way:

> The usual definition: hegemony equals ideological domination. Gramsci adds an essential qualifier: domination by consent. Without consent hegemony fails. For the most part consent is granted ideologically. . . . As long as interests are met, and as long as general senses of morality and ethics are assuaged, consent continues to be granted. Hegemony survives. (1992, 20–22)

If we extricated the public transcripts from the hidden transcripts presented in this chapter, we would find ample evidence of ideological consent, of individuals apparently buying into the terms of their oppression. In fact, code-switching could represent the worst form of "domination by consent," where Mirena and Lucy appear to adopt the language of landlords and DSS representatives, even though it may not be to their advantage to do so. But we can only make this claim if we are willing to ignore the hidden transcripts that present themselves in private communications among community residents that take place before and after their interactions with wider society's institutional representatives. For, in the hidden transcripts, we see that individuals critique, question, seek paths around, and attempt to subvert the racist and classist ways these institutions work. Consent, then, is only a facade, a mask for dissension, worn in public to appease. To admit this is to also admit that hegemony falters, stammers, and has to work hard in order to maintain itself against people who are always testing its possibilities, probing its limits, and seeking its loopholes.

But a few will look at the bottomline results of Mirena's and Lucy's evictions and say that, as Villanueva does, "their interests are met. . . . [but] hegemony survives." A point I do not dispute. Lucy and Mirena have, in the best of possible interpretations, only gained small victories here, and still they remain in social positions where they do battle daily for resources and respect. Yes, hegemony survives. But that isn't the point. The point is that hegemony survives, but not easily, not in taken-for-granted ways, and not in monolithic, unyielding terms. These vignettes and literacy artifacts have shown us that in the broad space between domination and resistance we find bitter laughter, negotiation, trial and error, insults, compromise, and, above all, critical awareness. In the next chapter, I'll overview the ways critical consciousness pervades residents' socialization process into institutional language.

5   Institutional Language in an Inner City

*In large complex societies, such as the United States, the . . . extent of
intrusion of government agencies in the daily lives of citizens may have
combined to set up conditions in which literacy no longer has many of the
traditional uses associated with it. . . . These shifts in large societal contexts for literacy are easily and frequently talked about, but their specific
effects on communities . . . though occasionally inferred, are very rarely
examined.*

—Shirley Brice Heath, "Protean Shapes in Literacy"

In the last chapter we saw how often the men and women in this
neighborhood had to deal with the literacy and representatives from
wider society's institutions: philanthropic organizations, the Department of Social Services, HUD, and landlords. To negotiate these and
other institutional interferences, residents developed complicated
meaning-making techniques. These techniques included the ability to
question the language used in documents, to selectively read for information necessary in order to circumvent a problem, and to insightfully
determine the power structure of situations and institutions from the
barest shreds of contextualization cues and texts. From a young age,
Quayville's inner city residents were socialized into and learned the
linguistic strategies needed for working through oral and literate forms
of institutional language. To date, little research has been done on
institutional language, as Heath notes, leaving us with a couple of
questions: What oral and literate skills does institutional language
include? And how do individuals learn and acquire these skills? This
chapter surveys the types and kinds of rhetorical tactics developed in
communities where the intrusion of government agencies reaches most
aspects of living.

And I do mean most aspects, for example, *the basics*: food, shelter, clothing, and utilities; *the relational*: living arrangements (RIP and HUD did not allow extended families to live together), marriage (DSS typically revoked funds to those who married), and child welfare (the policing branch of DSS regularly conducted in-home assessments); as well as *the possible*: employment (if an adult woman worked for poverty wages, DSS cut her benefits, even though her wages would not cover child care), education (DSS cut benefits to those who attended college, but maintained some benefits to those who attended vocational school), and job training (DSS benefits only covered training for work in service industries). Individuals continually honed oral and literate proficiencies attendant upon these areas of influence. In their institutional language uses, community members both resisted and accommodated dominant structures as they withstood daily material and ideological struggles.

Residents often discussed with each other their interactions with institutional representatives. When they did so, their critiques modeled analyses of daily political struggles for younger generations sitting and playing nearby. The youths and teens, therefore, acquired a sense of the language used in contending with wider society's public agencies. Area residents instructed each other on ways to linguistically grapple for respect and resources. Residents taught and learned from each other through intentional reflection on language use that was saturated with critical and oppositional values. To illustrate these points, I refer to two vignettes, one interaction, and one extended literacy event. First, two short sketches reveal how a child and a young adult both set and police boundaries of influence with social workers. Next, two more vignettes demonstrate older residents speaking about the complexities of working with the Quayville police and the NAACP. Then, I describe how four children, ages 9 to 11, made meaning from a parking ticket I received. Finally, a teen's doodle written on the back of a diner placemat reveals how she explored the power structure of her community using the metaphor of a popular card game in her neighborhood, Spades. These examples all reveal ways that children, teens, and adults spontaneously display and practice their institutional language skills.

Some scholars attempt to place literacy events like these into neat categories. For example, in her ethnography of inner city literacies, Denny Taylor defines literacy events as instrumental and creative. "Instrumental writing—writing to meet practical needs and to manage or organize everyday life—was of primary importance to the families of Shay Avenue. It included writing to gain access to social institutions or helping agencies" (182). Given this definition, the children's negotiation of a traffic ticket would fall under the category of instrumental literacy. The teen's doodle would fall under Taylor's category of "creative writing," when "writing became an art form, as the doodling of names became a means of self-expression" (186). Her sketches across the page and flowery lettering on this diner placemat would indeed look like a doodle if extracted from the context of its creation. But, if I called the literacy events I'm about to describe merely instrumental or creative, I would do a disservice to the elaborate knowledge present in the linguistic events surrounding these artifacts. These oral and literate events I'm calling institutional because of their highly political nature, and through them children and adults learn to assert themselves in the face of long-standing institutional influences in their daily lives. Because I've located these literacy events in the often unseen symbolic systems of community residents, we're able to appreciate how these individuals learn to construct the power relations between themselves and wider society's organizations, and how through these constructions they develop politically strategic plans and skills to both accommodate and resist. In other words, we begin to comprehend how critical awareness develops in this inner city through daily language use.

"She Ain't Got Permission"

Marquis (12), Richard (13), D'Andre (11), and I sat together in the office of one of the social workers at the center. They wanted to compose and perform a rap using a notebook for drafts, my tape recorder for practice, and two books for ideas and phrases. Marquis opened the office supply closet looking for a pen and came across a small stack of neatly folded bandannas. He took one, opened the door to the office, and walked out apparently to ask if he could have one.

"Where'd you get that? That's not yours," Sue said to Marquis.
"Can I have it?"
"No," the social worker put her hand on his arm to turn him back toward the office, "go put it back."
"Get your hand off me," he jerked back away from her. "You can't touch me." Sue folded her arms and watched as Marquis walked back into the office. With all the commotion, the three of us had stopped our work and Marquis addressed us loudly.

"She shouldn't be holding me. Tryin' to touch somebody." He opened the closet and put the bandanna back as he continued to speak in a conspicuously loud voice. *"She ain't got no permission touchin' nobody in here 'cept for her own stupid little baby."*

"I Can Call Him Nigger, Girlfriend, But You Can't"

Teen night in the center. Misty (15) and Megan, a social worker, stood next to each other making ice tea for the teens in the center. I stood a little behind them chatting with two other teens, Betty (17) and her younger sister Asia (16). Misty talked about a young man in the community which drew Betty and Asia's attention.
"He a nigger," she said, "he took her money and said Groan did."
Megan quickly replied, "You shouldn't call anyone a nigger."
"I can call him nigger, girlfriend, but you can't."
"I would never call anyone a nigger."
"And you best not. But I can."
Asia turned to Betty and said under her breath, "I heard that."
Betty nodded.

In both examples, community members called attention to and policed the boundaries delineating the influence and authority of caseworkers. Specifically, Marquis directly challenged Sue with the imperative "Get your hand off me," then he called her to task ("You can't touch me") on her breach of a standard operative in this neighborhood: social workers could not physically interact with a young community resident without parental permission. Marquis also loud-talked Sue to draw further attention to her overextension of her influence. Loud talking includes speech "which by virtue of its volume permits hearers other than the addressee, and is objectionable because of this. Loud talking requires an audience and can only occur in a situation where there are potential hearers other than the interlocutors" (Kernan 1971, 96). When Marquis entered the office and spoke with a marked increase in volume, ("She shouldn't be holding me"), the three of us became the audience he needed to publicly upbraid Sue, who had stepped out of line. "The loud talker breaches norms of discretion, his strategy is to use the factor of the audience to achieve some desired effect on the addressee" (97). Knowing Sue stood within earshot, Marquis used the three of us as a foil for (in)directly confronting Sue's vie for authority. "The loud talker is to assume an antagonistic posture toward the addressee. When it is used to censure, it reveals not only that the loud talker has been aggrieved in some way, it also indicates by virtue of making the delict public, that the speaker is not concerned about the possibility of permanently antagonizing his addressee" (100). Short of the bandanna that he returns to the closet, Marquis had nothing to lose by publicly chastising Sue. His direct imperative, coupled with his loud talking, ensured that the boundary of her control remained in check.

As his audience, Richard and D'Andre had modeled for them a fairly effective form of institutional language. When Marquis shame-faced Sue with his loud talk, Richard and D'Andre smiled, indicating their approval of Marquis's rhetorical moves. (They sat out of Sue's line of vision and so risked nothing in showing their support to Marquis.)[4] When Marquis closed the office door, I asked what that was all about. D'Andre said, "Hardly nobody like Sue." Richard shook his head and smiled at Marquis, "Man, you bad." D'Andre legitimized Marquis's skill in keeping Sue in line, while Richard appreciated the quality of Marquis's rhetorical moves. Through Marquis's example, D'Andre and Richard acquired several linguistic tactics to help them delineate and regulate the extent of social worker's influence over their actions.

Turning to the next vignette, Misty's strategy boldly halted the center worker's assertion of authority, at the same time as it flattered Megan's status in the community. Megan attempted to censor the types of language Misty used: "you shouldn't call anyone a nigger." In saying this, Megan endeavored to broaden the range of her authority: as a caseworker, she advocated for residents, but this position never entitled her to oversee residents' language use. Misty clearly demarcated ("I can call him nigger, girlfriend, but you can't") and limited ("You best not") the worker's status in the community. As Misty did this, though, she also paid homage to Megan's insider status by calling Megan "girlfriend," a term reserved for those who were close to each other. By doing so, Misty mollified Megan as she rebuked her.

Because Misty is Black, she legitimately used the term "nigger"; her claim to the use of this word indexes her status as insider in the community, a fact about her social status of which she's happy to remind the social worker. She's also in a social position to remind Megan of the limits of Megan's power and status in this community: Megan was her "girlfriend," close to her, but not close enough to use the word "nigger." The threat, "you best not," and the gloat, "but I can," reiterated the limited extent of Megan's power in this community.

Asia, Betty, and I stood close by as this exchange unfolded. Asia and Betty attended to the ways Misty set limits with Megan, and the ways Megan respected those limits ("I would never . . . "). When Asia turned to Betty and said softly, "I heard that," she endorsed Misty's actions behind the scene. ("I heard that" harkens back to call and response rhetoric where an audience shows strong support for what the speaker says.) Betty nodded in agreement. Behind the scene, Betty and Asia recognized the tussle taking place and confirmed Misty's linguistic means to keep Megan in her place as a both insider and outsider who should remain alert to her tenuous status.

Moving to the ideological level of these exchanges, we see how community residents become socialized into an oppositional value system. In both examples—with different linguistic means—young community members practice ways of checking undue intervention of social workers into their daily activities. In Marquis's direct challenge, the community's covert belief system manifests itself and indicates the attitude that approves outright resistance to a social worker's undue intrusion on personal space. When Marquis loud-talked, even as he complied with her request to return the bandanna, he indicated the hidden ideology that justified his chastisement of her actions. Given this community's value system, that is, his language use was necessary, appropriate, and justified if he was to keep the social worker from overstepping the limits of her authority.

Misty's language use points to the community's attitude that residents who identified as Black could legitimately critique a community resident using the word "nigger." When Misty first used the word, she meant to criticize a young man's actions, even as she signifies their shared identity ("He a nigger," she said, "he took her money and said Groan did"). And yet, Misty's use of the word placed Megan in an uncomfortable position. Smitherman shows the contradictory beliefs implicit in this exchange: Misty used "nigger" to "show disapproval of a person's actions" (62), "nevertheless, it bothers many Whites when Blacks use the word in their presence" (255). We see, then, a clash in values unfolded in this example; Misty highly valued the word "nigger" because it evidenced her freedom to use this word as a critique of an African-American resident; and Megan devalued the use of the word. In the end, Misty's values prevailed.

"Ain't Got Nothing but Rumors"

A Saturday morning and kids played outside the center, doors wide open to encourage a spring breeze. Just inside the doors, Salliemae and Major sat on opposite ends of one couch; Lucy sat across from them on the other couch. They discussed the new police program of drug sweeps in the neighborhoods close by theirs. They alternately feared and hoped the program would soon work into their area. While they hated the drugs and dealers up from the city, they also worried that their own kids might be targeted by association. Major's position was staunchly pro-police.

"Yeah you ain't got kids down here that might get caught up in the wide cast of their net," Salliemae sternly pointed out. The young boys stopped what they did outside, and leaned into the door jam of the center. One girl jumping rope told her friends, "Hol' up. Hol' up. Hol' up." The girls stopped playing, fell silent, and strolled over to the front stoop of the center. "They only targeting Blacks too, but you know, Major, them Scott boys [White family down the street] be selling more than any Blacks."

"I'm saying they all should be locked up. Get them all off the damn street."

"Why don't the cops really investigate who doin' what and then make their arrests?"

"Maybe they already have been. Maybe neighbors have been complaining and the cops are finally listening."

"Look here, Major," Salliemae's brow furrowed, "None of us really know who doin' what, who sellin' what and how much. Ain't got nothing but rumors and kids on the corner with new clothes."

"We should set up a meetin' with the police program. Tell them we like what they doin' but also let them know how they can do better," Lucy offered. At that point Megan said she could arrange one, and that they all could use the center. As the discussion ended, the boys left for the corner store, and the girls went back to Double Dutch.

"They Come In and They Don't Listen"

Tony and Lucy sat on their living room couch talking about the drug sweeps. After four rounds of arrests in other neighborhoods close by, residents called the NAACP to complain that the all-White police department targeted Blacks more than other groups, even though Whites dealt too.

"NAACP come in here like they gonna save us and they never talked to no one except for Bootsy," Tony talked fast, smoked furiously. As we talked, Lucy's children filtered in and out of the living room. Sasha sat in an armchair, her earphones around her neck.

Chaos asked his mom for a cigarette, and he sat next to me on the arm of the love seat.

"Bootsy?" I couldn't believe they only talked to her when her son was precisely the person in the area whom many had hoped would be arrested.

"I'm sayin'. Of course she gonna tell them a bunch of shit. But what gets me, they didn't even talk to her," tilting his head toward Lucy, "and she the one who started Neighborhood Watch." Sasha shook her head.

"They [the NAACP] come in and they don't listen. They think they already know so only talk to the one or two families who sure enough want the cops stopped. So now the cops stop the program and NAACP ain't doing nothin' about the drugs."

"And most people on the block want to get rid of the drugs," Tony exhaled in disgust.

These interactions took place only a few days apart and center around the same subject. Quayville's police had developed sting operations in the inner city where they closed down drug dealers' operations and crack houses. The police had begun at the northeastern section of Quayville's inner city and methodically worked their way down the hill to this neighborhood. In the first exchange, adults discussed the impending police action in their part of town, and in the second interaction, Lucy and Tony described why and how the NAACP stepped in to stop the police sweeps.

In both vignettes, adults critiqued the institutions that, in their zeal to serve and protect community residents, ended up paternalistically dismissing residents' concerns. In the first, Salliemae noticed a pattern in the arrests made during other raids ("They only targeting Blacks"). After noticing this trend, she asked, "Why don't the cops really investigate who doin' what and then make their arrests?" Her question could have resulted in more careful attention being paid to who was arrested and why. Her question clarified the situation; she complicated the Major's too easy call to arms without disregarding the Major's point—she too wanted the dealers off the street, but she wanted to ensure the police and residents carefully identified the dealers. ("None of us really know who doin' what, who sellin' what and how much. Ain't got nothing but rumors and kids on the corner with new clothes.") Salliemae put a stop to faulty assumptions being made on the basis of stereotypes—a young Black man standing on the corner wearing new sneakers may not be a drug dealer and should not therefore be arrested. One last linguistic device presented itself in this interaction: Lucy said, "We should set up a meetin' with the police program. Tell them we like what they doin' but also let them know how they can do better." Once they identified a problem in the ways an institution works, they took action to address it with a meeting intended to negotiate with the institutional representatives. Their critiques moved them to find ways to show their support for the police action and to intervene in it—to comply and contest.

In the second example between Tony and Lucy, the institutional language skills present different rhetorical moves. Tony named the assumptions pervading the missionary behavior of NAACP representatives: "NAACP come in here like they gonna save us." Since the NAACP failed to canvass the community for more perspectives on the police action, they took charge of the situation before they were invested with the authority to do so ("they never talked to no one except for Bootsy"). The organization assumed the prerogative to represent area residents based on the information provided by one family—the very family that had a vested interest in thwarting the police. Residents held a dim view of Bootsy as I found out at one of Mirena's get-togethers: "Bootsy be usin' her own son to support her and her habit"; "That bitch stupid. She ain't got enough sense to get her sorry ass down to welfare to recert [recertify her application]. Of course she got to look to Groan for her money"; and "You see her teeth? She been suckin' the glass dick [smoking crack cocaine]. Shit, they need to put her ass in Rehab and get Groan back to school." Bootsy solicited the help of the NAACP in order to prevent the police from picking up her son, her source of income and drugs. ("Of course she gonna' tell them a bunch of shit.")

Tony pointed out the irony of the NAACP's actions—they did not even talk to the person who founded and ran the crime prevention program. ("But what gets me, they didn't even talk to her," tilting his head toward Lucy, "and she the one who started Neighborhood Watch"). With such a narrow scope on the issue, the NAACP represented a slanted perspective on the topic, threatened legal action against the police, and effectively halted the police program. Lucy criticized the NAACP for behaving with top–down assumptions, "They come in and they don't listen." Both institutions work under paternalistic attitudes that overlooked the complexity of the situation and bypassed local perspectives. Both Tony and Lucy named the insidious presumptions and distinguished the political positions of public servants and community members as they unfolded in the course of events, and they called into question the predominant ideologies residing beneath the words and actions of institutional agents.

In the background of these interactions, young children and teens formed an attentive audience. When the Major, Salliemae and Lucy debated the police actions, children stopped their play to stand by the door and listen in. They hushed the newcomer to the group, so they could hear the adults come to terms with each other over a pressing issue. In Lucy and Tony's living room, Sasha and Chaos became the audience to the debate. Sasha shook her head when Tony noted the oversight in the NAACP's actions, indicating that Sasha listened with disapproval of the NAACP. In the larger scene of dialogues between adults, youths listen in as adults analyze the politics at work. Through the adults' model, youths learn rhetorical devices needed to define, redirect, and sometimes stave off altogether unwarranted institutional influences. The living room and community center transform into local classrooms for critical consciousness, where adults teach through example and youths learn through watching and listening.

As Heath found, children learn through the observation of, as opposed to participating in, adults' discussions. "Adults did not consciously model, demonstrate, or tutor. . . . Instead, parents talk about items and events of their environment. They detail the responses of personalities to events; they praise, deride, and question the reasons for events . . . They do not simplify their talk about the world for the benefit of their young" (1988, 352–53). Adults in Heath's study socialized the younger ones into the nuances of using language in daily living, without formal instruction. Yet in Quayville an interesting tension emerges from the socialization of younger generations into institutional critique, a tension best described using Freire's metaphors for education.

Even as the adults modeled critical consciousness, or dialogue in a liberatory sense, they did so based on a presumption similar to the banking model of education where "the teacher teaches and the students are taught; the teacher knows everything and the students know nothing; . . . the teacher talks and the students listen—meekly; the teacher acts and the students have the illusion of acting through the action of the teacher" (Freire 1970, 59). Adults in Quayville rarely valued the points of view of younger generations because they viewed their children's perspectives as hopelessly uniformed by virtue of the children's lack of experience. Children could watch and listen to adult conversations, but only on rare occasions did they interrupt their elders' flow of discussion. If they did so, they pulled an adult aside to ask a question for clarification without drawing attention away from the heart of the deliberations, without inserting themselves into the conversation. Since the younger generations had little authority to talk about subjects, their interruption of an adult conversation garnered hard stares and silence from the adults who would eventually resume the talk as though the teen had not spoken. The community symbolic system demands that when adults talk, youths listen, period. Thus, when language socialization took place through the modeling of skills by adults, the value system established a lecture hall atmosphere where young ones received knowledge in seemingly passive ways.

But the teens often listened actively to find the conflict in positions between adults. When teens had thoughts on the adults' exchange, they would recap with each other the heart of the adults' conversations and ask an adult to give them the gist from an insider's perspective. So when Lucy came away from the talk with Major and Salliemae, her daughter and other teens pumped her for information: "Why Major want everyone on the street to be picked up?" Lucy explained that Major was old and tired and didn't want to have any trouble. Another teen asked Lucy, "When you all gonna talk to the cops?" Lucy said she wasn't sure, but soon. "Well, who gonna make sure Megan call them in?" Asia asked. Lucy said she was "in there right now on the case." Then a tough question: "Why work with the police when they be all White and racists?" Here, we see a more separatist value system indicated in the teens' question. "Well how else you think we gonna get rid of the dealers?" The teen suggested that maybe they shouldn't even get rid of the dealers, and Lucy interrupted, "you say that cause your man be dealin.' " The teens all laughed, conceding Lucy's point. Since the teens risked being ignored or dismissed if they entered into the conversation of the adults, they created their own forums for judging events. Teens can be critical of institutions, but the adults' analysis holds the center stage because only the adults have the authority to present their assessments publicly. Language socialization through modeling just may be the banking model of critical pedagogy.

"You Gotta' Pay"

Marquis (age 11) was making a Valentine for Delilah (10) when I walked into the Neighborhood Center. I pulled out a parking ticket I had gotten earlier that day (and asked them what it was. Marquis tisked me and said "You know what it is." I said I did, but that I didn't know what to do with it since I was fairly new to the area. Samson (9) grabbed it out of my hands and walked to the door with it. He held it away from his face then up to the light.

Marquis asked me where I found it. I said I found it on my windshield. Delilah knew: "Oooh, you got a ticket for parking where you shouldn't have!" Samson came running back and teased me about the ticket saying I was going to go to jail. Marquis said, "She ain't going to jail for no ticket. She gonna pay somen." Then they asked how much, and Delilah read it off the ticket: "$25 for parking right here," she pointed to the address where I parked. I said that I didn't think there was anything wrong with parking there, and Samson leaned in and pointed to the violation that was circled from the list of possible violations. "Says here you owe $25 for parking in posted pro, prohi, prohi." Here Delilah leaned in and tried to sound it out with him: "Probation. Prohibition. What's that?" I pointed to the first part of the word, "Prohibit" and asked them if they ever heard that. I began giving them a bunch of sentences where they might have heard or read forms of it. "Swimming prohibited. Alcoholic beverages are prohibited in malls and places." Marquis said: "That means you can't do it. You mess up!" They all laughed at me then handed me back the ticket. I had one more question. "See, I'm not from around here. How do I take care of this?" Delilah tisked me and said I needed to go downtown. I asked where, and Samson took the ticket again. "Look, you can send it in. Just turn this end over and you got yourself an envelope." We were all surprised to see that the ticket itself was an envelope.

"Just put it on someone else's car," Marquis said.

Delilah said, "Yeah, on another Mazda."

"But won't they know it's my car?"

"It have your license number on it. [took ticket from Samson] Yeah, right here [pointed]. You got to pay it," Marquis said. But Samson was still thinking about it. "How they gonna know? See she can just put it on someone else's windshield or she can just forget about it."

"They got a copy of the ticket at the office, and if she don't pay she'll go to jail." I said really? And I started to read the ticket aloud, acting surprised that such a harsh punishment would be leveled on me. "All fines will double in two weeks from date of issue. Three unpaid tickets within eighteen months will constitute a scofflaw [lawbreaking] violation and may lead to suspension of registration."

Marquis and Delilah put the final word to it: "You gotta pay."
Delilah shook her head: "Twenty-five dollars too. You got it?"
"Yes, but not much more than that."
Then Marquis told us a story. "One time Shakil (his little brother,
8) gave me a ticket. I parked my big wheel out front of the house, and
he wrote me a ticket for a hundred dollars. Said I had to give it to
him too, or I was going to jail!" We all laughed at that, Shakil too.

Samson learns from the older kids how to troubleshoot this parking ticket as though it represents a problem to be solved. In fact, when
Samson asks questions to help me get around this ticket ("How they
gonna know? See she can just put it on someone else's windshield or
she can just forget about it"), he is instructed by Marquis, who has
more information about the matter ("They got a copy of the ticket at
the office, and if she don't pay she'll go to jail"). Marquis adds to the
discussion through his comic story of his little brother ticketing his big
wheel. This story not only showed how much practice Marquis and
Shakil already have with the literacy related to the justice system, but
it also models for Delilah and Samson a funny example of how to
transfer this literacy artifact from one context to another.

As they begin to think of what this artifact is, how it got on my car,
and what I should do about it, they construct it as a material problem
to be solved, a challenge, an issue ("Twenty-five dollars too. You got
it?"). They pass the ticket back and forth between themselves as they
collectively address ways out of its constraining discourse; it changes
hands five times within this short interaction. Each time it changes hands,
someone selectively looks for and locates information on the ticket that
would help me: Delilah looks to see what the fine was; Samson locates
the specific violation; Samson shows me how the ticket functioned as an
envelope; and Marquis checks if the ticket did indeed have my license
plate number on it. Such collective knowledge illustrates problem-solving skills needed when faced with pervasive material hardships.

Marquis and Delilah know not only what this artifact is, but know
how to ask questions about it in order to find ways to make it more
permissive, more open ("It have your license number on it?"). Asking
questions during problem solving is of course what teachers do to
help move students forward in their thinking. But Marquis's question
helps his friends think about the ticket differently; he models for them
a way to enact their agency when faced with an unwelcomed institutional influence. As he tries to find a way out of the ticket, he considers

the hypothetical consequences of such choices, as though he is playing chess. His question reveals Marquis's critical awareness of the social position I had to the city's traffic bureau. I had no way out.

They try to construct this ticket in enabling ways, looking for ways around its influence. Every literate and discursive strategy they use contributed to this goal—selective reading, collective problem-solving, constructing the ticket as a problem to be solved, and questioning options. Rather than passively assuming that the ticket needed to be paid, these children use institutional language skills to actively negotiate this literate artifact. In the end, they decide "you gotta pay," but only after they satisfy themselves that they had considered other alternatives to obviate this institutional influence.

Over and over again, community members collectively practice strategic readings of letters, applications, notices, and information packets, often pulling in family members and neighbors. Heath (1983) describes comparable collaborative literacy events to show the interplay between orality and literacy during literacy events. But what's interesting to me is how these individuals collectively construct the power relations between themselves and wider society's organizations, and how through these constructions they develop plans and skills to move through institutional influences in their daily lives. Sitting around a kitchen table for instance, individuals read aloud to a group all sorts of letters, bills, and receipts, and, as a group, they troubleshoot the unwanted institutional influence. As the adults talk, the children filter in and out of the room, sit on their laps, or play nearby, and all along they acquired these institutional language tools through their exposure to them. Someone would read a letter from DSS aloud:

> "They say I didn't recert [recertify], so they gonna sanction my ass for three goddamn months."
> "Did you recert?"
> "You know it. That day Shantel with me and we saw you coming out of Cost Hacker?"
> "Well haul her ass down there and tell them there a mistake. You got a witness to prove it."

Or someone would bring in a past due bill from the utility company:

> "Now where I gonna get the money for this?"
> "Just pay what you can. They won't cut you off if you given' 'em a little somen'. They just like men!"

"You know it, girl. I'd just call them and say you're in a tight situation and can you please set up a payment plan with them? Number's right there [pointing to the upper left-hand corner of the bill]."

Or someone would show the printout from the grocery store that indicates her benefits were declined:

"Get your ass down to DSS. And you best hurry up and get there before noon, 'cause you know they keep you waitin' during their lunch."

"I'd try to call 'em first. Sometimes that works for me. But you know they got a phone tree now, and your ass on hold for half an hour."

"You sure you got your benefits today? Mine's won't be here for two more days."

From decades of having institutions intervening in their daily lives, these community members model for their children ways to read into an organization, to find an access route to opportunity, to find a way out or around or through.

When viewing the children's interaction centered around my parking ticket, some might say that these children's effort to subvert the law is one of many urban pathologies—inner city residents trying to shirk their legal duties. They would claim that their language patterns represent evidence in support of the culture of poverty; children learn to mistrust the public institutions created to serve and protect them. However, solving the problem with the parking ticket represented an economic obstacle rather than a mistrust of the legal system. Figuring out what to do with this parking ticket became an occasion for deploying language skills in the service of saving money. These children view the parking ticket as much more than an inconvenience; it represents a material problem to be solved, an obstruction to get around if possible. While some have the luxury to simply pay a parking ticket with little more than an irritating second thought, these kids consider it deeply. That is, we may perceive an institutional literacy artifact like a parking ticket as a mere bother, yet this same ticket can infringe upon the limited monetary resources of inner city residents and so claim a good deal of their problem-solving time. These four kids construct this parking ticket as a material struggle in which having $25 *cash* in your pocket is more important than paying that money to the city.

Cash is rare in this inner city. Tenants pay rents using vouchers or direct payments from welfare to landlords; direct payment from DSS to the utility companies meets part of the bills; food stamps, certificates or WIC checks buy groceries; but cash in someone's hand or pocket or purse is a rare thing not to be taken lightly. If cash is on hand, it's out of hand just as quickly to pay for lay-aways, diapers, babysitters, soap, feminine hygiene products, and clothes. Considerable thought and energy goes into how to maximize each dollar. Sales sheets, coupons, advertisements for yard sales, trading stamps—these tools help residents maintain some cash in their pockets, and thus they're read, saved, clipped, shared, talked about, and collected. With so little cash, priorities change. Rather than a reflection of the pathologies of inner city residents, though, this principle reflects the often unseen luxury needed to work within many of society's mainstream institutions. Through the literacy needed to negotiate a traffic ticket, then, we gain insight into a whole web of literate and problem solving practices of urban life. As they become older, urban youth hone their abilities to form interpretations of social power structures and their position within these structures.

"The Game of Power"

With huge green eyes and light skin, Afriganzia often became the object of ridicule in her neighborhood; she just didn't look Black to her neighbors, and she'd fight them if they said that to her. Lucy Cadens confessed to me that when Chaos and Afriganzia were born, she wanted to leave them at the hospital: "I'm Black, their daddy blacker than Black, why I got these kids with blue and green eyes? Shit, I told the nurse to take them back and go get my own." I thought about this as I looked into Afriganzia's eyes, were they blue, or green? She and I were sitting in a diner talking about what we were going to do in the next meeting of the literacy program we were co-directing. Our conversation turned to the card game, Spades, we had played the night before with two of her friends. I asked her if she noticed any similarities between the community and the card game. The object of Spades is to collect books with your partner. One person leads with a card and the other players follow suit and discard; the highest card takes the book. All Spades are trump, meaning they can "outrank" other cards and take a book. This means there's a hierarchy of cards consistent across every game, but the ways in which players earn books change with every hand.

As we talked about this game as a metaphor for her community, she turned over her placemat and began to doodle. In the top left corner of the placemat, she ranked the cards from highest to lowest, and next to these ranks she wrote names. We talked about why each person was listed next to each card—the two most powerful and active Black women in this neighborhood were first. As she spoke about why people had the status they do, I asked if I could quote her on the placemat. Because the women were "giving, caring, teachers, educators, philosophers, doers, hardworking, responsible, and respectful," they were "everyone's mothers" and the most powerful in the community. Next she listed the supervisor of the two social workers in the neighborhood center, then she listed the social workers. Their power in the community was most often challenged by other older women. When these social workers "worked for the community, they move up the rank."

Men held the rank of queen of spades. Their contributions to the community came from resources they were able to gather for individual families. The younger men "running drugs have skills and knowledge and money, but they can't get jobs. Not many mens can get jobs."

She moved further down the hierarchical list, and just under the young men, she wrote the name of her neighbor, Gertrude, a White single mother of four who bought her home through a HUD-financed loan some years before. Gertrude had status because people knew and liked her, and because, "She shoot high when she has to," Afriganzia said when she wrote Gertrude's name next to the jack of spades. Figurative translation: Gertrude will discard a high card only when she has to in order to take a book that's important to her game. Literal translation: she'll use her social status to forward an agenda about which she felt strongly. Afriganzia continued: "She don't often get involved, unless it concerns her or her own, and then she got some pull." Besides these trump cards, the other women, children and teens held the ranks in other suits. Afriganzia sat back in the booth, put her pen down, and looked thoughtfully at the doodle as she drank her soda.

She wrote across the page in large flowery letters: "The Game of Power." She realized, "It's like this all over too, ain't it? Not just in the hood?" I agreed and said she already knew this. After all, she recognized the supervisor had more power than the social workers in the community center. "So they're playing Spades at United Ministry, RIP, welfare. . . . " As she listed places, she drew one large circle around her community and many smaller circles overlapping this and each other. The overlapping circles triggered another reflection for her. The women in the neighborhood "are really good talkers, good with language. They cut all across these," as she said this she drew an arrow through the circles. "Using this," and she drew a sheet of paper at the end of the arrow with scribbled lines representing words on a page.

Afriganzia uses her knowledge of Spades to describe the social and political structure of her community. In making a hierarchical list of community members, she knows how a person's authority and status depend upon the types of knowledge and resources one contributes to the community. For example, the young men "running drugs have skills and knowledge and money, but they can't get jobs. Not many mens can get jobs." These men have to know at a glance who to sell to and who to avoid; how to deal without leaving any evidence of dealing, that is, dropping the "buy" on the ground, walking away from it, and collecting the payment in a handshake further on down the block; and they have to know how to calculate a deal and keep track of good customers. Many people, however, found all dealing morally reprehensible and socially lethal to their community. Of course, dealing produced a bit of money that young men give to their families, or a pregnant girlfriend, or the mother of their children. Yet Afriganzia realizes one limitation to these young men's social status: the instability and illegality of their work. Because their stability as providers is uncertain, their status within the community is lower, even though she respects them for what they try to contribute and what they know.

In other words, she assigns a social role to each of the area residents, a role with a certain status depending upon the resident's knowledge and resources given to the community. In the *Social Construction of Reality*, sociologists Peter Berger and Thomas Luckmann argue that "institutions are embodied in the individual experience by means of roles," and that, "by virtue of the roles s/he plays, the individual is inducted into specific areas . . . of knowledge" (1966, 74–77). Part of Afriganzia's language skill represented in her "Game of Power," reveals her understanding of how people get positioned in institutions according to their social roles and the knowledge needed to fill these roles.

Afriganzia also suggests that a person's social status in this community rests upon his/her ability to cross institutional boundaries using many types of language skills in order to gain resources. The women with high status in the neighborhood "are really good talkers, good with language. They cut all across these." As she said this she drew an arrow through the overlapping circles that represented institutional organizations, their borders, and their interrelations with each other. Further, when I asked why Salliemae held such a high status (ace of spades, the third highest card), Afriganzia replied "she know a lot about how the system works—who to talk to at welfare or at United Ministry to get what you need. She been telling people what to do for years." Some women in the neighborhood enjoy a high rank on her hierarchy because they act as linguistic border crossers, that is, able to speak and write in sophisticated ways to institutional representatives across a variety of contexts.

Finally, Afriganzia's doodle shows her understanding of the ways a person's social rank can fluctuate up and down the hierarchy according to his/her civic deeds. If someone contributes to the well-being of others, they garner more respect and honor for themselves among the residents. The women in the neighborhood are "doers"; when I asked Afriganzia what she meant by this two days later, she said, "You know, they clean the garbage on the block, organize parties. They do things for the other people, make the whole place better." But if a person inconsistently contributes to the community s/he loses status. For instance, when the social workers "worked for the community, they move up the rank," the implication being that their contributions to the community are inconsistent, and therefore their social rank fluctuates.

Afriganzia applies her construction of social positions and status in the community to the ways people use their status to intervene on someone else's behalf. Note how she indicates Gertrude's role in the neighborhood: Gertrude "shoot high when she has to," as Afriganzia said when she wrote Gertrude's name next to the jack of spades. "She don't often get involved, unless it concerns her or her own, and then she got some pull." Gertrude asserts her limited status in this community when she has an agenda of her own. In fact, I only saw her do this twice, once when she supported the police drug sweep on the block, and once when she wanted the neighborhood center social workers to do more door-to-door work. And both times, the older Black women supported her agenda by "shooting low," in effect, they handed over their authority to Gertrude as an endorsement of Gertrude's actions. Afriganzia drew an enlightening parallel between every play in a hand and every interaction among community members and institutions. In these gatekeeping encounters, a community member's social position invests them with certain types of resources; and one person's goals could be advanced even more when someone with the social status to do so intervenes on that person's behalf.

Thus, from Afriganzia's doodle, we see that institutional language tools include both the ability to determine a person's rank (position or role in a community), as well as the ability to apply this knowledge to social structures besides her community: "It's like this all over too, ain't it? Not just in the hood?. . . So they're playing Spades at United Ministry, RIP, welfare." Each circle she drew around United Ministry, RIP, and welfare represents gatekeeping encounters that the smartest women in this inner city deftly negotiate with their language. Afriganzia, in short, demystifies institutions that affect her daily life. The metaphor of Spades became a backdrop for comparison of the positionality of residents. With it, she described who holds what authority, why, and how one uses his/her authority to help someone (or not). As we'll see in the next chapter, demystifying a social structure, as part of institutional language, helped one woman negotiate the application process to a local university.

During this literacy event, Afriganzia overlaid her knowledge of games onto her interpretation of her community's politics. She modeled the community on the placemat without formal instruction about how to do so. Once I asked her if she noticed any similarities between the neighborhood and the card game we had played the night before, she consciously reflected on her experiences in this local community. Thus, she also learned as she doodled. She even continued her socialization and learning later that evening when, again playing Spades with her girlfriends, Afriganzia spoke with them about "the Game of Power." (Although I was not there, I spoke with two other teens who verified they all had talked about the community's power structure and Spades. Lashana told me that she even chided Afriganzia for not seeing it sooner: "I says to her, 'I been seeing that game.' "). Given these teens' reactions to Afriganzia, we see that this type of conscious reflection on power structures is characteristic behavior in this community. In acquiring and learning institutional literacy, these teens put words to their latent knowledge of the political and social structure of their neighborhood.[5] Afriganzia's doodle revealed the intricate cultural logic behind the linguistic tools needed to negotiate many gatekeeping borderlands that crossed through daily living in this inner city.

These analytical, oral, and literate events reveal area residents' extensive and ever-developing knowledge of the ways to deal with institutions that impact their lives. Even though some would characterize these linguistic patterns as rudimentary, or basic, these behaviors actually encompass many literate abilities taught in school: such as analysis of text and other signs, comparison of one learning situation to another, transference of knowledge from one context to another, and questioning the taken-for-granted. To acquire and learn institutional literacy, then, individuals

- questioned each other and looked for answers in their observations and the literate artifacts before them;
- modeled, on paper and through narrative, ways of transferring knowledge to other contexts;
- collectively read and assessed a situation or literacy artifact;
- problematized the actions of institutional agents or artifacts;
- constructed these problems in the most enabling ways possible;
- discussed the outcomes and effects their language choices possibly have;
- named and safeguarded boundaries of influence for institutional representatives.

But these language events also offer us an understanding of just how politically strategic institutional language can be. To be well versed in the politics of institutional language, in short, means that a person uses a variety of signs

- to construct power relations between one's self and others, particularly institutional representatives;
- to determine who has what types of knowledge, resources, and social status in an organization, in other words, to demystify an organization's social structure;
- to develop plans and skills to negotiate unwelcomed institutional influences;

- to name the assumptions underpinning the actions of public servants;
- to use language persuasively in trans-institutional contexts, that is, to be linguistically strategic in encounters with many of wider society's institutions.

From a young age, children learned the language necessary in order to recognize and obviate the long-standing material and ideological struggles in their daily lives. Using a highly developed knowledge base of institutional language, these kids and young adults weighed the authority and status behind other people's statements, both oral and written. They determined the power structure at work, and where they stood in relation to this structure as well.

This community's knowledge and learning was based on a tacit assumption: all actions are potentially meaningful signs. Afriganzia "read" community members' social status from what they did and said. Remember, the women in the community who were "doers" had the highest social rank. Their actions were part of the moral and civically minded gestures that gave them a high rank in "The Game of Power." In previous chapters, we've seen this as well: recall how Lucy read the social worker's smirk as a sign of disrespect in chapter 1; remember how the long list of ideological struggles mentioned in chapter 3 stemmed from these men and women's interpretations of gestures (i.e., a women clutching her purse tighter, or someone crossing the street); and remember in chapter 4 how Lucy felt comfortable speaking directly with a manager instead of through me, simply because he addressed her with respect and used her full name. In upcoming chapters, we'll also see how community members interpreted people's choices as meaningful signs during gatekeeping interactions.

My point is this: a hand gesture, stance, facial expression, tone of voice, or turn of phrase, any of these and other signs factor into community members' construction of the political significance of a situation or document. In institutional literacy, people make meaning from interpreting words and actions. "Reading" a situation, a highly valued analytical behavior among adults, means individuals construct the power relations of interactions given the cues observed in people's words and deeds. Often area residents would ask a friend to validate their "read" on a situation: "What your read on that?" or "How you read that?" or "What you make of that?" This reading allowed them to interpret the ways in which they were construed as other by people they considered others. As a means of navigating gatekeeping encounters, individuals do what ethnographers do as a means for creating scholarly work: they see human behavior as "symbolic action which, like phonation in speech, pigment in painting, line in writing, or sonance in music, signifies" (Geertz 1973, 10). Part of institutional literacy, then, is being able to differentiate between a twitch or a wink in order to name your struggle.

The orality and literacy in this community indicate residents' striving to gain control over institutional influences. Heath described numerous literacy events in Trackton schools, work places, and churches and finds that:

> members of each community have different and varying patterns of influence and control over forms and uses of literacy in their lives . . . In institutions, such as churches, they may have some control. In other institutions such as their places of employment, banks, legal offices, etc., they have no control over literacy demands. (1988, 370).

By control, I believe she means access to and interaction with the literate forms and oral customs associated with each institution's brand of language use. In Quayville's inner city, individuals know language skills that allow them to gain a measure of control over the institutional literacies they have access to and interact with. These skills include selectively reading a document, asking insightful questions to make a document enabling, or constructing a document as a problem.

The knowledge associated with institutional literacy in this community developed from years of material and ideological struggles with wider society's institutions. Residents' value this knowledge because it allowed them to circumvent unwanted pressures from organizations outside of their community, but the extent to which they value linguistic cunning shifts across generations: the younger generations value separatist and direct challenges to the authority of society's organizational members. They can do so because they have little to lose. Older generations, though, understand that often institutional forces can work to their advantage; and when institutions fail to work to their advantage, residents strategically shape their language to sway these institutional workings at the local level. Both generations recognize the struggles with public organizations, but the adults have less room to throw off these struggles outright. Adults craft language skills to play a deeper game.

6 "Racism Always on the Front of My Mind"

"To be accepted into a place you got to sound like them without changing who you are. But once you in and they see who you are, you're Black, then maybe you can be your old self. But at first, you got to look and act like you one of them . . .

I'm so used to flipping into their talk, I do it real easy.
But the racism always on the front of my mind."

—Afriganzia Cadens, on her use of
language with institutional representatives

Learning institutional language skills sometimes compromised and often complicated community residents' cultural beliefs. The examples presented in this chapter show how one teen, Afriganzia, practiced her institutional language during the short time she was employed in the Neighborhood Center. As she learned to co-direct a summer literacy program, she often reflected on the social and cultural challenges of working with people in White society. The goal of this chapter is to show how she conceptualizes the challenges to and pressures on her own community-based beliefs as she practiced her linguistic knowledge used for gaining institutional resources. While I show Afriganzia becoming even more socialized into institutional language skills, this chapter also considers the cultural and social implications of her socialization.

I opened this chapter with Afriganzia's reflection on speaking within dominant discursive patterns when trying to access institutional resources.[6] In this quotation, she refers to the skill of masking one's identity in order to gain entry to resources and institutions—

without ever giving up a sense of self-identity and culture. Mask wearing as an institutional language skill means retaining a sense of self and cultural beliefs even as one veils these beliefs with language that appeals to White society's norms.

Mask wearing suggests a critical awareness of and intervention in day-to-day politics that demand of individuals much more than a simple change of communicative patterns to fit into different situations. John Baugh, a linguist who studied African-American street culture and language, found that "people tend to adopt styles of speaking that are suited to their social needs and aspirations" (1983, 6). In reference to the speaking and literacy skills needed to integrate into mainstream organizations, he asks: "if there are pressures for group loyalty and pressures to stop using street speech, how does the individual cope with this constant tug-of-war?" (8). A sensitive question, a question many have asked if in different terms (see, for example, Smitherman's discussion of push/pull pressures to linguistically integrate; Du Bois's discussion of African-American's double consciousness; and Fanon's psychoanalysis of having a Black face while wearing the White mask of linguistic integration). Unfortunately, Baugh undermines the acumen of his question by saying that the tug-of-war really amounts to little more than a need for street speakers to be in contact with mainstream language users. The individual's tug-of-war: "is actually less of a problem than might be expected, because the various dialects seldom overlap in the same speaking context. . . . If street speakers face a dilemma it is one not so much of being torn between two forces but of learning how to move from one extreme to the other with ease and proficiency" (8). The residents of Quayville's inner city did move with proficiency and from one context to another—but the process was never simple as Baugh implies. Granted, Baugh studied "the speech of blacks who have had limited contact with whites" (5) and who, as a result, may not have had the daily practice to develop proficiency in institutional language. Yet, even with proficiency, individuals in this study never simply switched between codes; instead, they continually attended to predominant racist and classist assumptions that influenced their need to code-switch. Residents in Quayville's inner city certainly show competence in their linguistic abilities to move between community and institutional contexts, but we need to characterize the ways their linguistic dexterity developed in relation to an oppositional ideology.

Learning institutional language was socially complex for the residents. It often brought into the open their struggles with insidious

value judgments and prejudices that typically rested beneath the surface of their interactions with society's institutional representatives.
Anthropologist John Ogbu characterizes some of the conflicting cultural values involved when African Americans deal with institutions.
As members of an involuntary minority group, or a group that did not
chose to come to America, African Americans "distrust white Americans and their institutions to a greater extent than immigrants" (1995,
90). Because dominant groups have consistently demeaned and devalued Black language and cultural practices, Ogbu says, African Americans "develop a cultural frame of reference that is in opposition to the
white cultural frame of reference" (1995, 96). Given these oppositional
cultural values, those individuals who "speak standard English and
behave according to standard rules of . . . conduct and practices, are
often accused by their peers of 'acting white' or of . . . being 'Uncle
Toms' " (96). Ogbu's characterization, while sensitive to oppositional
politics and cultural beliefs, tends to overlook the elaborate ways in
which conflicting values can be masked to appear as consensual values. In day-to-day lived experiences, individuals find linguistic means
to appear as though they comply to predominant institutional language norms—even as they maintain their oppositional beliefs. More-
over, Quayville's inner city residents openly analyzed the social
complexities of learning oral and literate skills that occupied the middle
ground between these conflicting value systems.

Learning institutional language means learning to be critically
conscious of the politics and presumptions that lead one to use these
skills in the first place. Part of this political awareness stems from
grappling with the tension between remaining loyal to one's home
culture when using a "standard" English that homogenizes race and
class. Achieving fluency in both Black and White English was easy
because interactions with Whites occurred nearly every day; but
biculturalism, where a person's cueing and linguistic devices reflect
both Black and White cultural and symbolic systems, was more complicated to accomplish.

As soon as area residents considered the implications of using
institutional language (and they often did), the tension of biculturalism
manifested itself. In his book *Bootstraps: From an American Academic of
Color,* rhetorician Victor Villanueva speaks of his own linguistic integration into mainstream institutions such as schools, universities, and
the military. He says, "biculturalism does not mean to me an equal
ease with two cultures. That is an ideal. Rather, biculturalism means

the tensions within, which are caused by being unable to deny the old or the new" (Villanueva 1993, 39). When learning the oral and literate moves needed to work within institutions, individuals contend with the tension of justifying language use against two cultural standards. For community residents, the tension of becoming fluent in institutional language rested primarily in *avoiding* the "racelessness" Villanueva speaks of (a term he learned from Signithia Fordham). Racelessness "is the denial of other-cultural affiliation, a denial of the collective, any collective; it is the embracing of America's dominant ideology, the ideology of individualism" (39–40). Learning institutional language skills meant wearing a mask of compliance, appearing to adopt predominant language varieties, and making oneself appear raceless. At the same time, learning institutional language also meant consciously separating oneself from the mask, maintaining loyalties to Black language and culture, and critiquing the social order that makes mask-wearing necessary in the first place.

In public interactions with institutional representatives, community members covered their own cultural beliefs in order to appeal to the social and symbolic systems of wider society. However, in private contexts, out of earshot or sight of institutional agents, individuals would reflect the sociocultural complexities involved when masking. When comparing the public and private transcripts (Scott 1985), we see that in the public transcript people code-switch with proficiency and adeptness; but in the hidden transcript they reveal their elaborate conceptualizations of the conflicting value systems implicit in their public exchanges. Yes, individuals deftly switch back and forth between codes depending on the situational context—this skill is so familiar to Afriganzia, she can "do it real easy." However, individuals in this inner city never *simply* changed their linguistic codes to fit situational contexts. When Afriganzia says, "racism always on the front of my mind," she refers to the politics involved in contexts where she uses institutional language skills, such as masking. She understands that because of racist attitudes that devalue her own language and culture, she has to take up the prestige language. In the "front of her mind," she remains aware of the racism in assumptions about what counts as appropriate language when engaging with larger society. Individuals in Quayville's inner city associated the institutional linguistic devices they learned and used with the racism they faced when dealing with public servants.

When being socialized into institutional language skills, then, area residents also had to figure out for themselves the extent to which using prestige dialects in asymmetrical relations would compromise their own sense of cultural identity. That is, they grappled with the boundaries that delineated how much they were willing to mask their identity and cultural values when using institutional language. In wearing the White mask associated with institutional language, then, area residents consciously and carefully avoided changing their face to fit the mask. They intellectually separated the mask from their cultural identity in order to insure some measure of sociocultural integrity, but also in ways that brought to the surface the insidious assumptions they encountered in their daily activities. When learning to mask language in order to work within institutions, in other words, individuals' implicit assumptions about race and politics often move to the realm of the explicit, the front of the mind, where they consciously determine the point at which using prestige dialects will compromise too much of their cultural identity. Instead of viewing linguistic masking as a taken-for-granted, easy behavior, we need to see linguistic masking as a behavior that often requires and brings to the surface political commentary.

The sociocultural complexities of acquiring and learning institutional language skills can best be seen when teens' lives alter and they're thrust into taking full responsibility for themselves. Such a change in lifestyle resulted from moving out of the parents' home, pregnancy, employment, or graduating from high school. These transitional periods are marked by increased experiences with wider society members and a corresponding increase in the types and kinds of social networks the individuals could draw upon for resources and support. When teens suddenly shift into the roles of young adults, they quickly learn to play a deeper game with their language, language they've acquired and learned in the community. Understandably, the lifestyle changes teens underwent prompted considerable reflection among themselves as they came to terms with, on the one hand, honoring their own oppositional ideologies, and on the other hand, working with gatekeepers in order to meet daily needs. Their reflections help us characterize the dynamics of cultural politics and social identity related to their growing competence with the oral and literate devices needed to access resources from organizations.

Although Afriganzia had not yet experienced the life changes that force a teen to interact more with wider society, she co-directed with me a summer literacy program, called Voice of the Children (hereafter Voice), that required her to work closely with center staff members and other institutional agents from universities and libraries. Voice invited a half dozen children in the area to read, discuss, research, and write about issues important to them. Over twelve weeks, the children generated ideas, interviewed other community residents, located books in the local public and university libraries, and drafted short essays on computers in the library of the university where I studied. When I proposed the summer literacy program to United Home in early April of 1993, they offered to pay $4.25 an hour to a teen in the area to act as a co-director. The teen would help organize the lessons, secure resources, as well as tutor children in writing and the use of computers. As co-director of Voice, then, Afriganzia became an institutional representative who also worked between institutions in order to provide area children with a meaningful experience.

As her social role brought her into contact with institutional representatives, Afriganzia acquired and learned institutional language strategies that challenged her sense of identity and cultural values. As a community member, center volunteer, and project co-director, she occupied multiple social positions producing not so much the double consciousness Du Bois speaks of, but a multifaceted identity. In the following excerpts from my fieldnotes, Afriganzia continually shifts positions within competing value systems. These examples show an ebb and flow process of working between emic systems across time and contexts.

Afriganzia Telephones the Public Library

"Hello, I'm co-directing a summer literacy program for children on 34th Ave.? I work at United Home's Neighborhood Center. I was wondering if I could schedule a tour for sometime next week?" [person on the other line responds]

"Will this cost anything?" [some reply]

"Also, what do the kids need to do to check out a book? . . . A proof of residency? You mean like a bill?" [some reply]

"All right. Thank you and we'll be seeing you next week." She hung up the phone and I sat looking at her. She asked me what I was looking at and I said, *"Jesus. That didn't even sound like you."*

"I know, huh? I like to mess with people. You know, they think you one way when you talk like that. Like you have blond hair and blue eyes, but when they see you, they all caught off guard. [Here she imitates the reaction of the person who would be seeing her after talking with her on the phone] 'Oh, you're so-and-so? We were expecting someone, uhhh. Something uhhh . . . ' "

"Why do they act so surprised?"

" 'Cause they stereotype you. So when they see me, well, I blow their image all apart. I like to f——k with their minds like that too."

Minutes from a Staff Meeting at United Home, Recorded by Afriganzia

Bridge Plan and Evaluation

Topic	Discussion	Action
1. Ceramics money is missing. Center is being used more frequently by residents.	$57.00 is missing. Who has access to the file cabinet? Who has keys? Salliemae, Major, and Lucy.	Megan will talk with Lucy re: safety of key.
	Teen girls were in the center until 1 A.M. Some concerns about how late people are in the center.	• Megan will talk to teen girls about this. • Having meeting with neighbors to come up with rule. Date:
2. Confidentiality	Ellen reported that neighbors were concerned about the confidentiality of the log book.	Staff will tighten up where log book is left. Staff will try to get locked file cabinet.
3. Tutors leaving	Evette has planned a tutor appreciation 4/26—kids are making thank-yous	Evette will distribute flyers. Evette will purchase stuff for party.

Afriganzia and I Plan the Upcoming Sessions

As we ate, we talked over what we could do in the next Voice meeting.

"The kids need to have a say in what we do every day. 'Cause, we're trying to let them have their own opinions."

"Yeah, good point. Why don't we come up with a handful of options for them to choose . . ."

She interrupted me, "Like, we need to give them examples of what we're doing or could do, and let them decide. Then it's a half-and-half thing."

Afriganzia Fosters Discussions with Children in the Program.

Getting the floor is tricky because the children are falling all over each other to say their piece. Afriganzia stopped them at one point in the discussion when everyone had something to say about violence and drugs in the neighborhood. She asked them to raise their hands so she could pick on them. After Voice met, she and I sat down to talk about the day's events. About her calling on the children, she said: "I didn't want them thinking this was like school, 'cause we'd lose them, but they talking all over each other. How they gonna hear each other if everyone talking all at once like that? But did you see how I raised my hand to be called on? I wanted to make things more equal. It work too 'cause they started hearing each other, and Sandy even called on me."

Afriganzia, Asia, and I Talk Over a Glitch in the Program

I explained to Afriganzia and Asia that I had been getting the run-around between the computer center and the library at the university that I attended. The library representatives wanted clearance from the technical services staff to allow us to use the computers in the basement of the library. The librarian, though, didn't seem too encouraging about the possibility because, "really, [they're] only making those [computers] available to the students taking summer courses."

"If they don't want to do it for the kids, f——k them," Afriganzia said.

"You gotta work them," Asia replied. "Can't we go to someone higher up and ask?"

"We ain't gonna kiss their ass, Asia. We shouldn't have to. We tryin' to do something for these kids."

"When did you hear me say I'ma kiss some White person's ass? I said we should go over the person's head."

We got to the technology services and it turned out we could use the computers, as long as we did so in the early evening. We went to the lab and learned Microsoft Word 5.1. On our way back to the car we walked slowly across campus in the heat of late afternoon: green lawns, flower beds of petunias and marigolds, wood chip mulch, a wrought iron clock in the middle of a bed of red and white striped petunias.

"This place a fairy land," Afriganzia said as Asia stopped to hand her a cigarette. Asia leaned over and spit on the sidewalk. "Tired of seeing all these White people, Ellen, can we go home now?"

Afriganzia and Megan Talk about the Former's Paycheck

"You have a paycheck up at United Home. Why haven't you picked it up?"

"I will."

"It's been ready for two weeks, Afriganzia, what's the problem?"

She smiled at Megan, "You sound just like my mother." Megan changed the subject and the conversation petered out. Afriganzia and I walked out of the center and sat on her front stoop. "Your mom mentioned your paycheck to me. She says you're too lazy to walk up the hill to get it."

"It ain't that at all. I just can't stand Sarah [the supervisor]. Last time I went up there she asked me to tell her what's going on down here. Spy on my peeps [people] like that, and tell her what's up? No way. As soon as I go up there she gonna ask me all kinds of shit that I don't want to answer."

"Yeah, but what about your money?"

"I'm doing this for the kids, not for the money." She picked up her pay one month after the program ended.

To begin with, Afriganzia's socialization into institutional language takes various forms. She acquired the literate skills necessary to transcribe minutes with the tone of professional distance and the organization of a social worker. A short time before Voice started, Afriganzia had found the center staff's logbook open. She found in it a record of private business and told community members, but she also noted the format and organization. Through this exposure to the literate practices of the center's staff, Afriganzia had obtained a model on which she could base her taking of the minutes. In addition, as Afriganzia progressed through the program, she learned how best to promote discussions in ways that kept an orderly flow to discourse. At first, children debated issues important to them all at once, a learning behavior that she soon realized fell short of facilitating listening skills. She then tried another way of fostering listening and speaking skills; when the person who wanted to speak raised his/her hand, she called on that student. Finally, she had acquired code-switching abilities through the continual modeling of this skill by adults in the area. But what are the social and political ramifications of learning institutional oral and literate practices? How does one strike a balance between institutional language practices and one's own cultural practices?

Many complex issues related to language and cultural identity manifest themselves in these examples, yet how they emerge deserves attention. In on-stage interactions, where Afriganzia publicly performs her duties as co-director of Voice, we might be tempted to characterize her actions as too easily buying into prevailing norms attached to particular codes and modes of language use. For example, she dutifully and "objectively" records the minutes for the staff meeting, using written techniques comparable to the ones staff workers use to record notes in their daily logs. She seems to relish her authority as a teacher, and quickly learns how to control the flow of discourse by calling on individual children. She code-switches quickly and easily in those encounters where she believes White English conventions hold sway. In other words, these excerpts are all shot through with evidence to support the claim that Afriganzia's actions blindly comply with institutional practices. Her on-stage, public performances, however, stand in stark contrast to her off-stage, private criticisms and insights. Off-stage she risks little in revealing her subversive beliefs about institutional language and race politics. Her off-stage social commentaries indicate the cultural and political tensions present when someone learns the necessary rhetorical tools for negotiating with and in institutions.

In both her public encounters with institutional agents and her role as a staff member of the center, Afriganzia threads her way between competing value systems by simultaneously accepting and evading types of authority. For instance, when she teaches and reflects on her teaching, she adopts and adapts the authority vested in that position. As we planned the upcoming sessions, she suggests that instead of just telling the children what we would do for the day, we should offer children a range of activities from which they could choose. Her suggestion indicates not only a faith in the abilities of children to direct their own learning activities, but also a belief in sharing the decision-making process about the curriculum. Afriganzia also recognized a problem with the flow of discussion. The Voice participants spoke all at once and were not listening to the points made by others. By asking them to raise their hands and then calling on them, she took control of the means by which children could contribute to the discussion. But she also raises her hand to gain the floor in an effort to help equalize the ways in which everyone there could enter into the debate ("But did you see how I raised my hand to be called on?"). She tries to take the role of both teacher and student, in effect. Her gesture indicates, as she said later, "[she] wanted to make things more equal." Part of her socialization into institutional language includes her trying out various linguistic means for handling the authority attendant upon her post as co-director of Voice, as a center representative. In the public display of her status, she does more than simply exercise the influence of her position as teacher.

Her community-based attitudes toward schooling surface when she leaves the center and reflects on her public performance as a teacher. She says, "I didn't want them thinking Voice was like school 'cause we'd lose them." Based on young community members' values, she predicts that students would avoid Voice if they began associating our actions with those they encountered in school. If the curriculum mirrored schooled activities too much, students would devalue the Voice program just as they did schooling. To avoid this, Afriganzia taps into the local cultural values about learning where collaboration is highly valued and often practiced in "half-and-half" or "more equal ways." She wants to foster an atmosphere where the program participants have "a sense of responsibility for developing their own opinions." Drawing from these presumptions, she develops teaching methods to handle the flow of discussion and implements a curriculum that would likely appeal to the Voice participants. Even as her relation to community children shifts as a result of the institutional mask she adopts, we learn from the hidden transcript how she adapts her authority position in order to honor her own community-based dispositions toward learning.

In similar fashion, the minutes to the center's meeting might seem, on the surface, to adhere to the institutions' values of policing the community. (Recall from chapter 3 the center's mission "to maintain the social fabric" of the neighborhood.) As a public transcript, literally and figuratively, the minutes take the form of other logbook entries.

They are divided into three sections: "Topic," "Discussion," and "Action." The topic section glosses the main ideas; the discussion uses short sentences to summarize the points made in the meeting; and the action section describes who will do what as a result of the discussion. The logbook format reduces the complexity of situations into a concise report for the superiors at United Home. Between the discussion and action sections, the rhetoric used indicates a straight line of cause-effect reasoning. For instance, the teen girls stayed in the center until 1 A.M.; as a result, restrictions on use of the center will be implemented. In these minutes, the duties of the center staff appear straightforward, uncomplicated, and clearly demarcated. This literacy artifact rests on the surface of politics where the staff's services are represented as taking place in a smooth course of events. Yet conflicts between the center's staff and community members rest just beneath the surface of the words on these pages.

Since Afriganzia's notes comply with this linear format, she appears to embrace the institutional values that do not necessarily represent the best interests of area residents. Turning away from the public transcript, though, we can begin to uncover the conflicting symbolic systems that inform this literate piece. We already know that, using subversive means, Afriganzia acquired the model for her literacy skills evident in these minutes. Since Afriganzia told other community residents what she read in the center's logbook, a sense of distrust and serious misgivings had arose among neighbors. Mirena's apartment became known as the center across from the center, in part, because Afriganzia told residents that their private affairs had been recorded for strangers to read. In the minutes, though, she wrote, "Ellen reported that neighbors were concerned about the confidentiality of the logbook." The content of her message effectively draws attention away from her own significant role in generating the conflict among neighbors. Afriganzia has written her own resistance out of the official transcript and appears to be a neutral party who simply records what was said at the meeting.

She covers up her own illicit behavior again when she describes the ways the "teen girls were in the center until 1 A.M.," when she herself attended the get-together. Megan had heard from Major that the teens stayed in the center late into one night, even though he didn't mention precisely who was among them. Afriganzia could have volunteered that information, but instead of pointing fingers, she diffused responsibility for the wrong-doing among all the teen girls in the area. After the meeting, she told a group of her friends gathered at Asia's that the center staff planned to limit their access to the center. Asia curled her lip: "They be sayin' how they want to keep us off the street. But when we use the center's VCR and keep our asses off the street, then they say we can't?" Another teen said they should just get their parents to support them; so when Megan canvassed the neighbors for opinions, she would hear parents endorse the teens' use of the center late into the night. The teens enacted their plan and solicited the support of the adults, and, as a result, they foiled Megan's hopes to limit their access to the center. Overall, the divergence between Afriganzia's public role as an institutional member and her hidden role as an area resident is striking. In the word choice of the minutes, Afriganzia appears to conform to the policing actions of the United Home employees, but on the block, she subverted their policing inclinations and sabotaged their plans to limit the teens' access to resources.

In a third way, her transcription of the meeting's minutes both acquiesces and undercuts the institutional presumptions of policing the neighborhood. Early in the meeting, the social workers tried to figure out what happened to the missing ceramics money. The staff members listed the residents who have access to the file cabinet when it's left open, and who has keys to the cabinet. Without a word, Afriganzia recorded the names of three respected community members who hold keys to the cabinet, one of whom was her mother. But when we left the office together, Afriganzia expressed her offense: "I bet one of them took that money. But they never mentioned looking to their own people for an explanation. They gotta go and blame my own mother. What is that shit?" The center staff workers assumed that the older residents with keys needed to be watched by the younger caseworkers. The insult was both to residents' integrity (as it relates to their honesty) and to their honor (as it relates to their generation); yet Afriganzia let the insulting presumption slip by. She recorded the conversation in a seemingly objective tone, even as she seethed about their insinuations. When I asked why she didn't speak up at the meeting about their disrespectful presumptions, Afriganzia said, "Why should I? They only gonna talk to my mom, and she'll just un-huhn them. And they'll leave her be." Despite their disrespectful presumptions, she realizes that Lucy would likely placate the workers and no more would be made of the missing money; so a fight would not have been worth Afriganzia's effort.

Taken on the whole, the minutes work well as an example of the masking devices an individual used in institutional literacy. First, it masks Afriganzia's position as a community resident whose own cultural beliefs remain hidden behind the public view of her transcription. Second, the minutes hide the political complexities of relations between center staff members and neighbors. And third, the transcription diverts attention away from Afriganzia's illicit behaviors even as it tries to address these behaviors. The minutes present Afriganzia's acquisition of discourse that wears the thin disguise of compliance, a guise that obscures undercurrents of defiance. She manages to resist a totalizing endorsement of the center's values by attributing confidentiality worries to me, dispersing the teens' responsibility for being in the center past hours, and undermining the center staff's plan of action. She manipulates this piece of writing so that it admits her own values, and thus, she safeguards her cultural identity as community member.

She played that middle position, even if it cost her, because she believed in helping the children in the program. When Megan asked Afriganzia why she had not yet picked up her paycheck, Afriganzia replied she would, which didn't satisfy Megan's curiosity. Megan pressed the point to try to find out what "problem" the teen had with picking up her paycheck. Afriganzia staved off her influence by saying to Megan, "You sound just like my mother." Read literally, this could mean that her mother had also been asking her about her pay. Read figuratively, this could mean that Megan is hounding Afriganzia in ways that Megan has no business doing. Either way, Afriganzia's smile indicates that although Megan overstepped the boundaries of her influence, she had not yet done harm, although Megan quickly approached offending her audience. Afriganzia had acquired a cueing device (smiling) and a rhetorical move (making an unflattering comparison to a nagging mother) that held Megan off without pushing her away.

For Afriganzia, though, the problem wasn't so much in handling Megan's encroachment, the problem was handling Sarah's. Because Afriganzia held a position on the center payroll, Sarah asked her to help the center staff with their advocacy. In order to effectively advocate for someone, social workers had to be privy to problems. Yet most of the adults in the area refused to interact with center representatives for many reasons, not the least of which had to do with the question of invasion of privacy. But if United Home could bankroll a local informant, staff members could advocate without an invitation from the concerned person. Sarah hoped to make Afriganzia into this paid informant: "Last time I went up there she asked me to tell her what' s going on down here. Spy on my peeps [people] like that, and tell her what's up? No way. As soon as I go up there she gonna ask me all kinds of shit that I don't want to answer." Sarah's questions flew in the face of Afriganzia's community-based ethics that dearly respect privacy. And so she found herself in a conundrum. Her betwixt-and-between position demanded that either she compromise the extent of her affiliation with the center, or that she compromise her own sense of loyalty to her friends and family. Rather than finding other language skills to outmaneuver Sarah's invasive questions, Afriganzia opted for silent withdrawal, a device that avoids the situation altogether. While her silence bypassed a perceived ultimatum, it had both material and social costs: not only would she forsake her money, but her mother, who needed the cash, pressured her to pick up her pay and attributed her actions to mere laziness. When thought to be lazy, residents quickly lost social status in the neighborhood. But Afriganzia stands her high moral ground, because as far as she was concerned, "I'm doing this for the kids, not for the money." In the kind of seemingly no-win predicament she was in with Sarah, the teen acquired a foot-dragging tactic, a tactic that created space for her to wait for a change in her position. Before she eventually picked up her paycheck, she stonewalled Sarah and Megan until she was technically no longer a member of the center staff.

Afriganzia's mask of compliance could only be taken so far before it would begin to mold Afriganzia's face to its shape. Sarah asked the teen to deeply immerse herself in United Home's value systems that needed to police the daily lives of neighbors if it hoped to maintain the social fabric of the community. Afriganzia could not, and would not, compromise her cultural values of privacy—she would not sell out her people to philanthropists who needed "cases" in order to keep their own jobs. This example shows one of the most difficult situations in which Afriganzia found herself, where yielding to the center's values would likely mold her face to the mask of an institutional representative.

If sometimes it proved difficult to wear the White mask associated with institutional language, sometimes wearing the mask proved bitterly entertaining. Many in the neighborhood modeled code-switching in front of their children when dealing with organizations over the phone and in person. Afriganzia was socialized in a culture where those who held status did so in part because of their talent in code-switching. She developed this linguistic faculty and employed it well in her phone conversation with the public librarian. For example, she uses complete sentences that suggest formality to her talk, as well as verb forms indicating White English ("What do the kids need to do?" In Black English she would have dropped the auxiliary verb and said "What the kids need to do?"). She consciously used her public performance of institutional language as part of a "psyche out" (her term) game often played in her neighborhood. Psyche outs happened when one individual leads another to think one way, then jerks the person in another direction.

Once she hangs up the phone, Afriganzia reveals her game in putting on this formal performance: "I like to mess with people. You know, they think you one way when you talk like that. Like you have blond hair and blue eyes, but when they see you, they all caught off guard. [Here she imitates the reaction of the person who would be seeing her after talking with her on the phone] 'Oh, you're so-and-so? We were expecting someone, uhhh . . . Something uhhh. . . .' " In this phone call, she plays up to and with the stereotypes wider society members typically hold—one can be identified as White solely through speech alone. If she fooled the librarian well enough, then she can delight in the librarian's awkward shock when realizing that Afriganzia, although sounding White over the phone, was actually Black. The person's surprise will indicate that Afriganzia succeeded in psyching out the person into believing his/her own prejudices about who speaks what forms of discourse. When we got to the library and approached the circulation desk, the person looked at me and asked if we had spoken on the phone earlier. I glanced at Afriganzia who looked amused by the success of her ploy. She smiled at the librarian and said "No, that was me." Community members take some delight in making others feel awkward about their stereotypes, especially when they burst apart these prejudices through their own language play (in chapter 8 we'll see another example of code switching to fool someone). Afriganzia toyed with the White mask associated with prestige dialects.

Even if a person trifled with the White mask of institutional language, their humor followed from the cutting reality that this mask represented. Turning to the final set of examples, we begin to understand how residents constructed their own classed and raced subjectivities when becoming adroit language users. When Afriganzia signed on to this project, we had to patch together resources from various organizations. This translated to hours of leg work that involved meeting with computer technicians, librarians, United Home representatives beyond the center staff, professors, and department administrative assistants—all of whom permitted access to the assorted materials we needed in order to prepare children for researching, reading, writing, and desktop publishing. Generally I would make initial contact with university representatives because I "already had an 'in.' " I would set a time to meet and talk over the possibilities of them helping our program. Then Afriganzia and I would meet them in person to firm up the details. The interaction, titled "Afriganzia, Asia, and I Talk Over a Glitch in the Program," stems from this context and shows how acquiring skills and resources related to White institutions can challenge preconceived understandings of race and class.

To start with, Afriganzia takes a firmly separatist stance on the problems I had in organizing computing resources at my university. "If they don't want to help us, f——k them." To her way of thinking, she cannot understand why anyone would obstruct a project that helped youths. In her culture, children represent hope, promise, and delight; they have attention and resources showered on them whenever possible. From her perspective, she's hard pressed to imagine why a librarian would forestall the children's development. Her blanket disapproval manifests itself in resistance through withdrawal.

Asia took a different tack on the problem. "You gotta work them. Can't we go to someone higher up and ask?" She believes that they should grease the mechanisms by speaking with the librarian's superior. But Afriganzia constructs this solution as selling out her dignity to a White person who hinders the children's opportunities. "We ain't gonna kiss their ass, Asia. We shouldn't have to. We tryin' to do something for these kids." Since the librarian's values seem to clash with her own, Afriganzia feels no compulsion to work with this person. Asia counters Afriganzia with, "When did you hear me say I'ma kiss some White person's ass? I said we should go over the person's head." Ass-kissing involved sycophantic behavior where one erases a sense of self and community so that his/her face fits the mask of deference. When a resident continually ingratiates him/herself to an authority figure for whatever reasons, the person became stigmatized as a "sellout" (their term).

This interaction offers a glimpse at how far a person will go when using language to appease a member of Whiter society in order to gain opportunities. If the gatekeeper appears to hold elitist values that diametrically oppose a community member's values, then the community resident will be less inclined to work with or even "work" (manipulate) the gatekeeper. Doing so, the person would forsake his/ her own cultural identity. As long as a community member maintained loyalty to and respect for Black ways, then institutional language could be legitimately used as both consensual and oppositional. But as soon as a gatekeeper dismissed values important to community members, then the task would be to find someone else to work with or to withdrawal completely. Total withdraw, though, typically came with a cost. In this case the cost was too high because we needed to get the children on computers if we hoped to make public their work. Teens often endorsed telling an institutional representative to "f——k off" as a form of resistance. But when trying to meet practical needs, this separatism turned into a self-defeating act that most tried to avoid.

This exchange heightens Afriganzia's awareness of class and race differences in another way. When she says, "this place a fairy land," she referred to the well-coifed lawn, the flower beds, red brick buildings with twelve-foot-high windows, the view overlooking the city below, the conspicuous signs of wealth, the indicators of prestige. The university's image reminded her of a land far away, only found in books, a land by and for Whites. "Tired of seeing all these White people, Ellen, can we go home now?" The process of engaging White institutional representatives left her feeling both weary and different. When we returned to her neighborhood, she sat on the front stoop with Sasha and her cousins. Sasha asked what was bothering Afriganzia who walked with her head down. Afriganzia asked if Sasha had ever seen the university on the hill. Sasha said no, and Afriganzia said, "White people got so much, it make me sick." Learning institutional language typically brought into the open disparities in wealth and differences in racial access to wealth, with despair gnawing at the edges of what seemed possible.

Her betwixt-and-between position meant that Afriganzia must both adopt and adapt, both comply and undercut, both play into and off of the dominant values of institutional representatives without ever forsaking her own cultural attitudes. Although the trial-and-error process of her learning institutional language suggests she has learned well, the difficulty rested in maintaining her own identity and cultural values, while she wore the disguise of deference and compliance. For Afriganzia, the primary importance of Voice remained in the ways it seemed to benefit the children who participated. Although she found the learning process frustrating, complex, and often difficult, she also knew why it held value by this community's standards.

Important challenges to one's own cultural beliefs result from the process of gaining fluency with institutional language. Area residents had to find means through which they could maintain their face (cultural identity) even as they donned linguistic and cultural masks. The continual tacking back and forth between competing emic and symbolic systems sometimes became a game, sometimes left residents feeling dejected, and sometimes allowed them to undercut uninvited influences. Even if the process of learning to switch into dominant linguistic codes appears facile in public transcripts, residents articulated the social complexities involved in this process in their own hidden transcripts. They critically reflected on the social implications of gaining proficiency with the oral and literate skills needed to work with public service agencies. Community members politicized the process of learning to use institutional language.

This chapter begins to give us an understanding of ways in which people avoid the racelessness of using mainstream English, even as they practice it and try to obtain fluency with it. Critical consciousness emerged in the challenge of learning institutional language well, the challenge of striking a balance between a counterhegemonic ideology and the structuring ideology of gatekeepers. Community residents' value system often stood in stark contrast to the value systems they saw indicated in the language of institutional representatives. Despite these contradictions, residents rarely found themselves in positions where they could directly challenge gatekeepers' values. Instead, they found linguistic skills needed to appear to comply, even as they resisted. The next chapter considers how community members perceived the predominant ideologies informing gatekeepers' words and deeds. I then show a handful of interactions where residents' and gatekeepers' competing value systems collide.

7 "An Everyday Fight for Us to Get Simple Respect"

If residents grappled with the social and cultural complexities involved in learning to work with institutional representatives, they did so because they perceived the negative and degrading presumptions present in the oral and literate language institutional representatives used. This chapter shows how inner city residents use orality and literacy in their daily challenges to the structuring values of institutional representatives. Close analysis of the literacy events and practices surrounding these shows not only the diminished and diminishing assumptions of many institutional representatives, but the sophisticated language strategies residents deployed to challenge these assumptions. Individuals deploy their institutional language skills not only to obtain material resources, but also to counter the denigrating tacitly held beliefs of institutional representatives. Community residents finessed the oral and literate demands of institutions in ways that both placated and undermined public servants. While the examples in this chapter point to systematic forms of domination, I want to draw attention to the linguistic strategies community members used to negotiate the asymmetries of these encounters. Doing so, we see how inner city residents desystematize oppression.

Compared to suburban communities, inner city communities face the pervasive influences of institutions in many day-to-day activities. As Berger and Luckmann (1966) note, "the private sphere that has emerged in modern industrial society is considerably deinstitutionalized as compared to the public sphere" (81). Because individuals in Quayville's inner city often were un(der)employed, lived in subsidized housing, and relied on public services, as we saw in chapter 5, public organizations intervened in how they obtained their basic necessities, managed their social relations, and cultivated their opportunities. Since bureaucracies influence inner city residents' lives, we need to examine institutional gatekeepers' roles and the ideologies that imbue these roles. If we understand the structuring attitudes of institutional representatives, in other words, we can begin to comprehend how community residents' language use challenges these representatives and their assumptions.

In Quayville, institutions tended to link their resources together. While that contributed to efficiency and could be beneficial, it more often appeared to residents that institutions colluded together in ways that severely limited their opportunities. So, for example, when a person received an eviction notice from a RIP landlord, RIP notified HUD and the Housing Authority. In effect, RIP blackballed the person they had evicted, which impeded the person's chances of finding housing through the other agencies. In another example, the Center's social workers reported parents to DSS if they suspected welfare fraud. In yet another example, the police department conducted surveillance in a centrally located apartment with the permission of RIP and the help of social workers. (In chapter 4, I detailed how housing officials and philanthropic organizations worked together to let Mirena "hit rock bottom" and go homeless for three months.) Admittedly, collusion between institutional representatives can be seen as a consolidation of scarce resources, a cooperative effort. But from the residents' perspectives, such collaboration pointed to the systematized efforts that mainstream institutions used to maintain the status quo of residents. They would say of gatekeepers: "They be trying to hold us down"; and "Their jobs depend on us being poor. Why they gonna help?"; and "Just can't get ahead. They give us more food stamps, then lower the welfare payments. I get work, and they take away my child care"; and "They get you coming and going and everywhere in between." These refrains could be heard on front stoops, around kitchen tables, at the corner, or walking to the store, whenever time and space permitted reflection on their situations.

A central theme to these observations threads throughout: community residents and institutional agents together maintained their interdependent relations. Area residents, that is, knew that institutional representatives remained employed so long as residents remained poor, unemployed, and in the ghetto. Residents conceptualized their roles within the models of cultural reproduction that least served their interests. Sometimes, men and women happened to be in a fairly secure position where they could use this interdependence to their advantage. Other times, the interdependent relation slipped into more of a dependency when residents reluctantly needed to rely on the philanthropy of public service agents because they had few other options. Community members remained aware of and attentive to their parts in perpetuating their living conditions—but their critical consciousness alone rarely helped them obtain the steady, meaningful employment, the educational opportunities, the respect and basic humane treatment they knew they were not getting from wider society. Even so, residents analyzed the oral and literate language uses of institutional agents. They uncovered the institutional agents' tacitly held assumptions that limited their life chances and overlooked their potential.

If a public servant agreed with the tenets of individualism, for example, the person would likely place poor people into two categories: the deserving and undeserving poor.[7] The deserving poor included those who could not work due to some physical challenge (age, disease, blindness) or social misfortune (widowhood). The deserving poor include individuals who would work if they only could find it. The undeserving poor included those able-bodied people who remained un(der)employed due to, it was presumed, some moral flaw or character weakness, such as sloth, indolence, vice, or promiscuity (that lead to pregnancies out of wedlock). Supposedly, these individuals failed to take advantage of the opportunities a meritocratic democracy offers, and, therefore, lacked the individual perseverance needed to succeed. After the 1960s, mainstream attitudes toward the poor widened somewhat to include the notion that poor people perpetuated their own lots through cultural practices and beliefs. The culture of poverty belief pointed to poor people's behaviors and attitudes produced when they responded to their conditions. For example, the theory maintained that poor people had more children with the belief that children would work to help support the family, even though having children actually slashes a poor family's resources. The children would grow up seeing only the behavioral patterns of their parents and would themselves have many children, often out of wedlock. Thus, the culture of poverty belief moved into a more socially determined understanding of impoverished individuals: poor people, by virtue of their cultural practices and beliefs, perpetuated their own poverty. To varying degrees, individualistic and socially determined assumptions pervade the oral and literate means by which public servants work today.

The Structuring Attitudes of Institutional Representatives

Community members often interpreted the demeaning attitudes of institutional agents by assessing the oral and literate language used in day-to-day proceedings of public service organizations. The first example shows typical forms required to access programmatic services. Whether a DSS, Medicaid, or HUD application, they all came with a list of documents required in order to validate the completed form, an information sheet describing the program, and the actual application. Applicants completed the Home Emergency Assistance Program (HEAP) forms when they needed to offset their high utility costs. In January of 1996, Lucy Cadens picked up a HEAP application when she received a notice of termination of service from her utility company (see figure 7.1). Although she paid $45 or more a month on her bill, the high costs of gas and electric heat for a poorly insulated three bedroom apartment continued to add up over the cold months. Her bill for January alone was close to $400, bringing her total owed to just over $960 for the winter of 1996. Lucy had heard about HEAP from a neighbor. Working on a limited budget of state funds, the HEAP office was opened only through January and mid-February before its funding ran out. Lucy and I looked over the ten pages of the application materials in my car.

"Jesus, these things are long," I flipped through my copies before I started the car. We were headed to our favorite buffet.

"They try to scare you out of applying. Try to discourage you. And it do for some folks. They see all these forms and all the shit you got to bring with you and they think, 'Hell, it gonna take me four or five hours just to pull this shit together.' And they don't do it. You spend all that time and what do you get in return?" We reached the buffet, parked in the slushy snow and buttoned our coats against the wind and flurries. I brought the application with me hoping she would talk more about it. We got our first round of food, chicken and rice soup, salads, and rolls, and we sat a booth. Lucy took the "documentation requirements" sheet off the top of the stack and shook her head.

HEAP

Home Energy Assistance Program

APPLICANT NAME	DATE

HOME ENERGY ASSISTANCE PROGRAM
(HEAP)

DOCUMENTATION REQUIREMENTS

☐ WHEN YOU APPLY FOR HEAP ASSISTANCE IN PERSON, YOU MUST PROVIDE PROOF FOR **ALL** ITEMS LISTED BELOW.

☐ IF YOU HAVE ALREADY APPLIED FOR HEAP ASSISTANCE, YOU MUST PROVIDE PROOF OF THE ITEMS CIRCLED. BRING THESE STATEMENTS NO LATER THAN _____ OR YOUR APPLICATION **MAY BE DENIED.**

ADDRESS (Where you now live)

You must provide **one or more** of the following:

- Current rent receipt with name and address
- Copy of lease with address
- Water, sewage, or tax bill
- Mortgage payment books/receipts with address
- Homeowners insurance policy
- Deed

ALL PEOPLE IN YOUR HOUSEHOLD

You must provide **one or more** of the following for each person in your household:

- Birth certificate
- Baptismal certificate
- School records
- Social Security card
- Driver's license
- Marriage certificate

FUEL/UTILITY BILLS

- If you pay a fuel or utility bill, bring a copy of your most recent fuel/utility bill.
- If you pay for **neither** heat **nor** utilities, bring a statement from your landlord that indicates heat and utilities are included in your rent.
- If you have a utility emergency, bring your utility termination notice.

INCOME

You must provide proof of **income** for all household members who receive any type of income, earned or unearned, including but not limited to:

- Pay stubs for the most recent four weeks
- If self-employed, or have rental income, business records for the most recent three months
- Child support or alimony checks
- Bankbook/dividend or interest statement
- Statement from roomer/boarder
- Other _____
  _____

COPY OF MOST RECENT CHECK OR AWARD LETTER:

- Social Security/Supplemental Security Income (SSI)
- Veteran's Benefits
- Pensions
- Worker's Compensation/Disability
- Verification of Unemployment Insurance Benefit amount
- Educational Grants/Loans

RESOURCES (For emergency applications only)

- Statement claiming zero resources
- Bank Statement showing current balance for checking, savings, and credit union accounts, IRA's, etc.
- Stocks, bonds, dividends

Depending on your circumstances, additional documentation may be required.

If you have any questions, please call

Figure 7.1 Home Energy Assistance Program (HEAP) Application

145

DSS-3421 (Rev. 6/96)

HEAP
Home Energy Assistance Program

HOME ENERGY ASSISTANCE PROGRAM APPLICATION

IMPORTANT NOTICE

YOU SHOULD BE AWARE THAT THERE IS LIMITED MONEY AVAILABLE FOR HEAP BENEFIT PAYMENTS. ONCE AVAILABLE MONEY IS USED UP, NO BENEFITS WILL BE ISSUED AND THE PROGRAM WILL CLOSE. THEREFORE, IT IS STRONGLY RECOMMENDED THAT YOU COMPLETE AND RETURN YOUR APPLICATION AS SOON AS POSSIBLE. BE AWARE THAT IN PAST YEARS THE PROGRAM HAS CLOSED DOWN AS EARLY AS MARCH 12.

ANSWER **ALL** QUESTIONS EXCEPT THOSE IN THE **SHADED** AREAS. PLEASE PRINT CLEARLY, AND SIGN THE FORM ON PAGE 5.

AGENCY USE ONLY

DATE RECEIVED

CONTACT THE AGENCY ABOVE IF YOU NEED HELP.

| OFFICE | APPLICATION DATE | UNIT ID | WORKER ID | CASE TYPE | CASE NUMBER | REGISTRY NUMBER | VERS. |
| | | | | 6   0 | | | |

CASE NAME

NUMBER REUSE INDICATOR □ REGULAR □ MAIL IN □ EXP □ EMERGENCY □ WALK IN

SECTION 1: HOUSEHOLD COMPOSITION

| CD | LN | | | | CLIENT NUMBER | | | SSCD |
| 1 | 01 | | | | | | | |

1. MY NAME, DATE OF BIRTH, SEX, SOCIAL SECURITY NUMBER AND ADDRESS ARE:

FIRST   M.I.   LAST

DATE OF BIRTH MO. DAY YEAR   SEX M/F   SOCIAL SECURITY NUMBER   IND DISP CODE   CAT CODE

2. NO.   STREET   APT #

CITY   STATE   ZIP CODE   COUNTY

3. MY MAILING ADDRESS (IF DIFFERENT FROM ABOVE) IS:

NO.   STREET   APT #   CITY   STATE   ZIP CODE   COUNTY

4. PHONE NUMBER WHERE I CAN BE REACHED:

AREA CODE   PHONE NUMBER

Figure 7.1 *(continued)* Home Energy Assistance Program (HEAP) Application

146

DSS-3421 (Rev. 6/96)

5. MY MAIDEN NAME AND/OR OTHER NAMES BY WHICH I HAVE BEEN KNOWN ARE:

FIRST NAME	MI	LAST NAME

OTHER NAMES

C O D E	FIRST NAME	MI	LAST NAME

6. TOTAL NUMBER OF PEOPLE WHO LIVE IN MY HOME/APARTMENT, INCLUDING MYSELF:

7. BESIDES MYSELF, THE FOLLOWING PEOPLE LIVE IN THE SAME HOME/APARTMENT (If no one else, write NONE):

CD	LN	FIRST NAME	MI	LAST NAME	DATE OF BIRTH MO	DAY	YEAR	SEX M/F	SOCIAL SECURITY NUMBER	S S D D	CLIENT ID NUMBER	IND DISP CODE	CAT CODE
1	02												
1	03												
1	04												
1	05												
1	06												
1	07												
1	08												

8. IS THERE ANYONE LIVING IN YOUR HOME/APARTMENT, INCLUDING YOURSELF, WHO IS:

BLIND OR DISABLED □ NO □ YES   IF YES, WHO? _____

60 YEARS OR OLDER □ NO □ YES   IF YES, WHO? _____

UNDER 6 YEARS OLD □ NO □ YES   IF YES, WHO? _____

9. DO YOU OR DOES ANYONE LIVING AT YOUR ADDRESS GET FOOD STAMPS?

□ NO □ YES   WHO? _____   FS CASE NUMBER [   ]

10. DO YOU OR DOES ANYONE IN YOUR HOUSE/APARTMENT GET PUBLIC ASSISTANCE?

□ NO □ YES   WHO? _____   PA CASE NUMBER [   ]

Figure 7.1 (*continued*) Home Energy Assistance Program (HEAP) Application

147

SECTION 2: HOUSEHOLD INCOME

CHECK (✓) YES OR NO FOR EVERY QUESTION. REPORT ANY INCOME FOR ALL HOUSEHOLD MEMBERS. ATTACH ADDITIONAL SHEETS IF NECESSARY.

INDICATE IF YOU OR ANYONE WHO LIVES WITH YOU GETS MONEY FROM:

TYPE OF INCOME	CHECK ONE (✓)	IF YES, GIVE AMOUNT	SOURCE OF INCOME	WHO RECEIVES?
INTEREST from savings, checking, CD's, money market accounts, etc.	☐ YES ☐ NO	Yearly Amount: $	Name of Bank and Account Number:	
DIVIDENDS from stocks, bonds, securities, etc.	☐ YES ☐ NO	Yearly Amount: $	Source of Dividends:	
SOCIAL SECURITY/SOCIAL SECURITY DISABILITY including direct deposit and Medicare B premium amount	☐ YES ☐ NO	Monthly Amount: $		
SUPPLEMENTAL SECURITY INCOME (SSI)	☐ YES ☐ NO	Monthly Amount: $		
PENSION/RETIREMENT private and/or government	☐ YES ☐ NO	Monthly Amount: $	Source of Pension:	
VETERAN'S BENEFITS	☐ YES ☐ NO	Monthly Amount: $		
UNEMPLOYMENT BENEFITS	☐ YES ☐ NO	Weekly Amount: $		
WORKER'S COMPENSATION	☐ YES ☐ NO	Weekly Amount: $		
DISABILITY private or NYS	☐ YES ☐ NO	Weekly Amount: $		
CHILD SUPPORT (received)	☐ YES ☐ NO	Court Ordered Weekly Amount: $		
RENTAL INCOME apartment, garage, land, etc.	☐ YES ☐ NO	Monthly Amount: $	Type of Rental:	
ROOM OR ROOM/BOARD (received)	☐ YES ☐ NO	Monthly Amount: $	Name of Roomer/Boarder:	
CONTRIBUTION from someone outside the household	☐ YES ☐ NO	Monthly Amount: $	Name of Contributor:	
ALIMONY including payments for mortgage, utility bills, etc.	☐ YES ☐ NO	Monthly Amount: $		
TAP, PELL, STUDENT LOANS	☐ YES ☐ NO	Total Amount For Semester: $		
WAGES	☐ YES ☐ NO	Weekly Amount Before Deductions: $ Weekly Amount Before Deductions: $	Employer: Employer:	

IS THERE ANY OTHER INCOME FROM ANY OTHER SOURCE? ☐ YES ☐ NO

IF YES, PLEASE EXPLAIN:

Figure 7.1 *(continued)* Home Energy Assistance Program (HEAP) Application

148

DSS-3421 (Rev. 6/96)

SECTION 3: HOUSING

1. Type of Housing
(Check One)

I am a:

☐ HOMEOWNER - Single Family House or Mobile Home ☐ RENTER - Public Housing Project or Senior Housing

☐ HOMEOWNER - Multi-Family House ☐ RENTER - Private Housing but receive government rent subsidy ☐ I live with someone else and share expenses

☐ CO-OP/CONDO OWNER ☐ RENTER - Private House, Apartment, or Mobile Home ☐ I pay for a room.

2. My monthly rent or mortgage payment is: $ _____ ☐ NONE

3. If applicable, the name of the apartment building or housing project I live in is: _____

SECTION 4: HEAT AND UTILITY INFORMATION

CHECK (✓) EACH BOX THAT APPLIES TO YOUR HOUSEHOLD. ANSWER A, B, AND C.

A. HEATING

☐ My Household pays for HEAT separately. **OR** ☐ My Household has HEAT included in the rent.

MY MAIN SOURCE OF HEAT IS:

☐ Fuel Oil ☐ Kerosene ☐ Propane or Bottled Gas ☐ Wood or Coal ☐ Natural Gas Heat ☐ Electric Heat

HEATING COMPANY'S NAME: _____

ADDRESS: _____

CITY, STATE, ZIP CODE _____

NAME ON HEATING BILL: _____

THE ACCOUNT NUMBER IS:
(Do **NOT** use the landlord's account number)

☐☐☐☐☐☐☐☐☐☐

B. UTILITY

☐ My Household pays separately for: **OR** ☐ My Household has ALL UTILITIES included in the rent.

☐ Lights ☐ Cooking ☐ Hot Water

UTILITY COMPANY'S NAME: _____

NAME ON UTILITY BILL: _____

THE ACCOUNT NUMBER IS:
(Do **NOT** use the landlord's account number)

☐☐☐☐☐☐☐☐☐☐

C. IS ELECTRIC NECESSARY TO RUN THE FURNACE? ☐ YES ☐ NO

Figure 7.1 (*continued*) Home Energy Assistance Program (HEAP) Application

149

If you apply to the New York Telephone Company for telephone Life Line Services, you authorize the Department of Social Services to disclose the information provided in your application to the New York Telephone Company for the sole purpose of assisting the company to verify your eligibility for Life Line Telephone Service.

I swear and/or affirm that the information given on this application is true and correct. I realize that any False Statements or other Misrepresentation knowingly made by me in connection with this application for assistance may result in my being found ineligible for the assistance paid to me or on my behalf. Additionally, any False Statement or Misrepresentation knowingly made by me for purpose of obtaining assistance under this program may result in an action against me which may subject me to Civil and/or Criminal Penalties. I understand that by signing this Application/Certification, I consent to any investigation to verify or confirm the information I have given and any other investigation by any Authorized Government Agency in connection with this request for Home Energy Assistance.

ALL QUESTIONS MUST BE ANSWERED AND YOUR APPLICATION MUST BE SIGNED TO GET ASSISTANCE.

SIGN HERE: X	Date Signed:
Name of Person, If Any, Who Assisted You:	Phone Number:

PERSONAL PRIVACY LAW - NOTIFICATION TO CLIENTS

The State's Personal Privacy Protection Law, which took effect September 1, 1984, states that we must tell you what the State will do with the information you give us about yourself and your family. We use the information to find out if you are eligible for the Home Energy Assistance Program and, if so, for how much. The section of the Law that gives us the right to collect the information about you is Section 21 of the Social Services Law. To make sure that you are getting all of the assistance you and your family are legally entitled to receive, we check with other sources to find out more about the information you have given us. For example:

- We may check to find out if you were working. We do this by sending your name and Social Security Number to the State Department of Taxation and Finance, and also to known employers, to tell us whether you worked and, if so, how much you made.

- We may ask the State to check with the Unemployment Insurance Division to see if you were getting unemployment benefits.

- We may check with banks to make sure we know about any income you may have received.

Besides using the information you give us in this way, the State also uses the information to prepare statistics about all the people receiving Home Energy assistance. This information is used for program planning and management. The information is used for quality control by the State to make sure local districts are doing the best job they can. It is used to verify who is your energy supplier and to make certain payments to such vendor. Your failure to provide us with the information we need, may prevent us from finding out if you are eligible for assistance and we may then have to deny your application. This information will be maintained by the Deputy Commissioner, Systems Support Information Services, New York State Department of Social Services, 40 North Pearl St., Albany, N.Y. 12243-0001.

Figure 7.1 *(continued)*   Home Energy Assistance Program (HEAP) Application

150

"Look at the hoops they make us jump through. Like we got nothing better to do than give them 'One or more of the following' " she read from the sheet. *"Why would they need more than my Social Security card anyways?"* She shook her head, poked at her pasta salad, and checked off the listed items she already had. She decided she needed to make more photocopies of everyone's birth certificates, but resented the assumptions behind the application: *"They think we give up easy. Or that if we really need it, then we better be willing to work for it. That's why they need two verifications of my address. They think all poor people be tryin' to get a free ride. Or, we poor so we got to be watched, you know? They be doublechecking us all the time."* She sucked on her teeth in disgust and pushed her soup and salad dishes away. Turning to the application, she glanced over the first page. *"I can go through this whole thing and tear it up. Every bit of it bullshit."*

Lucy interprets the class-based prejudices permeating the language of this application. She understands that this public service organization views her as an unethical, shifty person by virtue of her having to complete the application in the first place. While many bureaucracies have long and involved forms to complete, community members attached significance to this length. The number of documents indicates to Lucy that the institution has hidden agendas. With the length of the form alone, the institution daunts the applicants ("They try to scare you out of applying. Try to discourage you").[8] The application as a whole places high demands on those seeking services. First, the demand is on time and energy and can be seen in the number of hours it takes to complete these forms ("it gonna take me four or five hours just to pull this shit together"). Second, the demands are on literate skills. To make this application successful, individuals selected only information they could convincingly support. Without certain verification, such as one or more forms of identification, community members' applications would not present a compelling display of need. Residents understood that these demands were shaped from the belief that poor people need to "work" (read: appease gatekeepers) for their public assistance. "Look at the hoops they make us jump through," Lucy says. In order to receive their "awards," residents had to fill numerous institutional requirements.

Lucy also perceives the ways the institutions mistrust those they serve. Public service agencies view community members as often trying to manipulate the system of benefits in order to receive more ("they think all poor people be tryin' to get a free ride"). Because poor people are presumably unscrupulous, they will resort to illegal means more quickly, and therefore need to be policed: ("We poor so we got to be watched, you know? They be doublechecking us all the time"). These forms often asked for the same information to be presented in different ways. So verifications must accompany what the applicant lists, and when applicants handed in these forms, they often were asked verbally to recount what appears on the application. The caseworker would ask the applicant to recall specific lines of information (i.e., "so do you receive disability payments?") and doublecheck the verbal answers against the written. While one could argue that caseworkers are merely checking the internal consistency of the application, their verifications and questions indicated to residents that the institution perceives applicants as typically unethical and needing to be kept under surveillance.

My point here isn't so much that this literacy artifact represents the insidious values it does, but that Lucy critically reads this artifact, locates these insidious assumptions, and analyzes the politics imbued in this form. As she says, "I can go through this whole thing and tear it up. Every bit of it bullshit." She understands how public service institutions degrade those they seek to serve. She knows how institutional representatives view her using their own classist presumptions. She understands too that despite how much she balks at the insinuations present throughout this application, she will still apply because she needs to keep her apartment warm. She did apply for this program, and did receive the aid she sought—four months after she submitted the application.

Another example shows further debasing postures organizations can take in relation to those they claim to represent. A "Behavioral Contract" (figure 7.2) was written by social workers in Quayville's inner city Community Center and resulted from an exchange between Tawna, an eleven-year-old, and Megan, a full-time social worker.

At both long tables in the center, kids, tutors, and myself crowded each other for elbow space, sometimes making it a game. Tawna sat at the table with her tutor going over math problems. Megan and Joe floated past the tables and sometimes hovered over us as we progressed. I tutored Candy as she practiced writing her name on the tablet between us. She repeated each letter as she traced the dots

the teacher had drawn for her "Ceee. Aaaa. Nnnn." As Candy spelled
I became aware of Megan's voice: "Keep it down, Tawna."
"Tell Tyron to stop talking to me then." Tyron sitting next to
Tawna smiled big at getting her in trouble.
"I'm not talking to Tyron," Megan said with raised eyebrows.
"I'm talking to you."
"I'm trying to do my work. I'm talking to her." Tawna pointed
to her tutor.
"Just keep it down or leave."
"But I'm not the one talking." Tawna's voice was loud and every-
one watched in silence as the scene unfolded. "He been talking all
this time and you ain't said nothing to him." Megan walked out of
her office doorway where she had been watching the tutoring.
"Alright, out you go . . . " As she said this she put a hand on Tawna's
shoulder. Tawna threw the cookie she had been eating at Megan and
lurched away from her:
"Don't touch me. You can't fu——ing touch me." Tawna ran out
the door of the center. The rest of us put our heads down and went back
to work. Candy looked at me and sighed, "Dddd. Yyyyy." She was four
letters into her last name when Tawna returned with her mother, Trudy.
Trudy had many loud words with Megan while Megan tried to
explain that her daughter had been disruptive. Trudy's bottom line:
"You had no right to touch my daughter. Who in the hell gave you
permission to touch her?" Trudy didn't wait for an answer from
Megan. She simply walked to United Home, the parent organization
of the center, and complained to Megan's supervisor. After a series
of meetings between the supervisor, Trudy, and Megan, the social
workers drafted a "Behavioral Contract."

The contract embodies many of the values and assumptions institutional representatives hold about inner city residents. Mainly, the
Neighborhood Center assumes that Tawna's behavior is disruptive
and defies authority. The ultimatum that Megan gave Tawna ("Just
keep it down or leave") shows little tolerance for questioning the
decisions of institutional representatives. This contract attempts to
acculturate Tawna and her mother into the value system that etablishes
the unquestionable authority of institutional representatives over those
they "serve." The center assumes that before Tawna and her mother
deserve their services, they must accept and abide by the commands
of center representatives. Notably, this contract works in a top-down

Behavioral Contract

I, _____ do agree to the following terms; in order that I might be readmitted to the Center's program:

Obey the following rules:

1. The adults (which includes college students, volunteers and paid staff) are in charge of the children who attend the Center's activities. No child is allowed to ignore or disobey orders given by the staff.

2. When a child disagrees with a staff person's decision, the child cannot retaliate by cursing, yelling back at the person, hitting, or throwing things at the staff or other children.

3. No child is allowed to fight physically or verbally. When a problem occurs with another child, the child must tell the staff person in charge.

4. All Center staff agree on decisions, before the children find out about the decision. Therefore, it is unnecessary to go from one staff person to the other with the same question. The answer will not change, once a decision is made.

5. Each child is expected to follow directions that are given by staff.

6. No child is allowed to go in and out of the Center during afterschool tutoring hours. This means no one is allowed to go in and out of the front door or go to the store, unless permission is given.

7. The noise level must be kept down, so that all of the children can study and concentrate.

8. During the tutoring time (Mon. through Thurs., after school from 3:00 p.m. to 6:00 p.m.), all children are expected to come to the Center with homework, reading, or work on an academic assignment with the assigned tutor. Once the child has spent at least a half hour on their studies, then the child can do a quiet activity.

Figure 7.2 Behavioral Contract

Schedule

_____ is allowed to the Center only accompanied by her mother for the following time schedule:

Week 1:   One half hour, two days a week. Her days are Wednesday and Thursday. (Her counselor is _____)
            Time: From 4:30 p.m. to 5:00 p.m.

Week 2:   Same as above.

Week 3:   One half hour, one day a week accompanied by her mother.
            One half hour, one day a week by herself.

Week 4:   Same as above.

When _____ is at the Center, during the time without her mother, if any problems occur she must go back to the schedule of Week 1. If the problem is very severe, another parent/staff meeting will or may be required.
    I understand that I agree with the terms of this contract.

_____   _____

Signature of parent   Date

_____   _____

Signature of child   Date

Figure 7.2 *(continued)*   Behavioral Contract

fashion, so the behaviors of the center workers cannot be questioned and are not outlined as part of the contract. Other institutional assumptions present themselves in this contract:

• Tawna's dismissal from the center and her pending readmission reveal the center's belief in the punitive and disciplinary roles of the institution.

- The center, as a philanthropic organization, has the right to regulate patterns of behavior according to their own cultural standards for how people should act.

- The center assumes that Tawna has aggressive and violent attitudes toward the institution that must be checked at the door (see point #2 in above contract).

- The center believes that staff members should have complete authority over the children. This means Trudy must transfer her parental authority over to the center staff over a short period of time (note schedule of allowable visits at the end of the contract).

- The staff assume that a strict schedule of visits with a specific tutor will help regulate Tawna's acculturation. They assign her a counselor assuming that a counselor has more authority to control her behavior than a tutor.

Not surprisingly, Tawna and her mother refused to sign this contract. As a form of resistance, they withdrew their support of the center. Instead of viewing their withdrawal as a means to circumvent the staffs' heavy-handed attempts to manage behavior, the center staff considered their withdrawal as yet another example of community residents' antipathy toward the center. As one staff member told me, "they just refuse to work with us, even though they're the ones who need help."

Like Trudy, others in the community resisted the structuring presumptions of the center staff by avoiding the place altogether. Freesia once confronted Megan about why the center failed to hire more community residents to work there. When Megan told Freesia to "come back when her attitude changed," Freesia refused to ever go back even though she lived right next door. In an example from chapter 4 we saw that Mirena faced an eviction notice but refused offers of help from the social workers. Mirena had confirmed that the social workers turned her in to her landlords for violation of her lease, which lead to the eviction. Resistance through disassociation came with a high cost though. More commonly, residents found other ways to work around and through negative assumptions of service institution representatives. They deployed various types of language in their daily interactions with gatekeepers. As you read, keep in mind that far from being amoral, acquiescent, vessels of passivity, these individuals' conviction and agency is everywhere present in their language.

Reading through the Lines

Reading though the printed and spoken lines of gatekeepers, community members saw right to the frequently insidious values imbued in gatekeeping language. Once community residents noted these values, they crafted their own oral and written language in sophisticated ways that indirectly resisted the degrading attitudes of gatekeepers.

For example, Raejone hoped to be placed on a waiting list for Housing and Urban Development (HUD) funding called Section 8. Section 8 guarantees landlords rental payment. Because of this guarantee, landlords were often more inclined to offer apartments to families trying to move out of the inner city. In Quayville, the HUD office, particularly its primary representative, Kathy Oaks, had a reputation for foot-dragging and selective awarding of funds. Most families in the area had a Kathy Oaks story, but few stories had happy endings. In a phone conversation during which Raejone allowed me to take notes, she told me what happened when she, her sister, and her sister's friend went to Kathy Oaks's office. (In separate conversations with Raejone's sister and her friend, I validated the events Raejone described.)

> Raejone went to apply for Section 8, "and as soon as I sit down, she gonna read that application aloud to me. She said 'because some of the wordings are tricky.' The whole time I be thinking to myself, 'What? Cause I'm poor, I can't read, you f——ing bitch? Show you.' I read ahead to the part where they ask you your ethnic background, and I see where it say 'optional.' So I wait for her to tell me that question optional and she don't. She just went on ahead and checked the box that said 'Black.' So I ask her why she didn't read that part [fine print] to me and she said [here Raejone imitates Kathy Oaks's intonation] 'because most people don't care or don't read it.' I ask her what they want that information for anyway, and she said to report to the government so they can have their demographics. I say to her 'but if people don't have to report it, then how reliable is that number?' She say it's just an estimate. And I say, 'so you get funding by filling these applications out for people and filling in the information.' "
>
> "It's an everyday fight for us to get simple respect, Ellen. If someone going to look at me funny when I get my food stamps, I'm a give her the same look. I'm going to use her crap against her. I could say, 'Yo' what's your problem? Gimme my benefits.' But that just makes them think 'Oh, another lazy nigger,' and I ain't gonna

*give them that satisfaction. When it ain't like that at all. I'm a give
their own shit back to them the way they give it to me."*

The institutional representative insinuated disparaging assumptions about
Raejone which Raejone recognized, undermined, and then meta-linguis-
tically assessed. To begin with, the representative read aloud the application, assuming either Raejone could not read, or assuming that if Raejone
could read, the application demanded more sophisticated meaning-making skills than Raejone had ("She gonna read that application aloud to
me. She said 'because some of the wordings are tricky' "). Raejone immediately named this insulting presumption ("The whole time I be thinking
to myself, 'What? 'Cause I'm poor, I can't read, you f——ing bitch?'"), and
she decided on a subtle plan for challenging the case worker's stereotype
(" 'Show you.' I read ahead to the part where they ask you your ethnic
background, and I see where it say 'optional.' So I wait for her to tell me
that question optional and she don't"). When Kathy Oaks filled in the
information that Raejone did not want volunteered, Raejone saw her
chance to prove a point to the gatekeeper. Raejone noted that the
application's fine print said that the information about Raejone's race was
optional ("So I ask her why she didn't read that part [fine print] to me").
Raejone's question not only calls Kathy Oaks to task for disregarding
Raejone's rights to withhold information, but also implies that Raejone
does in fact have literate abilities. Raejone pressed Kathy Oaks to reveal
how information about Raejone's race would be used in this application
("I ask her what they want that information for anyway"). Then when
Raejone saw how the institutional structures of funding work, she challenged Kathy Oaks's gatekeeping activities ("so you get funding by filling
these applications out for people and filling in the information"). Taken
together, Raejone's linguistic resistance to this caseworker and HUD's
institutional structure works on many levels. First, Raejone had a point to
prove about her level of intelligence. Next, Raejone undermines the ways
HUD uses demographics to keep track of those to whom they assign
funding. Finally, Raejone moves back to critique Oaks's gatekeeping actions. From the beginning, she pushes at the demeaning presumptions in
the language of the HUD agent. "It's an everyday fight for us to get
simple respect" tells us what Raejone hoped to achieve from her analysis
and challenge: simple respect.

Further, Raejone metadiscursively assesses her own language strategies used when she encounters a gatekeeper's prejudice. She considers other language strategies ("I could say, 'yo,' what's your problem?

Gimme my benefits' "), but in her estimate such an approach only confirms the disregarding beliefs institutional representatives maintain ("But that just makes them think, 'Oh, another lazy nigger,' and I ain't gonna give them that satisfaction"). She shops for a linguistic tool similar to the ones institutional gatekeepers use, but different enough to undercut the gatekeeper's lurking attitudes ("I'm a give their own shit back to them the way they give it to me"). Raejone decides that she will use language that complicates the limited and limiting ideology resting beneath the surface of the caseworker's language use. Reading though the lines of gatekeepers, Raejone constructs the larger social implications of the representative's word choice, and she develops similar, yet different, lines for gaining the respect she fights institutional gatekeepers for everyday. In similar fashion, Salliemae undercut a landlord's disrespectful categorizations of her.

Defying Easy Categorization

If before the 1960s no category carried more stigma than pauper, as Katz found, then after the 1960s no category carries greater stigma than '"poor Black woman." The women in Quayville's inner city felt this stigma keenly when they searched for new apartments. Sitting on a front stoop one day, Freesia talked to those of us gathered playing cards about looking for a new apartment. "They look at your application, where you live, ask you if you on AFDC [Aid to Families with Dependent Children, commonly called welfare], and you know you ain't gonna get the place." Others agreed. "You got three strikes against you. You poor. You Black. And you a woman with kids." On another occasion sitting around a kitchen table, Salliemae talked about her apartment hunting. "You can't let them think you the typical Black woman on welfare. You gotta show them you something special." She had the classified section open wide across the table. "Look here, this one say 'AFDC need not apply.' I don't even think that's legal." To lessen the impact of the stigma they knew landlords placed on them, many community members crafted literate tactics to confound landlords' easy and reductive categorizations.

In *Stigma*, Erving Goffman, a well-known sociologist of institutions, offers an understanding of how people handle ill repute. "The stigmatized individual defines [her]self as no different from any other human being, while at the same time she and those around her define her as someone set apart. Given this basic self-contradiction of the stigmatized individual, it is understandable that she will make some effort to find a way out of her dilemma" (1963, 108–9). For the individuals in this study, the way out was often through language use, language use that landlords would recognize because it's imbued with their own cultural values. Goffman would likely call these linguistic tools a form of "covering." "Persons who are ready to admit possession of a stigma (in many cases because it is known about or immediately apparent) may nonetheless make a great effort to keep the stigma from looming large" (102). Women heads of households attempted to direct attention away from the stigmas attached to their housing applications by showing landlords their social connections.

Because they often needed a ride, and because they knew I would be interested in their interactions, community members frequently asked me to take them to look at apartments. More than this, most considered my presence an asset to their application process. "Having you with me will make them think I'm respectable. You being from the [university] and all," Mirena said as we drove to apartments. She recognized the denigrating ways landlords categorized her when she showed up to apply for the place. She also recognized that, by mere association with someone from a mainstream institution, her stock would go up in the landlord's estimation. Many women relied on lists of references to complicate the dehumanizing categorizations they believed landlords held.

Not long after I had arrived and sat at the kitchen table with Salliemae, she handed me a paper and asked me to type it on my computer for her. I asked if I could keep a copy, and with her permission I reprint it here (figure 7.3) with the names and numbers suitably altered. When I handed her the finished product (which filled an entire sheet), I asked her two questions and wrote her reply on my copy: (1) Why these people? and (2) Why on the computer?

Salliemae handed this list to every landlord who let her apply for housing. With each name she included either the person's occupation or relation to her. John Athens was an area fighter who enjoyed some success in the ring and in Quayville was a local hero. Stevie and Tracy both held positions at an area high school that Salliemae previously attended. And Salliemae's co-workers held jobs with DSS as child-care providers. By listing these professions, she indicated that her social networks included those whom landlords would likely find "respectable." Doing so, Salliemae pointed to her own respectability through association.

Salliemae Washington	Current landlord
5723 17th Avenue	Steve Kosnoski
Quayville, [State, Zip code]	XXZ-XX13
(519) 555-1212	

References

Stevie Wheeler	XXZ-XX14
(High School Guidance Counselor)	
Tracy Marinio	XXZ-XX15
(Quayville Teacher)	
Ellen Cushman	XXZ-XX16
(Ph.D. Candidate)	
John Athens	XXZ-XX16
(Boxer)	
Shulanna James	XXZ-XX17
(Co-worker)	
Willie Sam Church	XXZ-XX18
(Co-worker)	

Figure 7.3   Salliemae's List of References

Yet her list also complicates information asked for on housing applications. She had to turn in proof of her AFDC benefits when she listed her monthly income. Knowing Salliemae collected benefits, landlords would likely assume she didn't work. To counter this assumption, Salliemae listed co-workers to show she did work out of her home as a child-care provider. In many cases, landlords had to ask her about this apparent contradiction; as one said, "You're on welfare, but you work?" This opened an opportunity for Salliemae to explain her unique situation. More than this, the list of references offered a basis for conversation about Salliemae's goals to finish her General Equivalency Degree (GED) and to go to college. The first three names on her list showed her connections to local schools and a university. As Salliemae explained to me, "See, then they won't be thinking I just want to sit up and collect. They won't be thinking I'm 'dumb,' " (she put quotes around this word with her fingers). She conceptualized her audience's potential prejudices and devised a list of references that undercut the basis for these prejudices. If landlords asked for more context, Salliemae told them about her continuing education, a sure way to challenge the impoverished categories landlords typically assigned to her.

Finally, Salliemae asked me to computer-generate this list for her when usually community residents wrote them by hand. She had many reasons for this final rhetorical touch. "See, if it printed up neat and on a computer, they're gonna think I'm really trying to get a place, that I ain't 'your typical nigger on welfare' " (quoting with her hands again). Salliemae knew the stereotypes landlords have about people in her position: passive, lazy, don't want to work. She named these stereotypes and wanted landlords to perceive her as the hard-working, decent, intelligent person she is. She believed typeface, as opposed to handwritten print, showed that extra effort to impress them. "Besides," she added, "they may think I either got a computer or got access to one. Either way it's gotta be a plus for my side." With this list, she indexed beliefs she assumes landlords have about the interrelation of self-worth, social status, and technology.

This list represents Salliemae's attempts to confound the simplistic categorizations landlords often make when they see an application like hers. And her list of references demonstrates a larger pattern of literate behavior present throughout this community. In the three and a half years of this study, I saw and participated in seven lists of references for housing applications. Two families even asked for letters of recommendation to include with their applications. These applications went to the private landlords, the Housing Authority, and RIP. Simply stated, these lists catered to many mainstream attitudes about the importance of social connections, education, hard work, perseverance, and even technology—and in so doing, demonstrate no small political moxie. Residents refused to accept landlords' inscriptions of them; instead, they manipulated landlords' symbolic systems by reversing stereotypes and making them work to their own advantage. At the same time, this list plays on mainstream presumptions about poor people supposedly being isolated in ghettos, illiterate, lazy, nihilistic, and disenfranchised.

Because inner city residents like Salliemae are keenly aware of the various stigmas mainstream institutions attribute to them, they find linguistic means to point to "respectable" group connections. In Goffman's words again, "here surely is a clear illustration of a basic sociological theme: the nature of an individual . . . as we impute it for her, is generated by the nature of her group affiliations" (1963, 113). Through letters of recommendation and lists of references, then, community residents strategically challenged landlords' facile and demoralizing classifications of them. At first glance, this literacy tool appears deceptively simple, a mere recording of information. But, in the final analysis, we realize that this piece stems from an evaluation of the political situation, an interpretation of the audience's tacit beliefs, and a shrewd selection of words that both complies with and undermines the audience's preconceived notions. The final example also defies at-a-glance assessments.

Assigning a Proxy

Since Clifford and Marcus's *Writing Culture,* a popular critique of ethnographies and social science research says that researchers co-opt the voice of participants in their studies. In that famous collection, Stephen Tyler speaks of ethnographers who gather tape recordings, then huddle in their tents and offices and libraries to compose the final ethnography with extensive quotes from the tapes. "In order that the native have a place in the text, they exercise total control over her discourse and steal the only thing she has left—her voice" (1986, 128). Does this popular co-opt critique hold up so well when the reverse is true, when the participant *asks the researcher* to speak for her? In other words, do the researchers granted proxy by the participants still steal voices? Participants in this community often assigned proxies to speak for them as an oral tool they used to obviate highly asymmetrical power relations. Let me illustrate how proxies worked in this community before I push at this co-opt critique further.

Women in Quayville's inner city many times asked friends, relatives, social workers, or myself to serve as a proxy for them, particularly if the person had a well-placed foot in the door of a service institution. With a proxy to speak for them, women could survey the immediate political context and get a sense of the particular gatekeeper. For instance, when Jolinda had submitted an application to an apartment complex, she waited to hear about their conditions for accepting Section 8. Jolinda asked her sister, Lula to call and check on the status of her application because, as Jolinda told me, "Lula talk real well over the phone. She can act like she from HUD and then they won't be thinking I the one bothering them." Jolinda used her sister's voice and skill at code-switching as a front to get vital information about her application. In Jolinda's assessment of the political context, she risked too much to call for herself. In another example, one woman asked her psychiatrist to call her caseworker at DSS because the caseworker "ain't hearing me when I say I can't work." The psychiatrist made the call, and the caseworker responded favorably. Proxies could also be assigned to children. When one mother needed a small item for the house, such as tape, paper, or pens, she sent her child down to the center for it. Children were rarely turned away empty-handed because as children, they received the sympathies of center workers.

Assigning a proxy to speak and write, women in this neighborhood communicated through someone else in order to gather information or resources. Rather than forfeiting their agency and voice to a proxy, then, they used the proxy's linguistic tools for their own ends. In the following example, Lucy Cadens asked me to be a proxy for her in order for her to gather information.

> Lucy and I sat at her kitchen table. She held her cigarette in her left hand, took a long drag, and handed me a letter she received from DSS a few days before. She gave me a minute to look it over, then asked me what I thought of it.
>
> "I think you've been awarded money in some kind of lawsuit. Here where it talks about the DeAllaume lawsuit. [I pointed]. But what's a recoupment?"
>
> "They take money back from what I already owe them."
>
> I read some more. "So you got $510 from this suit?" She nodded and exhaled through her nose. "But 'fully offset from the outstanding recoupment?' I have no clue what the hell that means."
>
> "They took the money I won and use it to pay what I owe them." She looked at me real hard.
>
> "Can they do that? Don't you have a choice in how you spend your award money?"
>
> "Exactly. But if I call and ask, I may not get a straight answer. They'll know it me asking about my money. So they just gonna' tell me what I already read here." I nodded slowly, mulling over what she said. She went on, "but if you call like an outsider, they just think you want to know. Besides you can talk their talk."
>
> "Well, maybe, but since it's your letter, don't you have a right to know?"

"Not when they think I want to milk the system."

"Oh I get it. Their guard will be down, right?" Lucy smiled at me as if to say "Ellen ain't so slow after all."

"Now you with me," and she laughed. I got her phone and put it on my lap then looked at the letter again.

"OK. So you want to know if the lawsuit said anything about how your payment should be spent."

"Right. But ask them first if the lawsuit said that clients would get payments directly." After ten minutes tangled in the branches of the infamous DSS phone tree, I spoke with a live person. She told me that indeed "the court order stipulated that payments would be made to DSS, and we could put it toward any outstanding balances." I wrote her words verbatim on the back of Lucy's letter.

Lucy Cadens asked me to proxy for her because she saw herself as being in a politically precarious situation with a DSS gatekeeper. The caseworker had information about the lawsuit that Lucy needed in order to judge whether or not DSS had treated Lucy fairly. In Lucy's assessment, she risked too much to ask this question directly to the caseworker ("I may not get a straight answer. They'll know it me, a client, asking about my money, so they just gonna tell me what I already read here"). Although Lucy code-switched on many occasions, she recognized that she still risked sounding like a self-interested client to the DSS representative. She perceived that the representative would likely be on guard against giving information to Lucy, a client who "might be milking the system." To obviate this undue assumption, Lucy assigned a proxy to gather information for her. Choosing to remain silent, and handing over to me the authority to speak for her, Lucy achieved her goal in a highly asymmetrical situation with a gatekeeper.

Some might still say that Lucy forfeited her voice, her agency, to a person with a higher social status. Such an argument would have to ignore the power dynamic between Lucy and me as it unfolded in this interaction. Long before I had a clue, Lucy knew where she wanted our collusion to lead. When I finally realized what she was asking me, she smiled knowingly and said, "Now you with me." Lucy directed this interaction, given her advanced understanding of the letter.

In fact, because of Lucy's long-term experience with DSS, she constructed the meaning of this letter with the authority of someone in-the-know. She understood, for instance, the lingua franca of DSS and translated key phrases for me regarding her award ("But 'fully offset from the outstanding recoupment?' I have no clue what the hell that means." She replied, "They took the money I won and use it to pay what I owe them"). Without her instruction, I would not have understood key phrases of this letter. She is familiar enough with the institution that she sees a possible loophole in how her award was distributed. When I said, "Can they do that? Don't you have a choice in how you spend your award money?" she responded with "Exactly," as though she were waiting for me to come to this question. Yet she still needed to validate the existence of this apparent loophole. But if the caseworker thought the person asking for information might be a client out to work the system, the caseworker would in all likelihood refuse to offer up any information.

I formed an initial question to ask the representative ("OK. So you want to know"), and Lucy corrected and expanded upon it ("Right. But ask them first if the lawsuit said that clients would get payments directly"). With her correction, Lucy reveals her understanding of which question would lead to the information she needed. Had I asked my question first, we would have overlooked two possible ways by which Lucy could have had justification for lodging a complaint. Lucy has authority in this situation that she shares with me, authority from her knowledge of DSS's institutional assumptions, authority from her critical reading of the letter, and authority to sanction my speaking on her behalf.

Besides her agency in this interaction, we must note her language tools. Lucy questions the decision-making process behind a letter that many of us would simply accept without hesitation. She problematizes this letter using her understanding of how DSS works. She teaches me what the letter means and leads me to a critical reading of its message. In the end, Lucy deploys language tools to gain information she wants and to work around reductive assumptions gatekeepers likely have. My linguistic code, we could argue, was the only voice co-opted here, and Lucy co-opted it for her ends.

In reading this chapter, some may choose to focus on the bottomline results of these gatekeeping interactions: after considerable time, Lucy finally got an award from HEAP; Trudy left the center altogether; Raejone did not receive HUD funding; Salliemae did get housing, but we can't say if landlords actually changed their unfair renting practices; and Lucy never received cash for her court award. Tallying up these outcomes, we could easily argue that bureaucracies remain unyielding and paternalistically domineering. We could point to all of these as compelling evidence of systematic oppression. We would be hard-pressed to make an argument that the overarching social order changed as a result of the oral and literate proficiencies residents deploy. All of these interpretations certainly have validity, but this isn't the point.

These examples reveal the duels in dualities: where resistance meets oppression, where agency meets structure, where power to meets power over, we see linguistic strategizing. We see detailed analyses of power structures by those who negotiate them. We see dominant and counterhegemonic ideologies wrestle in the quagmire of daily politics beneath the concrete surface of what often appear to be taken-for-granted daily interactions. Perhaps the analyses and language skills residents deploy in gatekeeping encounters are small arms fired. But unless we make these exchanges stand up and be counted, we risk dismissing individuals' critical awareness.

8   The Transfer of Language in Gatekeeping Interactions

More often than not, individuals in Quayville's inner city encountered gatekeepers who obstructed their efforts to gain resources and debased residents as they did so. The last chapter surveyed the types of oral language deployed to both comply with and challenge the demands of gatekeepers. In this chapter, I consider a specific case that illustrates the oral and literate skills needed to facilitate the goals of community residents in their gatekeeping encounters. I take, for example, Raejone's college application process that extended over several months as she tried to gain admission to a local university. As with other gatekeeping encounters, texts and face-to-face interactions are central to the negotiation that takes place in her application. I will describe how, over a period of several months, Raejone systematically navigated this academic institution by transferring many of the language strategies I pointed out in the last few chapters. The transfer of language is a complicated linguistic and social process, but I believe that it can model for gatekeepers ways to use our privileged positions to benefit others.

The transfer of language has been studied on the rhetorical and ideological levels in order to show ways in which the process falls short or goes astray. Composition and rhetoric scholars have identified rhetorical skills students need in order to cross over the social distance that exists between universities and communities (Bartholomae 1989; Geisler 1994). Further, education scholars have studied conflicts in the cultural assumptions at play when students linguistically transfer community language skills to academic contexts (Moll and Diaz 1987).

James Collins and Jenny Cook Gumperz each have considered the rhetorical skills *and* the cultural assumptions at play when students transfer language in academic interactions. Collins notes the ways cultural assumptions play into the transfer of language when people speak and write in academe. Through an application of Bourdieu's notions of "habitus" and "fields," he suggests that both subjective and objective tensions contribute to linguistic production in any situation. Subjective tensions include the compromises people make in their own values in order to adapt to the value systems implicit in using a linguistic code different from their own. Objective tensions include the peer pressures individuals face from their family and friends who often want them to succeed at learning and adopting prestigious discourses. Simply put, the more experience the individuals have with prestige languages, the less subjective tensions they likely feel when transferring to a dominant code, even when objective tensions are high and the "social expectations are greater . . . that legitimate . . . language will be used" (119). In a case study of one African-American writer trying to enter a university, Jenny Cook-Gumperz also finds that transfer demands not only an "acceptance of another set of grammatical paradigms, rhetorical practices, and usage conventions," but also "demands a shift of [the writer's] basic social assumptions" (1993, 338). All of this research on the rhetorical and cultural components of transfer has been useful in defining when and under what social conditions the transfer of language occurs.

In these studies of transfer, though, scholars look at what happens when linguistic transfer is incomplete, goes awry, or compromises someone's values. We still need to account for those linguistic choices and assumptions necessary in order for the process of transfer to work well, and to potentially uplift the social and political position of people involved in gatekeeping interactions. How can gatekeepers and community members gather, select, and deploy the rhetorical tools necessary to promote the social and political equality of those seeking resources in the gatekeeping encounter?

In this chapter, I'll sketch what people on both sides of institutional encounters can do to make linguistic transfer a beneficial experience. From mid-September of 1993 to February 1994, Raejone researched area colleges and submitted an application to one, a local university (hereafter named State). During this time, she let me copy all of the literacy artifacts she produced, as well as tape-record one interaction she had with Mr. Villups, an Education Opportunity Pro-

why objective?

why objective?

gram, admissions counselor at State. She also allowed me to quote her directly on the small notepad I carried with me to our weekly meetings when we would discuss the progress she had made on her application. Let me begin with a look at the semantics she used in her application essay, her best effort to represent herself to the admissions counselors. Next, I'll look at the language the admissions counselor used to meet Raejone halfway in her admission process. Lastly, because Raejone was the first in her family and in her age group in this neighborhood to write such an essay, I want to show her process of gathering the linguistic tools she deployed in it. Certain types of linguistic savvy can de-systematize the daily workings of institutions and make organizational structures more enabling, less constraining. However, people on *both* sides of the gate need to adopt and adapt their language strategies to indicate mutual respect for each other's cultural positionings.

"I Know That I Will Be an Outstanding Student"

Statement of purpose essays funnel the best language strategies an applicant has into a concentrated representation of the self. This representation usually highlights students' attributes and contextualizes liabilities—all in an effort to convince university gatekeepers to admit potential students to the possibilities and opportunities higher education offers. To many students (and their families), the university promises intellectual development and social mobility, and they place hopes in these essays. In Raejone's statement of purpose essay, she writes in a fashion that strikes a compromise between what the university values as a good student and what she values as a good person:

> My name is Raejone Cadens. I am a twenty-two year old mother of two who is anticipating being a freshman at State majoring in liberal arts. My experience during the past four years running my informal child care has given me the confidence that I need to obtain my degree in elementary education. Through this confidence, I know that I will be an outstanding student who is driven to achieve new knowledge.
> My background experience has shown me how to teach children some skills including, counting, their colors, the alphabet, and heritage awareness. One week in every month we devote to the study of different ethnic cultures. This experience helped me understand

various cultures and heritages, as well as teaching me that instruction is complicated. I've learned how to deal with unexpected problems and to help children who are unpredictable. I've also found that if we develop children's skills (reading, writing, language, etc.) while they're young, they'll have a stronger foundation to build upon.

My short term goals include earning good grades towards my Bachelor's in liberal arts after completing my GED classes at EOC [Educational Opportunity Center]. I intend to finish my basic math, science, and social studies skills at EOC by May 1994. In addition, I'm receiving outside tutoring in English composition by a doctoral student. With these short term goals in place, I can better come to grips with my long term goals.

Within the next four years, I plan to educate myself so that I can help educate little children in inner cities to mold and sculpture their lives. I will maintain a grade point average that is required by the _____ State Department of Education in order to receive a degree in liberal arts. I also would like to minor in special education; I feel that with a major in liberal arts, as well as a minor in special education, I will broaden my opportunities as well as my abilities to teach and work towards more than one area of potential employment. My long term goal is to establish my own business in the education field which will bring a new excitement to learning for children who need motivation to achieve.

I sincerely hope you consider my application for enrollment. I believe with your resources and my strength to excel the community's children will benefit.[9]

Raejone felt good about this essay, "I like it. I like it a lot," she said as she took it out of the printer. After such a long time to research and draft, it comes from her heart and agrees with her principles. In it, she references many Black cultural assumptions and beliefs she subscribes to: the personal struggle to achieve in the face of immense obstacles; the community ethic of civic duty to return to her people what college will give her; the Black woman ideology to be strong; and finally, the highest esteem for children and the knowledge needed for their education. At the same time, it caters to the value system she believes academics share: the preference for diligent, goal-directed students; the partiality for students who want to be knowledge-makers; the esteem for those who also believe in the value of education.

Raejone bent the semantics of this essay until the meaning of the ideas most important to her indicate both her value system and the university's, even though these value systems stem from historically different centers. This semantic flexibility happens "when White English words are given Black Semantic interpretations, [and] their range of referents increases" (Smitherman 1977, 59). In other words, "since Blacks share in the consensus dialect of the American mainstream, on one level a word's referent is the same for Blacks and Whites. But since Blacks also share a linguistic subculture outside that mainstream, on another level (the Black Semantic level) the same word has multiple meanings and associations" (59). This said, a close analysis of the semantics Raejone selected and deployed in her personal statement reveals the hidden tension between her value system and the university's.

Raejone conflated her Black cultural value of self-help and personal struggle to achieve with her short-term goal to obtain her General Equivalency Degree (GED) at the Educational Opportunity Center (EOC). "My short term goals include earning good grades towards my Bachelor's in liberal arts after completing my GED classes at EOC. I intend to finish my basic math, science, and social studies skills at EOC by May 1994." A history of personal struggle rests just beneath this statement. Raejone dropped out of high school to have her first child just two weeks before her graduation. She reluctantly went on welfare when she realized that she couldn't hold a job with a baby, but found a program that paid her one small dollar an hour to watch the children of other welfare mothers in the area. Believing the only way out of this impoverished and impoverishing system was through education, Raejone tried to get her GED.

She scored a 232 on her first attempt to pass the GED (4 points shy of passing), so she was required to take basic skills classes before she could retake the test. To the admissions counselors, Raejone's short-term goal would mean that she has a neat timetable for the completion of her degree. For Raejone, her short-term goal reflects a different reality of daily struggle to achieve. To attend these classes, she would have to find a sitter for the kids, someone who didn't ask for cash, but would accept Raejone's promise to sit in return for the favor; she would have to get the kids to the sitter on time without a car in the dead of winter; the children would need to be fed and clean before she left; her homework and housework would have to be done; and even if all of this was in place, nothing out of the ordinary could happen, such as her son or daughter getting sick or a relative coming to stay with her. Her personal struggle to achieve is perhaps best indicated by her use of "come to grips with my long term goals" in the final sentence of this paragraph. To the admissions committee, this would probably read "*meet* my long term goals." From her interpretive standpoint, it reads "to *get over*," to reach her goals against tremendous odds. Her tenacious attempt to better herself stems from a deeply seated cultural belief in the value of self-help.[10] Interestingly, the Black cultural value of personal struggle overlaps with what Raejone believed the university values as the diligent student.

Raejone's long-term goals simultaneously index the Black value of maintaining reciprocity in the community, and the university's appreciation for a goal-directed student. "Within the next four years, I plan to educate myself so that I can help educate little children in inner cities to mold and sculpture their lives." Raejone's long-term goal rests on her fundamental belief that "Black people who make it, gotta' remember where they came from," as she so often told me when writing this essay. In fact, Raejone mentions her civically minded intention to contribute to her local community two additional times in the essay: "My long-term goal is to . . . bring a new excitement to learning for children," and "I believe . . . the community's children will benefit. Through this repetition, she not only adds to the coherence of her essay, but also implies her community's attitude that an individual's education should be for the community's benefit. She couched her cultural assumption in the semantics of her long-term goals, a statement that would appeal to the admissions counselors, who appreciate goal-directed students.

In another semantic double play, Raejone characterizes herself as "driven to achieve new knowledge," and she has "strength to excel." She uses the word "confidence" twice to describe herself. Before all of this, though, she is a "twenty-two year old mother of two." People in Raejone's community valued her as a strong woman who was a good mother and student and cook and daycare provider—her label as a "strong woman" was a hard-won social status in her neighborhood. Interestingly, her community value system implied by her word choice, appealed to the slightly different value system of admission counselors. To Raejone's mind, she will be an outstanding student because she's a strong woman; to the admissions counselors, she would likely be an outstanding student because she "is driven to achieve new knowledge." Her confidence and strength make her just the type of person a university would likely admit.

If the semantic choices of Raejone's essay flex to meet two different sets of value systems, a quick look at the pronouns she selected and deployed should reveal this ideological flexibility as well. Raejone wrote most of the statement with the first person singular pronoun, "I," yet she once chose the first-person plural pronoun, "we," and she twice chose the second-person plural, "you." Of course, a statement of purpose has to include "I" by virtue of the rhetorical task. Yet her use of "we" shows one place where she appeals to an overlap between her values and the university's regarding what counts as knowledge and experience. Raejone summarized her background experience that included four years of providing day care, then she detailed her pedagogical activities and what she learned from this job along the way. She concludes, "I've also found that if *we* develop children's skills (reading, writing, language, etc.) while they're young, they'll have a stronger foundation to build upon" (emphasis mine). She sees the worth of her community-based experience and knowledge about children's education, and her use of "we," links her value system to that of the university's. With one pronoun, she turns what might be perceived as a liability by the admissions committee (her working in daycare instead of finishing high school) into an asset.

She does so in light of the situational context between herself and the eventual readers: she is outside the academy trying to gain access from already educated gatekeepers. She recognizes the situational context by using the second-person plural pronoun "you" ("I sincerely hope *you* consider my application for enrollment. I believe with *your* resources and my strength to excel the community's children will benefit") (emphasis mine). This direct address to her readers points to their authority as decision-makers and as purveyors of educational resources. She flatters this authority by calling attention to it, not altogether ingenuinely, but certainly strategically.

From this initial analysis, we can see where Raejone's transfer of language actually bridges both the counselors' beliefs and her own because the semantics and lexical choices she deployed simultaneously reference two different, yet shared, sets of social values. Raejone's essay created a mutually rewarding statement of purpose by exploring the values and language of the university, and finding the common ground between these in which she could feel comfortable writing. The success of her essay depended upon both her choices of the views she expressed and the manner of her expression. Yet if we look at her text apart from the history of its production, we'll miss an important point:

in this situation, the gatekeeper was also willing to select and deploy language that signifies shared values between himself (as an African-American university representative) and Raejone.

"You Ain't Got to Say Nothin' Flowery"

Early on when Raejone first mentioned she wanted to go to college, she asked me to put her and her sister Sasha in touch with someone in admissions at State. I made an appointment, and later that week on October 12, 1993, the three of us walked in to Tony Villup's office. I asked if they minded my taping, and with their permission, I audiotaped the entire forty-eight-minute conversation. Mr. Villups first described why he thought the sisters were there and what the university had to offer. He asked them a little more about themselves and their families and told them what procedures they needed to go through to gain admission. He gave them each applications, a catalog, and informational brochures about the program. He went on to describe what the sisters might expect as students in the Education Opportunity Program (EOP). Except for a few questions and statements that Raejone and Sasha had, Mr. Villups did most of the talking. In this section, I'd like to focus my analysis on how he defined his role as institutional gatekeeper through his discourse and actions. If we agree that gatekeepers act as both judge and advocate (Erickson and Shultz 1982), Mr. Villups's code-switching and contextualization cues reveal one way a person can strike a balance between the role of judge and advocate in ways that promote social and political equality.

Mr. Villups simultaneously reproduced the language (and status) of the academy and subverted it in one setting. He situated the university's status within national, local, and inter-institutional contexts. When Sasha asked him if she could transfer into the Criminal Justice program from a community college, Mr. Villups located State's program among the country's best. "You'll need for Criminal Justice a minimum 3.25 gpa to be accepted into [this] program . . . very strong, very strong Criminal Justice program, very popular." Sasha said "Oh" quietly and looked down in response. By saying the program was very strong, which is why it required a minimum 3.25 gpa, Mr. Villups located this program in relation to all other programs in the country. In doing so, he moved the university, in particular this program, further away from Sasha's access.

Mr. Villups also situated the university's status among the highest of the fifteen colleges in this area. He told Raejone she might want to build up her GED score by attending a local community college before entering State. "But with a 252 score I have to suggest probably right off that we wouldn't be able to accept you in January in EOP. An option would be continuing at a community college. . . . Work on improving the grades, completing at least a 2.5 gpa while you're at MCC [the community college] and transferring into our program in the fall." Read one way, this statement functioned as information about the requirements for admission. Yet this statement also differentiates between the status of the community college and State. Because the admission standards for MCC are lower, she would be able to use the knowledge she gains at the community college to help her meet the challenge of the more intellectually rigorous, and thus prestigious, State. He further establishes the prestige of the university on the local level when he says: "coming to a place like [State] which is a highly competitive, large institution, a lot of students have to depend on lots of different skills." Here, again, he reproduced the status of the university by saying that it's "competitive" with the best universities in the area, possibly the country. He again distanced the university from the access of Raejone and Sasha.

Perhaps the most subtle element of Mr. Villups's reproduction of social status manifests itself in his descriptions of his own status within the institution. From a pool of 300 applicants for EOP, he decided who could be accepted to this program. Implicit in these types of functions is power over the academic future of students, a type of status to be recognized. In this situational context, this language functioned as informational for Raejone and her sister, as a reproduction of social relations, and as a signifier of each one's own power.

As one result of this discourse, these women felt dwarfed in the face of the university. "Damn. I don't know if I can cut it here," Raejone said as we left his office. His language also made them seek the community college option before they transferred to the "real challenge." These women represented themselves differently after talking to him. "Maybe we should start out small and work our way up to State. I want to make sure I can do it before I get to the really big place," Sasha said as we got into the car to leave. When they went into this interview, they were able to meet the challenge of this university because they had faith in their abilities. After this talk, they recast themselves in a role that was in a lower social, and less hopeful, position for success. With this we see the constraining function of gatekeeping discourse; the sisters had their opportunities shrunk, their goals reduced, their estimations of themselves reflected back to them in more limited ways.

However, taken alone, this analysis could not account for the favorable impression Mr. Villups made on Raejone and Sasha. When we left the office Raejone said that "he seem real. He didn't always talk real formal . . made everything understandable" and Sasha agreed. Later that week in another conversation, Raejone said that Mr. Villups "talked with us, not at us, or over us." Somehow, he impressed these women as a decent man who not only has the power to open the university's prestigious gates for them, but who sounded genuinely interested, inviting them in as equals, making the university accessible to them.

In the midst of recreating the university's status and prestige with his discourse, Mr. Villups departed from academic social language and invited Raejone and Sasha into the university's discourse community he was representing. He code switched from White to Black English, and in doing so, legitimized the use of their shared dialect in a context where White is the prestige language. Through a close analysis of just a small portion of their interaction, I hope to show how the ideology implicit in Mr. Villups's code-switching (Gumperz 1982) and paralinguistic cues (Erickson and Shultz 1983) functioned as an equalizing force. His discourse that reproduced the university was shot through with a subversive discourse of solidarity, Black English. The layers of social significance of Mr. Villups's code-switching can best be exemplified in the transcript.[11] Mr. Villups addressed Sasha:

And if you were to tell me something today . .

as to why you want to attend here / . . and why

the university should admit you . . . //

what would it be? //
[dec]

He sat back and folded his hands across his chest. Long pause. Sasha's head was down, and Raejone and I looked at each other, then down. Mr. Villups leaned across his desk, his arms extended to Sasha and smiled:

You ain't gotta think of nothin' *flowery* //
[acc]

Sasha chuckled and replied softly:

I wanna .. I wanna *make* somen' of myself //

Tony: OK
    [acc]

Sasha: Wanna be *proud* of myself //
    [dec]

Tony: How will education help you do that? //
    [dec]

He leaned in further and made eye contact with her.

Sasha: "It'll keep me . . . " (Here her voice trailed off, she shrugged and looked down.)

Tony: Well .. you know / I think you started out

real good // Alright / You can do this . . .
    [acc]

it's good that you decided you wanted to
[dec]

do that //

Mr. Villups initially asserts his authority with his question ("And if you were to tell me something today . . . what would it be?"). This question could have functioned as an open invitation for Sasha to persuade him of her abilities. Instead, it functioned as a bold assertion of his authority, all because of his contextualization cues. He increased his proxemic distance from them by leaning back in his chair and decreased his accessibility by folding his hands across his chest—thus firmly establishing the asymmetry of the power relations unfolding in this situational context. The sisters' responses to this question indicated they were uncomfortable with his authoritarian posturing. They averted their gaze and simply didn't risk an answer. His use of authority this way alienated them into the silence of resistance.[12]

Yet he quickly subverts his status and authority by "talking Black" to her. He invites Sasha to use their shared linguistic code: "You ain't gotta think of nothin' *flowery*." This syntactical construction indicates Black English with its double negative; also, "ain't" is typically used in Black English as a replacement for the auxiliary verbs "to be" or "to have," used in White English (Labov 1972; Kochman 1970). Further, the tempo of this utterance was accelerated and said in a higher-pitched register. He also called attention to the status of language by saying that her words don't have to be "flowery," or the prestigious language usually used in that context. His increased loudness and marked emphasis on "flowery" indicated his mockery of the formality of his initial questions. He both complies with and subverts the discursive conventions typical in this situtational context.

His code-switch invited Sasha to speak their shared dialect in a situational context where White is the prestige code. He legitimized their shared dialect by bringing it into this setting, and cleared a social space for her that allowed her to represent herself as a student. Once she began to speak, he encouraged and prompted her ("How will education help you do that?"). He asked this in a decelerated tempo, with a low-pitch register and tone. These prosodic features, coupled with his direct eye contact, added a significant measure of personal connection to his second question. Sasha attempted an answer but admitted later in the car ride home that she wished she could have thought of something more to say. By showing his respect for their shared vernacular, Mr. Villups's code-switching had the social function of affirming and subverting his authority as a gatekeeper. He cleared a rhetorical space for her to bring her community-based discourse to bear in a context where fluency in academic English is valued. Acting simultaneously as both judge and advocate, then, Mr. Villups encouraged the transfer of Sasha's home-based discourse, an action that supports Moll and Diaz's finding that "transfer, when it occurs, is usually socially arranged" (1987b, 309). Mr. Villups in many ways socialized Sasha into the rigors of the academy where one is questioned intently to create knowledge individually.[13]

Raejone's essay discussed earlier this chapter stemmed directly from this interaction. Mr. Villups asked for a personal statement from each of them, so he could better represent their case to the other admission counselors. Raejone knew what questions to answer when she sat to write ("And if you were to tell me something today... what would it be?"). As she spellchecked the final draft of her personal statement, she told me that she pictured herself writing to Mr. Villups and the other counselors on the admissions committee. She gathered information about her audience and personalized what is usually a bureaucratic process. His gatekeeping actions suggest the various means by which a person with the power and status to do so can act as both judge and advocate to the benefit of those seeking opportunities in gatekeeping encounters. The transfer of Raejone's and Mr. Villups's oral and literate language enacted the democratic ideology behind the establishment of EOP programs—to give equal opportunity to underrepresented students in the university with the hope of promoting social and political equality. Raejone transferred her language in an effort to work within this equal opportunity program; and Mr. Villups transferred his language in ways that invited her to obtain the equal opportunity this program promises. They linguistically navigated this institutional exchange together. Raejone not only used this interaction to inform her understanding of her audience, but she also poured over the literate resources Mr. Villups gave her to gather a language for presenting herself in the essay.

"I Been Thinking a Lot about Power"

Raejone researched the university's language, and what it values in students, knowledge, and academic standards. After dinner one Sunday evening in early September, she said, "you know, I been thinking a lot about power and I want you to tell me everything you did to get through the university. . . . I want the words too. I want to know what I'm going to hear when I get there. I need the words." I told her she might learn quite a few of the words as she actually worked with some theories and tried to summarize them. She agreed, and on my next visit I gave her a copy of a composition textbook that I used. Although I can't draw a full picture of how she interacted with the text when I wasn't there, she often would talk to me about what she had read, or she would show me a paragraph she wrote on a subject in the book.

Her research into the language of the university also included:

- Attending a history class to obtain her GED.

- Consulting with a friendly high school counselor who "always speaks professional" because as Raejone said, when "you around different people, well, you pick up how they talk."

- Obtaining a handout on writing personal statements from the Writing Center as a guide. She referred to it as she composed her personal statement on the university computers. When she looked over the second draft of her essay she said: "I still need to tell them more about" and then read from the text, " 'my expectations with regard to the program and career opportunities.' "

- Finally, when correcting her writing, she asked me to read it aloud: "I want to hear how it sounds from you." As I read it aloud, she corrected small grammatical errors, relying on her ear for spoken language to help her polish her written language. She decided her essay was done because it "sounded all right."

All of these strategies and resources Raejone gathered and deployed to help her prepare for and engage in the language of the university. She achieved the fluency of her personal statement through self-determination, discipline, and a deeply rooted desire to develop herself and gain entrance to higher education that has historically promised mobility to Blacks. She also charted specific ways in which she could "make it through State" by reading the undergraduate bulletin.

One Sunday after our initial meeting with Mr. Villups, Raejone and I tried to make sense of the State bulletin and all the application materials Mr. Villups gave us: brochures, EOP descriptions, applications, procedures, and the catalog.[14] After dinner, Raejone and I sat in the living room with all her information. She had been reading the materials and had specific questions for me. She handed me the catalog: "How will I afford this tuition? and How do I know what courses to take for my major?" The first question was easier to deal with because Mr. Villups had pointed out a table in the EOP program description ("Educational Opportunities Program: An Investment in Human Capital") that discussed the cost of education at State. Even though this listed the total cost for a single EOP Freshman as close to $9,000, "the university, in most instances, was able to provide large enough financial aid 'packages' to EOP freshmen to prevent them from having to borrow or work during their first year of study."

I read this aloud to Raejone, who was flipping through the bulletin: "That's good," she said. "Here's another list of costs. And here's something that says the cost for this year." She handed me a simple white sheet that projected the cost for 1993–94, "College Costs (Total Educational and Personal)." Raejone pointed out that while these costs were still high, compared to a private college they were inexpensive. Raejone held up the bulletin she had been pouring through: "Look at all these scholarships and grants. Shouldn't I be applying for these also?" She had marked with an asterisks all the grants and scholarships for which she thought she might be eligible. I said that she was automatically eligible for some of these when she filled out her financial aid form. She nodded and sighed. As we held open these handouts, brochures, and catalogs, she and I began to see paths of access as well as the enormity of the goal Raejone had set for herself. Considering Raejone's situation (the kids, costs of education and living, needing to move because of an unresponsive landlord, her arthritis and migraines, the needs of her siblings and boyfriend, and then all the complexities underneath these), we begin to see a context for these texts that demarcates more exacting costs. Raejone knew this and continued to conceptualize exactly what she needed to do and when in order to get into the university. Her questions functioned as navigation tools in the institution because they allowed her to actively shape her current responsibilities into those similar to a student's.

Her second question, though, stymied us. Raejone showed me the "Requirements for the Bachelor's Degree." The overall requirements for the BA were:

1. A minimum of 120 credits.

2. At least 90 credits in liberal arts and sciences.

3. The completion of general education requirements . . .

4. The completion of a writing requirement.

5. 30-36 credits in a major . . .

6. The completion of a minor . . .

7. 24 credits in professional courses for the candidate desiring state certification in education.

With this outline we still needed to understand which classes would fill which requirements leading to her degree and certification in primary education. She asked me to find the outline for that degree in the book. "I'm just not seeing it," she said. Flipping ahead, she found a list of courses for her general education requirements, but even this was confusing for us. "It says here I need 'six graduation credits in each of' these 'three categories.' But six classes for these areas means I'll be there forever. That's 18 classes and say I take 4 a semester. . . . " I thought about her math, and then checked how many units each class was. I said that each class was probably three credits, and flipped to the back of the bulletin to doublecheck. Some were three and some were four: "See here, it has a number in parentheses next to the name of the class? That's how many credits it is." She turned ahead, with pages 30-37 still marked with the fingers of her left hand. "I saw these. The course in African-American studies looks good." She had underlined this course and placed an asterisk next to it for her future reference.

"Yeah, but where are the requirements for my major? This catalog's so confusing. Look how we have to keep going back and forth in it. Where's primary education?" I said it was confusing, and it probably had to do with the size of the place that they needed to break it down this way because they have so many courses to offer. I went to the index, telling her what I was doing and why, found the page citation for the education department, and turned to 165. Here, just under the hierarchical list of professors, I read the description of the degrees offered. "The Department of Education Theory and Practice administers programs leading to provisional and permanent certification to teach academic subjects in secondary school in _____ State" (165). I read ahead for the section on primary education, scanning furiously. "Raejone? I don't think they have a primary education program."

"What? State's suppose to be this BIG place. They don't have a primary degree?" She sat back in her rocker and closed the folder of information she was holding in her lap. "Now where am I gonna go to get this?" I shook my head, part disbelief, part frustration at spinning our intellectual wheels in the mud of their bureaucracy. Raejone called to State the next day and confirmed that she would have to go to a private Catholic college to study primary education in this geographic area.

Our assumption was telling: we assumed that because of its size and prestige, State would surely have this program. "Where in the hell do we get primary teachers, then, if the biggest university in the area ain't puttin' 'em out?" Raejone asked. While we were negotiating the literature, collectively looking for access into the university, we ran into a closed door. This literacy event reveals how easily we got lost in academic bureaucracy. Just to try to negotiate the requirements for any major demanded a back and forth between three different sets of information: the list of overall requirements for the degree, the list of departmental requirements, and the list of actual courses. Working through the catalog was an exercise in trying path after path of access, pasting together various parts of information to navigate the options and obstacles in order to reach Raejone's educational goal. She eventually applied for a degree in liberal arts.

Raejone used her institutional literacy skills to demystify the university in much the same way that Afriganzia demystified her community's structure in "The Game of Power" described in chapter 5. Demystification of an institution is central to the process of navigating gatekeeping interactions well. Part of the process of transferring language, then, includes gathering together rhetorical skills and cultural assumptions that comprise the gatekeeper's positions in a situational context. Raejone, through her problematic reading of the catalog, gathered useful information that allowed her to unmask part of this university's organization. In reference to earlier sections of this chapter, we also see that Raejone gathered information from Mr. Villups about what the university values in students as well as where the EOP program and he as a counselor stand in relation to the rest of the university's hierarchy.

So through one part of her process of transfer, Raejone uncovered a great deal of information about the value systems and social hierarchy of State. Demystification, you'll recall, was one of Raejone's goals at the beginning of her application process. Remember what she said to me in September 1993 when she first thought to go to college: "You know, I been thinking a lot about power and I want you to tell me everything you did to get through the university. . . . I want the words too. I want to know what I'm going to hear when I get there. I need the words." To be institutionally literate in this inner city, residents had to think about power, research ways in which other people negotiate various institutions, and learn the precise types of language valued by the particular institution.

Conclusion

The transfer of language can promote social and political equality, an egalitarian ideology often implicit, yet not actualized, in encounters with social service institutions. Raejone and Mr. Villups both carefully transferred language practices in order to facilitate Raejone's striving. They both deploy specific linguistic strategies in order to enact the democratic principles that made this interaction possible in the first place; the mission of EOP programs is to provide infrastructure needed to give underprepared students a fighting chance in college. Let me summarize some of their institutional language tools below. (Though I list these side-by-side, I do not intend any correlation between the strategies.)

Raejone	Mr. Villups
• Flexed the semantics of her essay to meet two separate sets of cultural values.	• Modeled academic discourse for Raejone and Sasha.
• Evoked shared ethics by choosing a pronoun of solidarity.	• Provided literacy resources to the sisters.
• Flattered authority of gatekeepers.	• Invited the sisters to speak Black English. Legitimized their shared dialect.
• Questioned the university's textual representation of itself.	• Encouraged Sasha when she used academic discourse.
• Assessed the utility of her language strategies.	• Explained the university's requirements for admission.
• Researched the language of the academy and braced herself for the unknown.	• Made himself accessible for a significant period of time (48 mins.).
• Knew and addressed her linguistic shortcomings (asked me for "words").	• Got to know them personally.
• Justified her writing against successful models found in the handout.	• Invited their questions.

Raejone and Mr. Villups's linguistic strategies help us exemplify bell hooks's ideal: "To claim border crossing . . . as the deepest expression of a desired cultural practice within a multicultural democracy means that we must dare to envision ways such freedom of movement can be experienced by everyone" (1995, 5). Gatekeepers have to personalize equal opportunity in everyday interactions if we are to realize a "freedom of movement" among all citizens. By respecting the linguistic resources, values, and knowledge people bring with them from their communities, gatekeepers can be fair judges and informed advocates. When individuals on both sides of the institutional exchange adopt and adapt their language, social structures open up more opportunities.

Even though Raejone had a rich and fairly positive gatekeeping encounter, I will not be Pollyannish about language transfer. Inner city community members labor under harsh conditions that too often keep them from taking advantage of opportunities when they do arise. Raejone never did get into college—her application was lost in the mail, and she was evicted shortly after she sent it. She remained homeless for a year and a half, shuffling from relatives' homes to shelters, farming her kids out to other friends and relatives as she tried to find housing. Her son had lead poisoning. Since most of the buildings in this area were constructed before 1919, walls had been coated again and again with lead paint. Welfare officials would not let her move into an apartment that had lead present and tested each potential place before allowing her to move. Eventually she found a small apartment and after some months found herself a job as a nurse's aid. Calling herself a "professional ass-wiper," she places her educational hopes in her children now.

Raejone's institutional encounter was a relatively positive experience when compared to the ones in the next two chapters. Even with her disappointment over her major, she learned some of the language practices and social values of higher education. Even though individuals, like Raejone, conceptualize the intricacies of power relations, deploy oral and written language strategically, and locate opportunities in one arena of their lives, other institutional arenas rarely provided consistent support that would allow community members to take advantage of their opportunities and potential. The ultimate sad outcome of Raejone's application process serves to remind us—and to check the claims of this study—that multiple economic and social forces push hard on poor people.

9 Evaluating the Tools

The last four chapters have shown how inner city residents practice and acquire institutional language skills in their community, and how they deploy these skills in gatekeeping interactions. This chapter, and the next, bring full circle the process of linguistic development in this community. Residents learned, deployed, and, as we'll see, assessed their oral and literate skills. After gatekeeping interactions, many times area residents returned home to discuss with their family and friends the language used as the exchange unfolded. Sociolinguists call this kind of evaluative talk metadiscourse, or statements that critique, interpret, and analyze oral and literate strategies. Metadiscourse serves various social functions such as: controlling the flow of discourse and maintaining certain people's authority (Stubbs 1983; Philips 1996), constructing and evaluating culturally based interpretations of dominant cultures (Basso 1979), and shaping the proficiency needed to transfer and transform language in various settings (Briggs 1986). I'm interested in describing the metacommunicative evaluations that these individuals used to understand the language of their interactions with gatekeepers. Gatekeeping interactions became case studies of collective and collected knowledge that residents used to understand their linguistic and political struggles with wider society's institutions. I find that during gatekeeping encounters, individuals never simply "reproduced" social structures, as though they were blindly immersed in and acquiescent to routinized forms of domination.

Instead, individuals used metacommunicative assessments to teach each other ways to work with and against institutional representatives. They use metadiscourse as social commentary on gatekeepers' racist and classist attitudes resting beneath the surface of language

189

use. Finally, they used metadiscursive analysis to find small openings for opportunity in the language of institutional agents. In all, metadiscursive evaluations present community-based symbolic systems of resistance. The examples presented in this chapter and the next depict residents' antihegemonic understandings that are "always pressing, testing, probing the boundaries of the permissible" (Scott 1990, 200). Some readers may judge these examples as inferior when compared to forms of overt resistance. To do so, though, would overlook the political function of area residents' metadiscourse: namely, it allows them to objectify the social positionings of themselves in relation to gatekeepers, to interpret the daily politics contributing to these positionings, and to refine the oral and literate tactics they need to jockey for better social positions in everyday interactions. Their meta-analysis of language reveals their critical awareness of methods for both complicating and complying with social structures. To illustrate these points, this chapter presents a number of instances where community residents metacommunicatively discussed the oral and literate strategies used in gatekeeping interactions.

"You Gotta Be Polite"

Lucy had just returned home from a day of apartment hunting. Her sister, Jolinda, Jolinda's eldest daughter Rachel, and Lucy's children, Sasha and Afriganzia, all sat around Lucy's kitchen table. Someone asked how her search went.

"I put in an application up there at Lakeview by the K-Mart?" Jolinda nodded. "But the fu——ers at two different places didn't even let me apply because of my Section 8."

"And it's guaranteed money," Jolinda said.

"Yeah, guaranteed money for poor folks. They don't want poor folks living in their place though." The phone rang, and Rachel answered.

"Yeah? . . . Who this?" She handed the phone to Afriganzia. Jolinda furrowed her brow at her daughter:

"Why you answer the phone like that? Didn't you just hear her say she applied for a place? What if that a landlord?"

"It shouldn't matter how I answer the phone."

"Well it do. You got to be polite."

"More like pol-White," Rachel said under her breath. Sasha chuckled, but Jolinda looked at Lucy and shook her head.

This example shows two forms of meta-analysis; one focuses on the individuals' interpretations of the politics behind the landlords' refusal to let Lucy apply for housing; the other focuses on the politics of using "polite" English when answering the phone. Lucy and Jolinda point out hidden reasons why landlords refused to give Lucy an application. Jolinda notes the counterintuitiveness of the landlords' denial ("And it's guaranteed money"). Section 8 assured property managers that they would receive Lucy's rent from a federal subsidy. One would believe that such an assurance would encourage managers to allow recipients to move into their apartments. Lucy cites the class prejudices tainting this logic. ("Yeah, guaranteed money for poor folks. They don't want poor folks living in their place though.") Section 8 stigmatizes those who receive it as being poor, and landlords often outrightly rejected the applications of poor people. The apartment manager's refusal invites Lucy and Jolinda's social commentary about landlords' prejudices.

Even with their critique hanging in the air, Jolinda scolds her daughter for answering the phone as she normally does. She says, "Why you answer the phone like that? Didn't you just hear her say she applied for a place? What if that a landlord?" Jolinda recognizes that her daughter's regular way of answering the phone would likely put off a prospective landlord who might be calling Lucy. Even though Jolinda does not agree with the ways in which landlords demeaningly perceive them, she maintains the need for polite deference to them when they telephone. The schism between what she believes and how she advises her daughter to act show the place where the hidden transcript meets the public transcript, where subversive ideology becomes veiled in the public discourse of a phone call. In this context, "we are dealing with an unobtrusive realm of political struggle" (Scott 1990, 183). Said simply, Jolinda knows that real material consequences rest in the public display of politeness to landlords, and because of these material consequences, she tells her daughter to appear deferential when landlords phone.

Her daughter quickly points out that "it shouldn't matter how [she] answer[s] the phone." In a situation where all things were equal, the discourse she uses to answer a phone should not make a difference for Lucy's housing opportunities. But, as Jolinda points out, Rachel's ideal does not exist. The way a person answers a phone leaves an impression that could confirm the caller's stereotypes, and so, in Jolinda's read of the political situation, her daughter had "to be polite." Rachel sizes up that linguistic strategy and attaches to it a racial significance: "more like pol-White." She realizes that being polite was a polite way of saying she should adopt White English to appeal to potential landlords. In short, this interaction makes us privy to two forms of meta-analysis. The first form critiques the race and class assumptions of many of society's apartment owners. The second form assesses community members' oral language tactics used in the face of these assumptions. A mundane activity, such as answering the phone, generated social commentary and revealed their insights into language and politics.

"That's Sad, Those People"

> *Lucy invited me to her place for dinner: hamburger patties in dark gravy, mashed potatoes and corn on the cob. She, her boyfriend, Tony, and I chatted after we ate. Tony described how institutional representatives react to his code-switching to White English.*
>
> *"Yeah, when I don't use slang, people get shocked. They expect you to say, 'Yo, bro', whassup with you?' That's sad, those people. They aren't ready for me to talk like them. It changes their perception of me."*

Tony's metadiscourse points to people's preconceived notions related to identity and language. Because gatekeepers see an African-American male standing before them, they believe he will likely speak "slang" or Black English with them. Tony finds this presumption disturbing because it indicates their one-dimensional characterizations of African-Americans—they're Black so they only know Black English. Thus, when Tony code-switches, gatekeepers look shocked because, as he says, "they aren't ready for me to talk like them." For many, a person's identity indicates the types of language use they're likely to employ, which Tony finds reductive. This one-to-one association of language and identity limits the point of view of gatekeepers, because they judge a person on skin color alone. As a result, when Tony adopts the predominant linguistic code in front of institutional agents, "it changes their perception of [him]"; they adjust their preconceived notions of who Tony is, where he came from, and what language skills he has at his disposal.

His metadiscourse makes explicit what he understands to be the racists assumptions of gatekeepers. When interacting with institutional agents, identity, language, and politics combine together. When taken together with the last example, these two instances suggest three components of community members' attitudes toward code-switching: (1) they understand the pragmatic need to code-switch; (2) they conceptualize the asymmetrical power relations that exist when code-switching, and (3) they interpret the racial implications of code-switching. Afriganzia had similar perceptions of code-switching, as illustrated in chapter 6. She adopted the White mask of institutional language in order to confound gatekeepers' stereotypes, stereotypes similar to the ones Tony describes in the above instance. In all, their metadiscourse furthers understandings of the social import of code-switching.

Often scholars describe the social functions of code-switching without exploring the larger social implications attendant upon shifting linguistic codes. For example, among the many social functions of code-switching, one is to mark group identification in situational contexts (Gumperz 1982a, 65). In order to classify the social uses of code-switching, scholars refer to the "observable sequential or syntactic features of the interaction" (Gumperz 1982a, 83). That is, studies of code-switching look closely at sections of actual transcripts where code-switching manifests itself, and researchers determine *why* individuals code-switch on the bases of these interactions alone (Baynham's 1993; Heller 1982; Akinnaso and Ajirotutu 1982). Yet these studies presume that individuals are not able, or perhaps not willing, to describe their reasons for choosing to use one code over another in particular asymmetrical situations. John Gumperz describes how this methodology arose:

> While linguists, concerned with grammatical description as such, see the code alteration as highly salient, participants immersed in the interaction itself are often quite unaware which code is used at any one time. Their main concern is with the communicative effect of what they are saying. Selection among linguistic alternates is automatic, not readily subject to conscious recall. . . . For the most part participants have no readily available words or descriptive terms to characterize the process of switching as such. (1982a, 61–62)

Since participants apparently have little conscious thought about the social functions and ramifications of code-switching, the analysis is left to linguist who look to transcribed interactions for clues. While I do not know why participants in Gumperz's work were disinclined to discuss their reasons for code-switching, I do know that the meta-analysis participants in this study provided reveals their awareness of the political implications and cultural ramifications of their code-switching. To their mind, using White English provided a necessary tool against the discrediting notions institutional representatives often entertained about their language and culture. Rather than an automatic, taken-for-granted use of language, their choice to use White English in asymmetrical interactions was a forced choice, forced by pragmatic needs and an unforgiving social order. And they knew it.

"I Can Pick Up on a Place Real Quick"

> Kasha and Chaos just returned from a campus visit to a college in another city. They had been invited to campus through the Higher Educational Opportunity Program. I had just visited with Lucy and was sitting on her front stoop. Kasha sat on the stoop with me and showed me her application. Chaos stood at the end of the steps looking up and down the street to see who was around. She and Chaos talked about their visit, and how interested they were in fashion design. Their conversation turned, and Kasha said:
>
> "They talk all different up there. I had to listen hard to understand what they was saying."
>
> Chaos replied, "Yeah but we can do it. I can pick up on a place real quick. Hear how they talk, and talk like them."
>
> "I guess if we there long enough . . . " her thoughts trailed off as she glanced over her application. She looked up and said, "Yeah, 'cause when I'm around White people, I do catch on to how they talk. But it ain't gonna be that easy, Chaos."

These young adults assessed the foreign nature of formal, academic discourse and the means by which they could acquaint themselves with it. Kasha noticed how "they talk all different," from her own community-based language. She had to listen close in order to follow the conversation. The tone of her voice indicated to Chaos that she might be feeling daunted. He encouraged her with, "Yeah, but we can do it. I can pick up on a place real quick. Hear how they talk, and talk like them." Chaos reflects his strategies for learning to speak White English—listening and imitating. He states that he can appear to be "like them" by appropriating the dominant linguistic code and masking his own code. Notably, he does not say he wants to become those speakers, or even immerse himself deeply in their language. Instead, he wants to be *like* them without, he implies, forsaking his own cultural and linguistic identity.

Kasha adds another means through which she acquires a privileged discursive code. She interacts with Whites over a period of time to "catch on to how they talk." She finds that practice with those who speak White English provides her a means to gain some measure of fluency. Her caveat, "but it ain't gonna be that easy, Chaos," suggests her hesitation in making such drastic alterations in her social networks and living environment needed to immerse herself in academic linguistic practices.

Their metadiscursive assessments reveal a conceptualization of how one learns to use institutional language in contexts where White people represent the majority. Yet Kasha's thoughts also indicate some reluctance in moving so far away, literally and figuratively, from their community when having to learn this form of institutional language. Their observations complicate John Baugh's description of the linguistic and social distances between inner city residents and White society: "Minorities, by virtue of being minorities, have been isolated from the social environments where the 'majority' dialect thrives" (1983, 3). As young adults, Kasha and Chaos felt this isolation more because their daily lives centered on tightly knit social interactions with friends, teachers, parents, and center staff workers. Adults who had responsibilities for children, though, frequently interacted with institutional representatives.

One result of Kasha and Chaos's relative isolation from White society is that, "for Blacks as a whole, the question of dialect loyalty has been cast against a backdrop of poverty and other isolating cultural factors. For many the first step out of the ghetto came in the form of adopting the norms of successful Americans" (Baugh 1983, 7). These teens resist the easy adoption of White English. Out-and-out adoption of privileged discourse has negative consequences for residents, who face possible ostracism from their community for acting "whitewashed." Residents often sought the middle ground between adoption and adaptation in order to achieve a modicum of social mobility. Overall, these teens' metacommunicative assessments reveal some of the complexities involved in grappling with the shift from Black to White English and the foreignness of contexts where White English prevails.

"What I See and What They See Are Two Different Things"

> When Afriganzia co-directed a summer literacy program for United
> Home, Sarah, the director, asked Afriganzia to divulge information
> about community residents. Sarah hoped Afriganzia would become
> a neighborhood-based informant who could help the center staff in
> their advocacy efforts. After her final meeting with Sarah, I asked the
> teen how it went.
> "If I was up here [at United Home], I would say the same thing.
> I'd want someone down there [in Afriganzia's neighborhood] to tell
> them what's going on. What I see and what they see are two different
> things. Guess you gotta live in that environment."
> "What do you mean?"
> "See, at the end of their day, they drive off in their car and go home
> to Westminster [suburb of Quayville]. They don't know what happens
> after dark. They may be really tryin' to help, but they can't because
> they're not _down_ there. You have to be experienced to help. Can't
> really tell what's happening when they hear it from someone else."

Afriganzia problematizes the ways center workers position themselves in relation to the neighborhood and neighbors. The center staff
need to gather information about residents if they hope to fulfill their
roles as advocates. In Afriganzia's assessment, the social workers remain too distanced from those they seek to help, in part because of
their class standing ("at the end of their day, they drive off in their car
and go home to Westminster [suburb of Quayville]"). Because they're
middle class, the social workers remain socially removed from the
ones whom they hope to represent in their advocacy.

Afriganzia interprets this social distance when she says: "They may
be really tryin' to help, but they can't because they're not _down_ there."
She emphasized the word "down" to indicate both it's White and Black
English meanings. In White English, the word "down" means physically located in the inner city, as in down the hill from United Home.
In Black English, the meaning of "down" refers to a social closeness in
relations with community members. To be "down with" someone or
something, in Black English, signifies that the person has an insider
status, a status that allows him/her to understand the perspective of
someone or the symbolic meaning of something. Since the social workers aren't down there in the inner city, physically or socially, they "can't
really tell what's happening when they hear it from someone else."

Instead of this first-hand experience, the social workers rely on second- and third-hand information about a family's problems. To Afriganzia's mind, "they hear it from someone else." The social workers do their jobs based on gossip between neighbors. Interestingly, though, Afriganzia admits that if she were in Sarah's position, she too would be courting an informant from the area: "If I was up here [at United Home], I would say the same thing. I'd want someone down there [in Afriganzia's neighborhood] to tell them what's going on." She critically conceptualizes the existing social positionings between area residents and center staff, and she finds these positions hinder the social workers, who "may be really tryin' to help."

Afriganzia's metadiscourse, then, illustrates her understanding of the interdependent nature of the relations between the center staff and community members. The center staff need to be involved with community members in order to perform their roles and maintain their job security. The community members may want, and sometimes need, the center's help, but they do not want the center to survive solely on their problems. On the contrary, neighbors wanted a hand in running the center, wanted to be hired by United Home. (In chapter 7, I briefly explained Freesia's challenge to Megan about hiring more residents to work in the center.) Earlier that summer, when Sarah met with both Afriganzia and me to discuss the progress of the literacy program, Afriganzia asked Sarah "why can't people from the community help run the center?" In the teen's view, the community would be better served if the center staff were not only more involved in the neighborhood, but if the community residents were paid to be involved in the center as well. Her analysis of the relations between the center and residents indicated the one-sided nature of involvement: the staff preys on the hardships of community members. She considers, instead, a shift in the social positionings of the staff that may open up the possibility of more reciprocal, mutually beneficial interactions.

"They So Nosy over There"

Sasha had just come in from watching an interaction between a center staff member and a woman on the stoop. Sasha sat at the kitchen table with her mother and me. She was annoyed with the way the center worker had approached the woman on the stoop and asked a personal question. She ended her rant with, "They so nosy over there. I bet she won't never ask for their help again."

Lucy had lit a cigarette as her daughter talked. She exhaled: "I don't like them knowing my business. When I want something, I'll go to them, but they tell everyone my business. RIP. Megan told RIP Disco [Lucy's son] dealing. I had told her that myself because I wanted them to help him get a job. She told RIP, and they got on me. She just don't know where to stop. I tell them something and it run right through them to someone else. So I just don't tell them nothing about me."

Lucy and her daughter judge the ways in which center staff members handle the information they receive on community members. When the center worker asked the woman on the stoop a personal question, Sasha interpreted this gesture as flying in the face of the community ethic that values privacy and discretion. The invasive questions earned the center representative the label of "nosy," a label that indicated not only residents' suspicion about why she was asking, but also their withdrawal from center workers who encroach upon their private lives. Lucy had a similar story to the one Sasha told, but she had also found a way around their intrusive behaviors.

To begin with, Lucy believed that telling Megan that Disco had started dealing would prompt Megan to help her son find a job. Instead of helping Disco find a job, though, Megan reported Lucy to the landlords, who harassed Lucy to make him stop dealing (see chapter 4 for the entire story). Megan wasn't necessarily being nosy in this instance, because, after all, Lucy had told her about Disco's dealing. But when Megan told RIP what she had found out about Disco, Lucy criticized her because she "just don't know where to stop. I tell them something and it run right through them to someone else." Thus, in Lucy's meta-analysis of the staff member's language use, nosiness may not be the worst problem. The worst problem rests in what the social workers do with the information they gather. Often center workers used community members' requests for help against them. Lucy's solution attempts to strike a balance in the inequitable relation: "When I want something, I'll go to them . . . [but] I just don't tell them nothing about me." She still uses the center's resources, but censors herself in the presence of the social workers in order to control the types of information to which the workers have access. Lucy reflects on her strategy of keeping mum as opposed to completely withdrawing from the center.

Her sense of the power relations with the center staff resembles her daughter Afriganzia's, discussed in the vignette before this. Lucy wanted to have a reciprocal relation with the center staff members. She sought their help for her son Disco, which would ensure their job at the same time as it helps Disco find one for himself. Yet the staff's· position as policing agents in the neighborhood limits the types and kinds of service they can provide. Instead of a mutually beneficial relation, then, the center staff members assume a watchdog, paternalistic position with neighbors. Lucy's metacommunicative assessment of the ways center staff obtain and handle information shows her critical awareness of and resistance to the top-down application of power by center staff members.

Some may fault Lucy and Afriganzia for entertaining idealist notions of reciprocally egalitarian relations with wider society. Yet the point of ideological dissent, as voiced in this example of the hidden transcript, is to aim "for an unobtrusive negotiation of power relations," since outright forms of resistance "would avail them little and risk much" (Scott 1990, 190). Individuals in Quayville's inner city believe that the possibility of some kind of equality resides in the careful negotiation of the language and assumptions present in daily gate-keeping encounters.

"I Think That's a Good Story. I Just Want to Know More."

Asia (15), Rachel (9), and I sat together in the center as Rachel read to us a suspense story she had written for a homework assignment. The story was about two young lovers, Merle and Jennifer, who were poor. Merle robbed a jewelry store in order to (get) Jennifer a ring, and most of the story centered around the action in the robbery. Her ending left her audience wondering what happened. After she read the story, she looked up for our reactions.

Asia had two questions about concrete details she couldn't yet grasp. "How long was he in prison?" And, "What did Merle and Jennifer's parents say?" Rachel wrote down her questions and looked up for more. "What was the whole theme of the story?"

"Huh? I forgot. I don't even want to think about it. I was just writing it," Rachel said.

"I think that's a good story. I just want to know more." Rachel turned the page in her notebook, sighed, and looked at Asia to go on. " 'Cause you know what, Rachel? You should have details, a theme, a plot. If you want to have the story as a suspense, you could write, 'he served this much time in jail,' and 'he'll never make bail.' Stuff

like that." They talked more about the types of details Rachel would need to build a suspense, and Asia summarized a thriller she had recently read.

In the end, Rachel looked at her story and said, "Needs some work. 'Cause we're going to ask 5th graders to make intelligent guesses" about the story as part of a peer review process. She sat at a table and began revising her story.

This example I include because it illustrates metacommunicative assessments of literate language use. Rachel asks Asia to evaluate the story from a reader's perspective. Asia asked questions that would likely lead Rachel to add more details ("How long was he in prison?" And, "What did Merle and Jennifer's parents say?"). Answers to these questions would help readers visualize more of the scene in which the characters, Merle and Jennifer, interacted. Asia's final question, though, pushed Rachel to rethink the story as a whole piece that needed some more direction. Rachel's story left us wondering why she was writing it ("What was the whole theme of the story?"). This prompt worked at the global level of the story and when addressed, would require a significant revision of the piece. Asia encourages Rachel, though, to continue with the story because, as she says, "I think that's a good story. I just want to know more." To facilitate Rachel's rewrite, Asia recasts the draft Rachel had composed into a large scheme for what stories include: " 'Cause you know what, Rachel? You should have details, a theme, a plot." Doing, so, Asia shows her meta-analysis of the structure and content of Rachel's story compared to what textual narratives typically do and contain.

While Rachel had perceived her story as merely an attempt to fulfill a school assignment, Asia perceives her story as being potentially meaningful to readers in general. Asia's analysis of the work leads Rachel to reconceptualize the audience for the piece ("Needs some work. 'Cause we're going to ask 5th graders to make intelligent guesses"). Asia's insights into Rachel's work urged Rachel to view her story as appealing to readers other than her teacher.

A closer inspection of their interaction, though, reveals an implicit devaluing of schooled literacies. When Rachel finished reading her story and gathered Asia's critique, Rachel shows her resistance to the teacher's task by saying, "I was just writing it." The story initially appeared to Rachel as a scholastic hoop to jump through, something that required little reflection to appease the teacher. When Asia asks about the theme of the whole piece, the work becomes recast as a story, not as a trite homework assignment. Initially, Rachel resists Asia's attempt to shift the perspective from which they view this work: "Huh? I forgot. I don't even want to think about it." At first, Rachel saw little intrinsic value in the story itself; she resisted filling the teacher's task with thought. But with Asia's question, Rachel soon became accountable to community-based readers, not just the teacher. Rachel's estimation of the importance of the story—for the story's sake—increased. She wanted to revise the piece, not because it was a school assignment, but because it could be meaningful to readers in her community. Her initial resistance to the schooled literacy turned into a meaningful compliance with both the school's and community's standards of what counts as a good story. In short, Asia's meta-analysis helps Rachel work more fully within both school and community belief systems.

Overall, these examples lend insight into community members' hidden belief systems and vernacular theory of language and the politics of cultural reproduction. As cultural studies theorist, Thomas McLaughlin defines it, vernacular theory "refers to the practices of those who lack cultural power and who speak a critical language grounded in local concerns" (6). He researched middle class individuals' interpretations of behaviors and found that "the activities of questioning the premises that guide practice is widespread and normal in contemporary culture" (150). Vernacular theory captures the intellectualizing present in area residents' metalinguistic assessments.[15] Their vernacular theory works on many fronts, as seen throughout this chapter.

    To begin with, their evaluations of language contain social commentary on the assumptions of institutional representatives. While they understood the belittling and unfair dimensions of gatekeeper's attitudes, they also recognized that their critiques could not be made public. Doing so might jeopardize life chances and yield few results worth the risk. Instead, their metadiscursive commentaries congealed their mutually shared symbolic constructions of their struggles—their social commentaries helped them define themselves as different from institutional representatives. With these metacommunicative techniques, they also identified which part of gatekeepers' language contained which assumption, objectified the structuring values of gatekeepers, and named their insidious enemy. In using metacommunication to name their struggle, they pinpointed places where they might find a glimmer of opportunity or a crack in the predominant value system that might offer a way out or around.

As illustrated in many of the preceding instances, residents maintained the belief that institutions and their representatives could be both complied with and undermined, both placated and used, both worked with and worked against. Kasha and Chaos discuss ways to appear as though they adopt academic discourse; Afriganzia suggests ways that the center staff and community residents might better work together in their interdependent relation; Lucy censors herself when she asks the center staff for help; and Asia recasts for Rachel the terms under which she should revise her story. Their metadiscursive evaluations offer means by which others can learn to negotiate institutions in ways that never wholly comply with and never wholly resist the structuring ideology of gatekeepers.

In order to suggest these means of strategic negotiation, though, residents also had to understand how power relations unfold in daily interactions. That is, they assessed the language used in those interactions that demeaned them and hindered their opportunity, and they also pointed out language use that might respect them and facilitate their goals. Tony describes the debasing belief present in those exchanges where social workers reveal their shock at his code-switching; Lucy and Jolinda describe the implicit beliefs of landlords who dismiss poor people out-of-hand; and Rachel critiques the racist assumptions associated with having to use polite speech when answering the phone. All these instances elucidate how residents understood the language and politics involved in their daily efforts to get ahead.

Alongside these examples, individuals also offered suggestions for the kinds of language and politics that might ameliorate their situations. Afriganzia points to ways that center workers might reposition themselves in association with area residents to facilitate more equitable interactions; Asia's critique of Rachel's story helped Rachel work more easily and completely within the norms for school literacy (although Rachel may not have seen it this way); and Lucy describes how her silence on certain subjects allows her to interact with the social workers in ways that best represent her interests. All three of these examples show how individuals interpret and revamp their interdependent relations with institutional representatives.

Finally, community residents' metacommunicative assessments of language display how they construct the complications related to adopting and adapting their linguistic codes. Rachel identified the linguistic norms that confer upon White English high status while Black English is devalued. Her critique pointed out that speaking politely was really in some contexts speaking "pol-White[ly]," and that if all things were equal, a person's discursive strategies would not matter. Tony noted how institutional representatives quickly judge a person's linguistic background based on his/her skin color, and as a result, gatekeepers act shocked to hear him "speak like them." Finally, Rachel implies her resistance to schooled literacies that seem as though they are empty tasks; but as soon as Asia shows Rachel the larger audience for her story, Rachel sits at a table to revise it. These critiques of oral and literate language use display some of the ways in which residents assess, and sometimes revamp, their language tools, as well as the social ramifications of doing so.

In all, we see individuals' hidden ideologies manifested in their reflections upon the oral and literate language used in interactions with wider society's institutions. Their antihegemonic belief systems contribute to their vernacular theories concerning how language and power fuse together in their daily encounters with institutions. Some may claim that even with these linguistic skills, residents change little the oppression they face. "At one level this is perfectly true but irrelevant since [the] point is that these are the forms that political struggle takes when frontal assaults are precluded by the realities of power" (Scott 1990, 192). In other words, such an interpretation would disregard the foundational forms of politics present in the metadiscursive evaluations of inner city residents.

Their meta-analyses of oral and literate discourse manifest their community based symbolic representations of oppression, and, therefore, help them develop and imagine ways to systematically test for weakness and define small advantages in the constraining language of gatekeepers. Their metalinguistic strategies, then, involve them in a process of continual struggle to resist the easy reproduction of repressive social systems. This chapter compiles more evidence of James Scott's claims: "The discourse of the hidden transcript does not merely shed light on behavior or explain it; it helps constitute that behavior. . . . [P]ractices of resistance and discourses of resistance [are] mutually sustaining" (1990, 189).

10 "Your Honor, I Just Can't Control Him Anymore"

The last chapter overviewed a number of types of metacommunicative techniques residents used to understand the language and politics related to their negotiations with institutional representatives. This chapter focuses on one specific gatekeeping interaction between two teenage males, their mother, and a judge, an interaction that had more than its share of irony. Ironies in gatekeeping situations, where the flow of events was the reverse of what everyone expected, often prompted residents in this neighborhood to assess the utility of their language strategies. As community members tried to understand why a gatekeeping encounter went awry, they talked about the institutional discourse and literacy used in that interaction. They considered: (1) when and how to resist a gatekeeper who is being unduly harsh; (2) which language styles they should have used given who was present and their authority; and (3) when and how to intervene in those gatekeeping situations that go poorly.

They use metacommunicative commentary on language with the assumption that the potential for altering an oppressive behavior exists at every turn taken during a conversation, every plea entered onto a sheet of paper, and every moment of silence. Giddens suggests "all forms of dependence offer some resources whereby those who are subordinate can influence the activities of their superiors. This is what [he] call[s] the dialectic of control in social systems" (1984, 16). Community members' metacommunicative commentary on the language used during gatekeeping encounters allows them a tool to objectify this dialectic of control—using metadiscourse, that is, community mem-

205

bers evaluate the ways in which their language might positively influence the actions of gatekeepers, actions that often are highly routinized and standardized.

In courtroom discourse the dialectic of control is firmly entrenched in the routinized communicative behaviors of participants. By routinized I mean precisely what Giddens does: "the habitual, taken-for-granted character of the vast bulk of the activities of day-to-day social life; the prevalence of familiar styles and forms of conduct" (1984, 376). Courtroom discursive conventions for judges are highly systematized—but still retain some flexibility—as Susan Philips found when she studied the discursive conventions used by nine judges across numerous cases as they entered pleas from criminal defendants.

Discourse becomes conventional when "speakers produce stretches of speech in interactions that may be experienced by co-interactants as new and spontaneous, yet may be an exact or almost-exact repetition of some or all aspects of a prior speaker's language form, or a repetition of the speaker's own speech from a prior occasion" (314). Her findings suggest the ways in which taken-for-granted courtroom discursive practices can be shaped differently, given each interaction and defendant. In her study, "nine judges had highly routinized discourse formats, so that each judge said exactly the same thing to each defendant exactly the same way each time he carried out the procedure. . . . This is in keeping with what we stereotypically expect from formal public planned speech" (1994, 319). Yet, even within the formal discursive etiquette of eliciting pleas from the defendants, some judges Philips studied flexed the boundaries of their discursive protocols:

> The other six judges . . . also had a routine discourse format for handling the procedure . . . But these judges were all committed on some level to the idea that each defendant was different in background and criminal act. They believed the procedure should be accommodated or tailored to each defendant to assure his/her comprehension of the procedure (319).

We'll see in this chapter that the judge who entered Disco's plea in this gatekeeping encounter had standard ways of interacting with defendants, and that Disco upset this courtroom etiquette by refusing to comply with the linguistic norms of the context. When Disco resisted the judge, he influenced the judge's routine behavior, which produced many surprising results, including metacommunicative evaluations of

Disco's linguistic strategies for resistance, as well as metacommunicative interpretations of the power dynamics in this situation.

Community members' metadiscursive commentary on language reveals much about the politics present in problematic encounters. To show how this is so, let me describe one encounter that took place between Lucy Cadens, her sons, and a judge. After glossing the types of metacommunicative evaluations of language present in this interaction, I'll survey the larger social issues indicated by these various forms of talking about language. But first, the interaction.

"Yes, Your Honor. No, Your Honor."

In the early evening of April 5, 1995, Lucy Cadens asked me to take her to night court in a town forty-five minutes away from Quayville. As we drove, she explained why her three kids and their friend (Groan, age 19) had been arrested. Disco, Chaos, and Sasha borrowed Groan's friend's car and went joy riding.[16] Disco bumped into the back of a car stopped at a traffic light. When the police came to write a report, they ran the plates and found that the borrowed car had been reported "stolen" by its owner, Groan's friend. Since Disco had been driving, he was charged with grand theft; Chaos, Groan, and Sasha were charged as accessories.

We found the town courthouse, a modern, well-lit building. I dropped Lucy off at the front door, parked the car, and walked into the court room, where the hearing was already in progress. I sat a few rows away from the judge's stand, took out my notebook and wrote what I heard. Lucy and her son Disco stood before the judge, a middle-aged man with graying hair. He spoke in a microphone that also picked up Lucy's and Disco's voice. The judge read the charges from the sheet in front of him.[17] Disco stood next to his mom, his arms folded and legs apart. He answered the judge's questions in monosyllables, "Yeah," and "No." Lucy's hands were folded in front of her and she leaned closer to the judge's podium as he read the charges to Disco.

> "How do you plead?"
> Disco quietly said "Guilty." Chaos, sitting across the aisle from me shouted, "You . . ." to his brother. Lucy turned quickly and glared at Chaos, her brow furrowed deep. Disco looked at his brother with raised eyebrows. The judge said he "wouldn't tolerate anymore outbursts" from the audience. Chaos sat back in his bench and shook his head to me.

The judge asked if Disco still wanted to plead guilty: "You have three options. You can enter a 'no plea' at this time, a plea of 'guilty,' or a plea of 'not guilty.'" Disco changed his plea to "not guilty." The judge sat back, pursed his lips and turned to Lucy. "Ms. Cadens, I'm getting fed up with your son's stance toward me. Does your son understand what I'm saying?"

"I don't know, your honor."

"Why is he being this way? Is it stubbornness, stupidity, or ignorance?" Lucy looked at her son hard. The judge continued to look at Lucy, who continued to look at her son. The judge turned to Disco, "If I was in your position, I would address the court with 'Yes, sir. Yes, your honor. No, your honor.' Stand with your arms down. Not crossed in front of your chest. You address the court with respect."

Disco stood the same with his arms crossed and said nothing. He turned slightly to his mother who shook her head at him.

In the few moments of Disco's silence the judge looked from Lucy to Disco, then back to Lucy. He sat back, took a long breath, then leaned forward and addressed Lucy. "Given your son's attitude and given the list of previous charges, I set bail at $2,500. Court will be the 19th of April." Disco put his hands behind his head and said, "Huh?" with his eyebrows raised and mouth open. He was cuffed and led away.

Once he was out of the room, the judge continued, looking straight into Lucy's face. "I was all ready to let him go home with you, Ms. Cadens. But it just wasn't getting through to him. I want to produce a better citizen. I want Disco to stay in school, and be on time to class, and respect the law."

"I know, your honor. I just can't control him anymore. I'm glad he's in jail where he can have some time to come to his senses."

They spoke together for some time about controlling children, and the judge handed Lucy a small stack of papers regarding her son's case and the phone number for legal assistance. "Call me directly if you have any questions. My number is right there," he pointed to the papers Lucy held. Lucy thanked the judge. As she turned to leave, the judge said, "I wish we had met under better circumstances. But it was a pleasure meeting you Ms. Cadens, just the same." Lucy smiled at the judge and said "likewise."

Chaos and Sasha were waiting out front for Lucy, and as we walked up I heard Sasha chuckle and say, "He shouldn't have even

been here in the first place. Groan should of said somen'." Lucy
folded the papers carefully and put them in her purse as Chaos
spoke. "Why didn't you say somen', Ma? He all set to let Disco go."
   Sasha offered a cigarette to her mother. Lucy replied, the cigarette
bouncing between her lips and proving a hard target to light: "His
stupid nigger ass is staying in jail. You don't talk to a judge like
that. Stupid motherf——er. You don't think I know the judge all set
to let him go?" We quickly walked to the car, Lucy still yelling at
Chaos, but managing to light her cigarette. "Alls he had to do was
be respectful. 'Yes, your honor. No, your honor.' Put his damn hands
to his side."
   "Yeah, but Ma, he did it on purpose. His bad ass . . ."
   "Well, his bad ass attitude got him two weeks in jail. And I ain't
getting him bail. Let his bad ass think about that." We piled in the
car and headed back to Quayville.
   "Yeah, but why the judge talkin' to him like that?"
   "You're a stupid motherf——er, Chaos. You just need to talk to
people with respect."
   "I'm just saying, Ma, why that judge come down on him like
that?"
   "I talked to the judge, Chaos. Disco think he so motherf——ing
cool. See what it got him? His ass stayin' there."
   "I can't wait till I'm a judge and can wave my big c——k like
that." Lucy had had enough and cursed Chaos out loud and quick.
We spent the rest of the car ride home in silence.

This gatekeeping interaction could have had different results for
the people involved, especially Disco. Much of the interaction was the
reverse of what people expected to happen—all because Disco refused
to speak in a certain manner. This interaction is particularly interesting because Disco enacted the hidden transcript of his community's
ideology even though, "many, perhaps most, hidden transcripts remain just that: hidden from public view and never 'enacted' " (Scott
1985, 16). Disco's defiance of the judge's authority pierces the fine
membrane that typically separates the expected public display of deference from community-based attitudes of resistance. Although Disco
believed otherwise (more on this later), he took considerable risk in
bringing his hidden beliefs into public view, especially in a way that
undermined the norms for behavior that structured that situation. And
since, "the first open statement of a hidden transcript . . . breaches the

etiquette of power relations," the judge and Lucy were facing a reversal in what they would have normally expected (Scott 1990, 223). In the face of such ironies, both the judge and Lucy used metacommunicative assessments of language to try to make sense of what Disco was doing and why. Some examples:

- If the judge had not imposed his expectations onto Disco regarding how someone should act in his court, Disco may have responded differently. But Disco's folded arms and monosyllabic answers were trademark defensive behaviors when a young man in this neighborhood felt threatened.[18] Disco's posturing worked fairly well for him on the street, but the judge simply became irritated with Disco's stance ("Why is he being this way? Is it stubbornness, stupidity, or ignorance?").

- After telling Disco how to act in his court, the judge expects Disco to change his behavior and language ("If I were in your position . . ."). When Disco acts the opposite way the judge expects him to, the judge used this as further justification for throwing Disco in jail ("Given your son's attitude . . . , I set bail at $2,500.). If Disco had acted differently, the judge said he would have released him to Lucy's custody ("I was all ready to let him go home with you, Ms. Cadens. But it just wasn't getting through to him").

- Lucy expected her son to address the court with respect. When he didn't, she stared at him hard instead of answering the judge's question. Lucy agreed with the judge, finally, and said "I know, your honor. I just can't control him anymore. I'm glad he's in jail where he can have some time to come to his senses."

The judged used metacommunicative commentary on speech as a form of damage control when Disco threatened the courtroom etiquette and discursive norms of the public transcript. The judge controlled his courtroom, much the way a teacher does her classroom. Stubbs examined the metacommunicative practices that teachers use to show "the radically asymmetrical situation of talk which typically holds in a school classroom" (1983, 53). Teachers asked questions similar to those the judge did when "needing to control the amount of speech," or when "checking or confirming understanding" (Stubbs 1983, 51). The judge also explains to Lucy why he put her son in jail, "it just wasn't getting through to him." I point out the types of metacommunicative commentary on speech the judge used in this gatekeeping interaction because it seemed he was uncomfortable with having to throw Disco in jail. Disco spoke and acted in surprising ways that left the judge unsure of the motives behind Disco's actions. Yet we can not simply categorize the types of metacommunicative evaluations taking place in this interaction and leave it at that. We still need to tease out the issues of power manifested in Lucy and Chaos's discussion, which took place after they left the courtroom. In trying to understand what should have been said, but wasn't, and why, Chaos and his mother unfolded the politics of this gatekeeping encounter.

Metadiscourse and the Politics of Integration and Resistance

From Chaos's perspective, Disco consciously chose not to use the "appropriate" language for that situational context. In fact, Chaos respected his younger brother's linguistic strategies for resistance. "Yeah, but Ma, he did it on purpose. His bad ass . . . " The "it" refers to Disco's refusal to say "Yes, your honor," and deploy other such indicators of deference. Chaos found it legitimate and necessary that Disco refused to adopt the discursive conventions expected in this interaction. Reflecting on the incident, Chaos said "the judge was trying to control Disco. But Disco knew the judge didn't have nothing on him." Disco knew that Groan's friend who owned the car had come into the court hours before and had dropped the charges. In Chaos's eyes, Disco earned the status of "bad ass," which, in his neighborhood, was high praise for young men who courageously stood up to others.

Lucy had a different read on Disco's refusal to linguistically integrate. Lucy believed that Disco's insubordination indicated her youngest son's stupidity: "His stupid nigger ass is staying in jail. You don't talk to a judge like that. Stupid motherf——er." But she also recognizes a certain validity in what Chaos believed, namely, that Disco resisted the judge and gained the community status of "bad." Lucy said, "Well, his bad ass attitude got him two weeks in jail. . . . Let his bad ass think about that." And here's where Chaos and Lucy part ways in their assessment of the utility of Disco's language strategies.

To Chaos, Disco protected his own dignity during a humiliating situation; not only was this a just battle for Disco to fight, but it was an honorable one as well. Chaos found Disco's language strategies profoundly useful, even admirable. To Lucy, Disco picked the wrong battle to fight—why would Disco refuse to say "your honor" and resist the judge, especially since he knew the consequences? Their metacommunicative assessment of Disco's language skills help us understand some of the complexity involved in linguistic integration. Important social questions rest just beneath the surface of their metacommunicative evaluations: How far do you go to linguistically work within the court system, or any institution? What do you have to give up? Integrity? Self-respect? What do you gain? Do the consequences of integration justify these, and other, personal costs?

Chaos saw Disco's language use as embodying a tension between identity politics and the pragmatic outcomes of integration. By refusing to linguistically integrate into the dominant linguistic conventions of that situation, Disco's street-slick, "bad ass" self was defined and redefined. Disco refused to give in, even when faced with what Chaos considered to be an odious and unnecessary assertion of authority by the judge (more on this in the next section). But at the same time, Disco went to jail because he didn't linguistically pay due homage to the judge, an undesirable outcome from Chaos's perspective no matter how much he admired his younger brother's language choices. As Chaos told me a few weeks later, "I see why Disco did that [refused to integrate], and he right. But, you know, he went jail. So was it worth it? I don't know." Disco maintained an important part of his identity by answering the judge in monosyllables, and yet the consequences of his actions suggest to Chaos that his brother's resistance might have been in vain.

Lucy's reflection on Disco's language use reveals to us the tension between speaking to others in ways that placate their authority, and speaking to others with the fundamental social value of respect. Note how Lucy flattered the authority of the judge ("I know, your honor . . . I don't know, your honor), and how she talked about addressing the judge ("You don't talk to a judge like that"); compare these statements to her fundamentally ethical and civically minded statement ("You just need to talk to people with respect"). Her metacommunicative commentary on speech suggests two different, yet overlapping, views on linguistic integration. For Lucy, language integration could mean you flatter someone's authority or could mean you speak to someone with respect. Depending on the situation, these were the same thing, but other times they weren't.[19]

Metadiscourse served Chaos and Lucy well as a tool to weigh the possibilities, outcomes, and difficulties in using certain language strategies. Their assessment of the effectiveness of Disco's language reveals their knowledge about the politics of language—what words do, how they're valued, by whom, and in what contexts. Disco's insubordination, or his "open refusal to comply with a hegemonic performance," stems from the hidden transcript (Scott 1990, 205). As shown in earlier chapters, the hidden transcript often centered on the politics of integrating into the dominant discourse of a situation and the paradoxes in doing so. Afriganzia's doodle, shown in chapter 5, attributed the high status of two women in the community, in part, to their facility with language, their ability to "talk with all sorts of people like the police and social workers." Yet, at other times, Afriganzia also spoke about the importance of "talking Black," and therefore being "Black." She had many pejoratives for those "niggers who gotta talk White all the time," and these people held a lower status in her neighborhood because "they sold out," so "you can't trust them they sound so White." The multiple stances residents took concerning the ramifications of linguistic integration mirror the residents multiple interpretations of Disco's act.

Disco's insubordination to the judge was met with mixed reactions in the community (I discovered these reactions when I asked, and when I stumbled into many conversations about Disco's story). Some attributed his actions to his gender, "He just doing a man thing. That macho shit"; others thought he was right to "get in the face of the judge like that," "not sell out," and that "He a bad ass nigger, all right"; others chalked his resistance up to his youth, "When you young you can do things like that," and social class, "What Disco got to lose? He ain't got nothing." Regardless of what community members attributed his resistance to, his insubordination stemmed from the hidden transcript, and then became part of the hidden transcript about the politics of integration, politics that factor in gender, race, age, and class. Metacommunicative interpretations of this gatekeeping encounter also helped residents interpret the power structure in this situational context.

Metacommunicative Interpretations and the Politics of Oppression

Chaos and Lucy sharply disagreed about their interpretations of the judge's assumptions and actions. Clearly the judge had authority based on his institutionalized position. Bourdieu would characterize the judge's influence as sanctioned by his post in the justice system. By virtue of his status, the judge has the "power to secure recognition of [his] power" (Bourdieu 1990, 131). Bourdieu's notion of institutional politics helps us define the judge's status, but we still have to consider the dynamic ways the judge's authority was (co)constructed, undercut, and manipulated by Disco and Lucy. Did the judge act in Disco's best interests? To what degree were the relations in this encounter asymmetrical? Let me consider these questions by focusing on the final part of the talk in the car ride home.

Chaos thought the judge spoke inappropriately to Disco. When the judge turned to Lucy and asked, "Is it stubbornness, stupidity, or ignorance?" Chaos thought the judge's question belittled and disrespected his little brother. As he told me the next day, Chaos wanted his mother to consider the judge's statement as evidence for the judge's onerous assumptions ("Yeah, but, why the judge talkin' to him like that?"). Lucy wasn't hearing it: "you're a stupid motherf——er, Chaos" (read: "You got your interpretation all wrong"). Chaos pressed his point that the judge usurped his authority, though: "I'm just saying, Ma, why that judge come down on him like that?" Chaos's metacommunicative interpretation of language with his mother helps him craft an understanding of the power dynamic of that situation. In effect, he's asking his mother to consider the possibility that the judge abused his authority and status by "coming down" on Disco.

Lucy countered her eldest son's interpretation by saying, "I talked to the judge, Chaos." Since Lucy actually spoke directly with the person, she had many more contextualization cues upon which she drew to create her interpretation of the situation; she thought that her interpretation of the power structure of this situation had more validity than Chaos's. In fact, Lucy understood and appreciated the judge's intervention on her son's behalf. Remember how just after Disco was cuffed and taken away, the judge addressed Lucy respectfully, looking straight into her face? "I was all ready to let him go home with you, Ms. Cadens. . . . I want to produce a better citizen." And Lucy replied, "I know, your honor. I just can't control him anymore. I'm glad he's in jail where he can have some time to come to his senses." Lucy agreed with the judge's use of authority; she appreciated his hardline stance because "Disco think he so motherf——ing cool. See what it got him?" For Lucy, Disco's problem was that he had drifted too far into the street culture that Chaos admires. Lucy holds Disco responsible for landing himself in jail; the burden to change was on Disco, regardless of how the judge used his status (more on this in the next section).

But Chaos still believed his interpretation of the judge's behavior was equally valid given his read of the situation. "I can't wait till I'm a judge and can wave my big c——k like that." This sarcasm reflects both Chaos's cutting analysis of the judge's behavior, as well as Chaos's assumption of what civic responsibilities gatekeepers should uphold. He indicated his belief that the judge was odious in word and deed, a "big c——k." Chaos inverted his meaning in that stinging remark and shows his contempt for domineering, manly, behavior in gate-keeping encounters.

Throughout the last few metadiscursive exchanges between Lucy and her son, we see how two equally valid interpretations of the politics of gatekeeping encounters can be sustained. From where Chaos sat, this entire interaction was based on the judge's usurpation of his status and authority. Later that week, Chaos said "that judge didn't have nothing on Disco, and Disco knew it. The owner of that car dropped the charges as soon as Groan called him three hours before Disco even went before the judge." Keep in mind, the judge's reasons for putting Disco in jail, "Given your son's attitude and given the list of previous charges, I set bail at $2,500." The judge sent Disco to jail because Disco refused to act the way the judge wanted him to act—the judge's need for control over the situation, his demand for respect, "just wasn't getting through to him." Bourdieu might agree with Chaos: "the point of honor is politics in the pure state." Because Disco wouldn't recognize the judge's honor, his honor was at stake. Honor is "valued as a means of manifesting power, as symbolic capital tending to contribute to its own reproduction, that is, to the reproduction and legitimization of prevailing hierarchies" (Bourdieu 1990, 131). To Chaos, the judge was onerous in his attempts to force Disco to linguistically recognize the honor of being a judge.

But to Lucy, the judge's "ruling" served as evidence of the judge's willingness to work with her to "produce a better citizen," to gain control and authority over her wayward son. Lucy allowed the judge to use his authority as an extension of her own maternal authority. In some ways, Lucy constructed the judge's authority as quasi-parental—she legitimized his use of it, because she "just can't control [Disco] anymore." Although the ideologies of honor, citizenship, and control stemmed from different places, the judge and Lucy's values overlapped in important ways: the judge's belief in honor and need to produce a better citizen stem from his role in the justice system; Lucy's belief in honor and the need to produce a better citizen stem from her Black cultural values. We can also attribute their overlapping values to similarities in the generations. After Disco left the room, the judge and Lucy spoke about the difficulties in controlling children these days. Because of the overlapping values between Lucy and the judge, Lucy constructed the judge's use of authority as legitimate and even helpful.

Two points are important to note: first, Lucy and her eldest son used metacommunicative interpretations on discourse to construct their understandings of the political aspects of this interaction; second, both of their interpretations of this situation had validity, a validity that each of them established as they discussed how the judge talked. Still, though, too many questions remain: Why would Lucy legitimize the judge's use of his authority, especially when the judge appeared so harsh and unyielding? Why didn't Lucy help her son more than she did? Finally, how could Lucy and her son possibly benefit from the judge's actions? Let me explore these questions in the next, and final, section of this chapter.

Metadiscourse and the Politics of Intervention

> *The logical connection between action and power [is the ability to] act otherwise, . . . to intervene in the world or to refrain from such intervention, with the effect of influencing a specific process or state of affairs.*
>
> —Anthony Giddens, *The Constitution of Society*.

When gatekeeping encounters have as many ironies as this one, often people witnessing the situation want to and choose to intervene on the person's behalf who seems to be at a distinct disadvantage, as Disco seemed to be to Chaos. When the judge asked Disco for his plea, Disco pleaded guilty. Chaos burst out with "You." Chaos, with this single word, told his brother that he entered the wrong plea. Thus, this utterance is a form of what I'll call metadiscursive intervention, where a person recognizes and calls attention to a problem in the taken-for-granted flow of discourse, in order to affect the results of gatekeeping encounters, to influence a "specific process or state of affairs," in Giddens's words. In this neighborhood, for instance, if someone saw that a good friend or a relative was speaking or writing ineffectively, the person would step in, call attention to the language choice, and alter the flow of the event. In chapter 1, remember how Lucy and her two sisters, Jolinda and Vivian, collaboratively filled out a welfare application? Jolinda was about to write her married name in the blank, but Vivian intervened and told Jolinda that such a choice might have a negative impact on the caseworker's evaluation of her application. Jolinda put her maiden name in the blank instead. This was an example of metadiscursive intervention—Jolinda's sisters objectified her language strategy and assessed its utility, all in an effort to positively affect the outcomes of Jolinda's application. For the remainder of this chapter, let me trace some of the social implications of metadiscursive intervention, loosely defined as discussions about when, how, and for what ends people intervene on someone's behalf.

When Chaos spoke up in court, he redirected everyone's attention to the linguistic choice Disco had just made. Chaos saw an error in his brother's plea and felt compelled to speak up. Chaos's language strategy for intervention, though, drew the scorn of his mother and the judge. In fact, the judge said he would not "tolerate any more outbursts." When the judge said this, he greatly reduced the likelihood that any of us in the court could have intervened further. In effect, the judge took back his control over the proceedings by handing down this edict. Despite the apparent inappropriateness of Chaos's comment, his intervention successfully interrupted the flow of events. His comment led the judge to lay out for Disco the language choices that Disco had available to him. The judge asked if Disco still wanted to plead guilty: "You have three options. You can enter a 'no plea' at this time, a plea of 'guilty,' or a plea of 'not guilty.' " At that point, Chaos's intervention was successful because it prompted the judge to use metadiscourse in a way that clarified the situation for Disco. Disco then changed his plea to "not guilty."

We still need to know why Lucy didn't intercede on her son's behalf.[20] As Chaos asked when Lucy first came out of the courthouse, "Why didn't you say somen', Ma? He all set to let Disco go." This question is particularly apt, because it appeared that the judge wanted Lucy to mediate this situation. Lucy was originally called to the court to have her son released to her. More than this, after Disco changed his plea, the judge turned to Lucy: "Ms. Cadens, I'm getting fed up with your son's stance toward me. Does your son understand what I'm saying?" The judge hoped Lucy would recast her son's behavior in a way that would appease him. She simply replied, "I don't know, your honor." And although Chaos thought this next statement was insulting, Lucy seemed to agree with it: "Why is he being this way? Is it stubbornness, stupidity, or ignorance?" Lucy looked at her son hard. The judge continued to look at Lucy, who continued to look at her son.

Here, the judge seemed to be exploiting multiple sources of authority: first, he seemed to want Lucy to explain why her son was acting that way; second, he insulted Disco in a way that could have embarrassed Disco into taking a more "appropriate" stance in the courtroom; and third, he seemed to be asking his questions to show his ever growing frustration with the unnerving ways in which Disco was acting. Instead of addressing the judge's question, Lucy looked at her son hard— in effect deferring her opportunity to speak up for her son.

But Lucy had good reasons not to use her language skills to keep her youngest son from going to jail. To show this point, let me turn away from this interaction, and focus on a conversation Lucy and I had the following day on our way to see Disco in the county jail. I told her I still couldn't understand why she didn't say more to get her son out. She explained:

> "I could have told the judge that I was going to reign him in, keep him controlled. On time to school. Out of trouble. But I told the judge I didn't understand why I couldn't control him. I could have convinced that judge easy to release Disco to my custody. But I didn't. I knew Disco didn't know what the f——k was happening to him, but I didn't convince the judge to let him go, and I'ma tell you why.
>
> The two weeks he'll be there, he'll have to clear his head. Don't even give you cigarettes there. Also, I can sleep easier because he there. I don't jump out my bed when I hear a gun and worry the rest of the night that my baby been shot. I don't go to the window when I hear yelling, thinking he's right in the middle of the shit. Maybe he'll start to realize that these people ain't playing with him. Also, by the time he gets out I will have moved out of that place. Jail'll keep him clean and safe until I can get my shit together and finish this move."

Lucy knew what she was doing when she chose to silently stare at Disco instead of intervening on his behalf. Her choice to remain silent helped produce, oddly enough, what she considered to be the positive result of Disco being in jail. Lucy carefully and strategically deferred her parental authority over Disco to the judge. By remaining silent, she gave the judge her permission to do what she knew he would have to do: come down on Disco. Lucy knows that Disco's insolence would be met with decisive defeat because the judge has his honor to protect, his authority to preserve, and his face to maintain. As she said, "Maybe he'll start to realize that these people ain't playing with him," when it comes to the maintenance of the public transcript. She understood and talked about all the things she "could" have said, knew the possibilities, weighed the consequences, and decided that silence was the best alternative. Her metacommunicative interpretations on discourse not only suggest her highly developed critical consciousness; she knew the justice system's power structure well enough to use it to her and her son's benefit—but this also suggests her multifaceted awareness of language strategies: she talked about silence as a rhetorical strategy.

When Chaos and I asked why she didn't intervene, we assumed that Lucy's silence *wasn't* intervention; we assumed that her language choice was ineffective. After all, Disco was cuffed and taken away. But the bottomline result for Chaos and me, wasn't the bottomline result for Lucy and Disco. Although not thrilled with being in jail, Disco returned home to a new apartment in the suburbs when he got out. Lucy's metadiscourse revealed that she was way ahead of Chaos and me in our thinking. She constructed the result of Disco's jail time as a positive possibility, a window of opportunity during which she could concentrate on getting out of a roach-infested, run-down, inner city apartment without being sidetracked by her youngest son's illicit activities.

When a person intervenes (or doesn't) in the linguistic flow of events taking place in gatekeeping interactions, he/she takes control over the language used in the situation, momentarily at least. When someone intercedes, the people in the gatekeeping encounter typically stop to reflect on their language, which can lead them to alter the flow of language use in positive ways. These moments of language reflection seem to be the places where people could possibly change their language behaviors in order to be less degrading. Metacommunicative interpretations assumed that the power of language can influence everyday interactions in potentially positive and/or negative ways.

If one is willing to reduce their political inquiry to outcomes, this interaction could be interpreted in the typical way: it would be seen as yet one more example of systematic oppression that sustains vast social inequalities. After all, Disco went to jail. However, such an examination of end results would fall short of revealing the complicated symbolic constructions pervading the language the participants used during this encounter. The typical interpretation would either have to ignore the ways Lucy used what appear to be oppressive structures to her own advantage, or it would have to reject Lucy's co-option as false consciousness. Either way, the complexity of the interaction would be flattened into a unidimensional portrayal where power moves from the top down, where community residents would come across as victims, and where hegemony would be seen as an impervious force of domination that squelches agency. However, we miss the fine weave of political maneuverings by making such claims, claims based on the assumption of ideological domination.

When men and women in this inner city assessed, discussed, and revamped their language strategies, their metacommunicative evaluations of language became a political tool. Sometimes prompted by bitter ironies, individuals in this neighborhood talked about the language used in gatekeeping interactions in order to massage a constraining bureaucratic obstacle into an opportunity. Metacommunicative tools are central to the ways community members construct their interpretations of everyday struggles with institutional gatekeepers. Their metacommunicative evaluations not only indicate their cultural logic about institutional language, but also reveal how this cultural logic continually develops from interactions across time and many contexts. With metacommunicative tools, these men and women assess the utility of language strategies they had previously learned, then they revamp these strategies accordingly. As with the last chapter, this one brings us full circle in the developmental process of institutional language skills. Their assessments of the problems of integrating into dominant discursive conventions, of the politics of a situation, and of intervention, all reveal faces of resistance we often aren't privy to. These findings are vital to those of us who believe we've cornered the market on critical theories of institutional power, language, and resistance.

Metacommunicative interpretations of this gatekeeping encounter assumed that social structures could be made more flexible during micro-interactions when people (1) evaluate their language use(d) in gatekeeping interactions, (2) interpret the power structures and consequences of actions in these exchanges, and (3) intervene in gatekeeping encounters that go awry. Reproduction of social structures is a fluid process where political standings fluctuate in the ebb and flow of language and contextualization cues, a process that can be effected by the entering of a plea like Disco's, an outburst like Chaos's, and a moment of silence like Lucy's. "Finally, a clear view of the 'micro' pushing and shoving involved in power relations, and particularly power relations in which appropriation and permanent subordination are central, makes any static view of naturalization and legitimization untenable. . . . The naturalization of domination is always being put to the test in small but significant ways, particularly at the point where power is applied" (Scott 1990, 197). The language and contextualization cues found in gatekeeping encounters reveal that dominant social structures are *not simply* reproduced and legitimized in routine ways. Residents manipulate the structures along the way, and afterward, evaluate their language used to work these structures. Their meta-analysis brings to the surface their tacitly held beliefs and reveals how their hidden ideologies are cultivated through critical reflection. With this in mind, scholars are much more likely to assume that individuals have critical consciousness built from their own reflections on day-to-day experiences.

11 Language and Power in the Everyday

A smirk. A question. An application. When imbued with demeaning beliefs, these and other mundane aspects of daily living amass together to form the arena of struggle for Quayville's inner city residents. Silence. A question. A list of references. When imbued with community residents' hidden ideologies, these tools and others form the basis of everyday acts of agency and critical awareness. The struggle and the tools take shape in the very places where scholars do not have access, or simply overlook. When we honor community residents' day-to-day lives and vernacular means of striving, we illuminate our own discussions of politics and literacies, as well as our own roles as gatekeepers.

Many institutional influences entered into the daily lives of these inner city residents and required considerable effort and time to negotiate. Some of these institutions included RIP, DSS, United Ministries, universities, HUD, the criminal justice system (courts, jail, prison, police), and the Housing Authority. These organizations, as we saw in chapter 3, were funded by the government and were established out of a concern for the well-being of citizens who were hungry, unemployed, homeless or living in dilapidated housing, or who lacked access to higher education. The civic intention of these institutions indeed responded to complicated social forces that shaped the daily living conditions of inner city residents. Over the span of 150 years, some of these historical forces included: waves of emigrants from the South and immigrants from Ireland and Italy; social movements for emancipation and civil rights; and massive shifts in economies from agriculture and shipping, to manufacturing and transportation, to service and high-tech industries (and interspersed between these, the wartime economic booms). The federal, state, and local governments responded to these social forces with programs. In particular, Johnson's War on Poverty weighed in heavily as a contributing factor to the programmatic goals and resources provided by DSS, HUD, and the philanthropic agencies mentioned throughout these chapters. Born, at least in part, out of a concern for the ways in which citizens lived, these institutions developed as a response to social and economic upheavals, and all these institutions and social forces helped shape the physical, cultural, and linguistic architecture of this inner city.

Residents in this area negotiated these institutions with such careful deliberation for practical and social reasons. Practically speaking, they needed food, housing, clothes, and heat for daily survival. Socially, though, they needed these resources to gain the status neighbors attached to those who took good care of their kids, family, and communities. Yet the wider society often overlooks these social motives. These residents took an active part in public service programs because they saw these programs as stepping stones out of the quagmire of evictions, unemployment, and undereducation they lived in daily. More importantly, they had to have their basic needs met if they were going to enact their own tacitly held hierarchy of civic duties to kids, kin, and community. Afriganzia talked about women who were "doers," respectful and responsible contributors to their community; Raejone wanted to go to college so she would be in a better position to provide day care and education to the children in communities like hers; and Lucy mentioned her fundamental ethic of "respect for people," and wanted to make her son "a better citizen." Community members worked within institutions in order to put the barest essentials in place, so they could then be in a position to take care of those around them.

Some readers may want to point to the residents' linguistic activities as perhaps necessary, but still troubling, illustrations of false consciousness and cultural reproduction. They could argue, with some validity, that community members complicitly engage in interactions that perpetuate their own poverty and lack of opportunity. And they could use most of the examples from previous chapters to craft a fairly convincing argument that we need to teach radical politics to the less powerful—to those dominated because of their subscription to prevailing ideologies. With more critical consciousness, and less passivity, individuals who suffer from demeaning attitudes of bureaucrats could start the revolutionary work of throwing off their burdens, or so the argument would go.

However, this position assumes that the onus to change oppressive institutions falls on the shoulders of community residents. In some ways, this radical position represents the flip side of the conservative position. Conservatives also want inner city residents to change their own living conditions. With different reasoning, conservatives might use the examples in this work to uphold their notions of "welfare queens" who, if only they would find a job, would be able to alter their own living conditions. Presumably, individuals have many opportunities in this meritocratic, capitalist society; if people don't live up to their potential, it's through some fault of their own. The conflating of radical and conservative positions here is, granted, a bit unfair, but it does illustrate how they both share a blame-the-victim attitude. While one faults individuals using the label of false consciousness, the other faults them using the label of individualistic self-help or the lack thereof. Both perspectives, nevertheless, fail to account for community perspectives on poverty, institutions, language and politics.

Certainly, the community saw those few men and women "who just sit up and collect 'cause they lazy and want the system to do for them, instead of them doing for themselves. They don't do nothin' to better themselves and sure don't do nothin' for no one else." This is the way one teen explained it. But the few individuals who "sit up and collect" were the exception to most residents' beliefs about how a community member should strategically interact with social service programs. This small number of individuals held a low social status in this neighborhood precisely because the majority of residents considered them to be lazy, abusing the system.

Most of these inner city residents, on the other hand, negotiated public service institutions with considerable deliberation because they wanted to better themselves, to work together with their neighbors to create a safe and clean neighborhood, and, perhaps most importantly, to provide their children a decent life. "If I do all right with them," Mirena nodded her head to her kids playing on the front stoop, "then they'll take care of me when I get old. They my ticket out of this little Harlem." Rather than viewing these social service institutions as owing them, most residents viewed these as a way out of poverty or a last resort in case of emergency, a stepping stone to something better, such as a full time job or admission to a college. With few exceptions, people wanted to be off welfare, wanted that union job in the local supermarket or meaningful full-time work that paid enough for a sitter, rent, utilities, transportation, and food—and that maybe provided medical coverage. And when individuals had the basics in place for a stretch of time, many actively looked for those jobs. Simple really, people don't want to be poor. Unfortunately, the social service institutions that residents hoped would provide a bridge to employment, secure housing, and educational opportunity seldom actualized the democratic values under which they were established.

Community residents recognized that social service institutions are "supposed to be here to help us." But, in practice, these institutions "just be keepin' us down," as I so often heard. The benefits the neighborhood members received were so meager that often they could not scrape together enough money to even dress appropriately for an interview, let alone get a sitter for the kids, or pay for transportation to the workplace. If they decided to go to school, as we saw in chapter 7, so many pieces of their daily lives had to mesh together tightly that if something went askew, such as a child getting sick, the entire day or week could be lost to getting routines and finances back in order. The resources provided by social services left little room for juggling everyday demands on time and energy, little room for mishap.

Often institutions worked in ways that maintained the status quo. For instance, the Department of Social Services cut benefits if someone got married, or found a job that paid poverty wages, in the belief that either one would eliminate a person's poverty. However, this assumes that the husband or job provided enough to live on and meet child-care expenses. Welfare also sanctioned benefits if someone lost a job because s/he couldn't find a sitter or transportation to work. A typical sanction denied two to three months of payments as a punitive measure for losing the job. Most institutional representatives appeared to these community residents to have a vested interest in *not* helping people to do for themselves—their job security rested in having a population of people dependent on them, which often prompted so many to say: "they lose their job if I get one"; or "they need to keep me down so they can keep food on their own table"; or "they only here cause it's a job. They ain't really trying to help me up and out." During everyday gatekeeping interactions, institutional representatives and the policies they maintained fell far short of fulfilling the democratic possibility and hope inherent in their institutional roles.

The schism between the democratic principles behind gatekeepers' roles and their actual practices could at times be deep and wide. For instance, the Neighborhood Center stayed open through grants obtained by the social workers at United Ministries. The grants paid, first, for the infrastructure of the center (wages of social workers, rent, utilities, supplies), and, second, for the programs run out of the center. When one social worker suggested they teach community members how to write grants for themselves, she was told in so many words that the community members were illiterate and couldn't write the grants in the first place. As proof of their illiteracy, the other social workers referred her to the case logbooks to show the grade levels of the individuals in the area (the assumption being that amount of schooling and level of literacy are one-to-one correlates, an assumption Scribner and Cole took to task years ago in *The Psychology of Literacy*). Incidentally, the case worker who suggested they teach residents to write grants was fired soon after she told me this anecdote, because she, I was told by the other caseworkers, "just wasn't a team player." The social worker, who was genuinely interested in handing over the means necessary for community residents to do for themselves, was trapped by the daily practices of other institutional representatives who underestimated the potential and abilities of the people they were there to serve. While community members understood the democratic mission of these institutions, they also fundamentally mistrusted the motivations behind many gatekeepers' actions and words.

These men and women negotiated interactions with institutional agents with desires to achieve a modicum of the social and political equality that society often denied them; and they negotiated these exchanges knowing that in some ways these representatives colluded together in a manner that severely limited residents' opportunities. We saw in chapter 4 how philanthropic and housing agencies united together in their efforts to let Mirena hit rock bottom once she was evicted. Because these institutions were internetworked, people in this neighborhood had much to risk and little to gain in a direct challenge to a particular institutional representative during any given interaction. One encounter that went awry could potentially block an individual's access to other institutions.

Instead of outward defiance, then, area residents used their linguistic savvy to both mollify and rebuke, play into and off of, adopt and adapt, placate and challenge, conform and undermine, accommodate and resist; they conceptualized how power unfolded in enabling and constraining ways; they deployed and evaluated their oral and literate devices in order to persistently fissure, crack, and test social structures. Their agency precludes us from believing that structures of domination are simply reproduced in monolithic terms.

The institutional language skills that area residents learned, deployed, and revamped represented the cultural logic of their hidden ideologies. On the one hand, adults valued those women and men who code-switched well and could proficiently use literacy from one institutional context to the next; on the other hand, individuals who overly relied on the prestige dialect, quickly faced the censure of area residents. In chapter 3, we saw how adults esteemed code-switching. In chapter 5, Afriganzia's doodle, "The Game of Power," described the most influential women in this community as linguistic border-crossers. These women earned their status in the neighborhood by being versed in the oral and literate skills needed to negotiate trans-institutional contexts. Not only could they apply a variety of their language skills across many sites, but also they translated institutional language for other community members. For example, Jolinda's sisters, both of whom were fluent border-crossers, helped her with her welfare application (discussed in chapter 4). Individuals appreciated the oral and literate devices needed to access public services. They esteemed these linguistic tools, not because they believed in the ideologies of institutions, but because they believed that strong individuals provide for their families. They strategically negotiated institutions with the critical awareness of when to use institutional language and for what purposes. They also remained attentive to the social implications of disguising their hidden ideologies.

While individuals had to be fluent in institutional language tools to gain status in this community, they could not become too immersed in the discursive conventions of any one of wider society's institutions, or they would be stigmatized as "selling out," or "going too far," or becoming and an "oreo." Afriganzia's experiences as co-director of a literacy program illustrate the means through which residents consciously wear the mask of deference when using predominant linguistic forms with gatekeepers. When neighborhood members code-switched to White English with fluency, they remained attentive to the cultural compromises they made in doing so. They insured that their mask of compliance remained separate and separable from their own cultural identities. When mask-wearing was openly resisted, as in Disco's refusal to honor the judge's authority, the defiant act made explicit many of the identity politics involved in negotiating institutions. Some community members thought he was simply a young male, acting macho; some thought he was a "bad ass nigger," high praise in street culture; others, like his mother, completely disagreed with his resistance and thought he was "a stupid motherf——er." For these inner city residents, then, institutional encounters always raised the question: How do I maintain some measure of personal integrity and Black identity when interacting with society's institutions? Even though institutions persistently attempted to inscribe neighborhood members' subjective positions (i.e., categorize them as the undeserving poor), residents consciously recognized, altered, manipulated, and resisted these attempts. They undermined the subjugating actions of institutions and endeavored to compose themselves differently, with more complicated identities and social positions.

Yet, occasionally, public institutions perceived individuals in ways that community members might also identify themselves. When gatekeepers worked with residents, the orality and literacy present in the exchange became a tool for enacting the democratic principles implicit in the interaction; and when gatekeepers stonewalled or demeaned residents, residents' oral and literate language presented subtle challenges to gatekeepers. In the best-case scenarios, community members worked with institutional gatekeepers, finding those values upon which both sides could agree, and building a mutually rewarding relation between everyone concerned. For instance, in chapter 8, Raejone strategically chose words that simultaneously indexed two different value systems—her own and the those of the university. Recall also from that chapter that both Raejone and her older sister Sasha liked the EOP counselor because he talked with them from a shared position, not at them or over them from a dominant position. And, though the outcome of Disco's judicial hearing was surely mixed, Lucy and the judge understood and shared each other's shared values of "respect" and "becoming a good citizen." Although infrequently enacted, institutional interactions could be places where civically minded gatekeepers and community members worked together to facilitate community members' social and political equality.

In the majority of cases, though, community residents identified troubling assumptions in an institutional agents' stance or language. In these instances, they deployed oral and literate devices that both placated and resisted gatekeepers' demands. Chapter 1 showed Lucy's signifying on a caseworker who hindered her application process. Her oral discursive technique both complied with and critiqued the caseworker's request that she bring in her daughter's birth certificate. Chapter 5 shows Salliemae and Lucy critiquing the paternalistic and racist assumptions present in the police department's drug sweeps; at the end of their discussion, they found a way to both support and intervene in the police action. Chapter 7 includes Salliemae's list of references that she attached to her applications for housing. Even though she recognizes the demeaning beliefs that landlords share about poor people, she both caters to and complicates these attitudes with her list of references. Finally, in chapter 9, Lucy metadiscursively named the ways the center staff believed in and practiced a policing function in the neighborhood. She censors herself when dealing with center representatives and, thus, evades their degrading actions. In all, their subtle dueling collapses the dualities often used to describe such public interactions. In complicating and replicating social structures with their language, residents played a deep and subtle game that tested the limits of what was possible.

Area residents' daily interactions with gatekeepers reveal the identity and cultural politics occupying the vast middle ground between domination and resistance. Individuals have critical awareness that imbues their daily activities; with this knowledge, they persistently problematize oral and literate language uses that some would view as rudimentary or pedestrian. Knowing the hidden ideologies attendant upon the oral and literate linguistic skills of community members, we're much less likely to label them as having false consciousness. We can begin to assume that critical awareness rests under the surface of seemingly complacent behavior, and based on this assumption, conduct research in ways that respectfully seek and describe community residents' oppositional ideologies. When we do so, we can challenge our presumptions that hegemonic social structures work in totalizing, one-dimensional ways. We can show the nuanced manifestations of dialogic power relations, where oppression and agency counterbalance each other across time and contexts.

In light of so many institutional influences in their daily lives, community members honed and refined their vernacular language tools in a cyclic process. The starting point for this process is, of course, arbitrary. We could describe the development of institutional language skills in three equally valid ways:

1. Community members learn institutional language skills, deploy them in gatekeeping interactions, and revamp these skills according to the outcomes.

2. Community members deploy their language skills in institutional exchanges, assess these, and then (re)socialize themselves into institutional language skills.

3. When community members assess and revamp their institutional language skills, they socialize those around them in oral and literate tools that can then be deployed in future gatekeeping encounters.

From these three descriptions of the developmental process of institutional language, we see that each phase in the process (acquiring, transferring, and evaluating) is informed by the other two. Further, institutional language could be found in both oral and literate forms in a variety of contexts. Each of these phases of the development of institutional language skills revealed numerous linguistic abilities:

Acquiring	Transferring	Evaluating
• questioned the literate artifact before them	• bent semantics to index two different value systems	• assessed the utility of language strategies
• modeled ways to transfer knowledge	• flattered authority of gatekeeper	• considered other linguistic tactics
• collectively problem-solved	• selected pronoun of solidarity	• questioned ethics of using one strategy vs. another
• constructed the mundane as problematic	• named and acted upon linguistic shortcoming	• determined why interaction went awry
• critically reflected on past experiences and future plans	• compared writing against successful model	• intervened on someone's behalf if necessary
• found people who could teach them more skills	• crafted linguistic representations of themselves	• altered linguistic strategies that worked poorly
• collected literate resources	• code-switched when thought appropriate for situation	• considered language and politics of situation

Orality and literacy sustained each other and, in their mutually sustaining relationship, provided analytical inroads into common linguistic occurrences. When community residents engaged literacy artifacts from institutions (as in the case of the traffic ticket and the welfare application), they verbally collaborated together in order to develop an analysis of the written piece. Conversely, when they discussed the community (as in Afriganzia's doodle), or impending interactions with landlords (as in Mirena's script on the Chinese menu), they employed literate representations of their talk in order to codify and hone their ideas and strategies. With the mutually influential relation between orality and literacy, in other words, community members fostered their analyses of the political complexities of situations. Further, the intertwining of oral and literate practices manifested itself in all three phases of their continual linguistic development.

These results show us that what we value as literacy may not be what people in communities value as literacy. Gere finds that extracurricular literacy includes those practices that take place outside the classroom and encompass "the multiple contexts in which persons seek to improve their own writing" (1994, 80). This reading and writing in the extracurriculum has, in Gere's words again, "very real types of economic and social consequences," and "one of the clearest messages of the extracurricular concerns power" (88). Of course, the type and extent of the power of extracurricular literacies remain for us to ferret out through continued ethnographic immersion in our communities. But the solution includes part of the problem. If we are to appreciate and understand the literacies that take place outside of the classroom, we must have an invitation into the daily lives of people outside of the academy—no easy feat, given the social distance between most universities and their communities, particularly inner city communities.

I have two concerns about this lack of access to extracurricular literacies. First, I think that when we do begin to explore reading and writing in the community, we too easily accept limited, and limiting, depictions of the level of literacy of people. I'm thinking of Bruce Herzberg's important work, which appeared in the October 1994 volume of *College Communication and Composition*. In this article, he describes an adult literacy program that bridges students from his composition classroom with learners in a homeless shelter. During class Herzberg's students "investigate the social and cultural reasons for the existence of illiteracy—the reasons, in other words, that the students needed to perform the valuable service they were engaged in" (316–17). I believe this work is necessary, important even. But I believe he settles with a description of these homeless people that undercuts the integrity of his goal—he terms these learners in the shelter "illiterate"; in fact, he uses this word eight times in the span of ten pages. Here is someone with laudable access to a site where extra-curricular literacies, I'll wager, take place in stolen moments of privacy in the daily lives of the people, but here is also an assumption of deficit from the outset. This assumption is problematic because it blinds us to people's potential and limits our investigation of possible literate practices.

My second concern about this lack of access to extracurricular literacies is that we too easily settle into our own value system of what counts as reading and writing. In other words, because we don't often know what types of nonacademic literacy are valued outside of the classroom, we slip into believing that our values are their values, that schooled literacy is esteemed by everyone. The sociolinguist Brian Street argues that instead of academics speaking of a literacy, we should be examining "literacies—the social practices and conceptions of reading and writing" as they take place in multiple cultural contexts (1993, 1). He finds, "the rich cultural variation in these practices . . . leads us to rethink what we mean by [literacy] and to be wary of assuming a single literacy where we may simply be imposing assumptions derived from our own cultural practice onto other peoples literacies" (1). Without adequate access to institutional and community literacies, then, we risk superimposing what we value as good reading and writing onto other types of literacy taking place outside of the classroom.

For example, the hidden ideologies that pervade the linguistic strategies in this community complicate scholarly categories that characterize and separate the functions of oral and literate skills. Residents in this inner city use both oral and literate tactics in analytical and mutually sustaining ways. One line of scholarly thinking, though, makes sharp distinctions between oral cultural and literate culture and infers a wide range of cognitive and linguistic differences based on this binary classification. In describing those theorists who truck in these binaries, Mike Rose finds these researchers also "make connections between literacy and logic and suggest that the thinking of some minority groups might be affected by the degree to which their culture has moved from oral to literate modes of behavior" (1988, 267). Strict delineation between orality and literacy, besides negatively affecting our perceptions of certain cultures, have little basis in actual practice. As Heath finds:

> The information to be gained from any prolonged look at oral and written uses of language through literacy events may... move us away from current tendencies to classify communities as beginning at one or another point along a hypothetical continuum which has no societal reality. (1988, 370)

Heath's crucial move here was to link oral and written language uses, showing the ways in which both activities reinforce each other. With Heath, the present work shows the necessary interplay between verbal and literate meaning-making activities. This research pushes the envelope of her finding, though, by underscoring the critical nature of residents' language uses. Again and again, we've seen instances of individuals naming the assumptions that pervade a literate text or an utterance. Recall, for example, Lucy's analysis of the HEAP application; or Afriganzia's assessment of the "Game of Power" played between community members and center workers; or Raejone's application for HUD funding; or Salliemae's list of references. Not only were orality and literacy mutually informing, but they revealed individuals' critical understandings of how institutional politics work, and how to shape their language uses accordingly.

Their critical literacy practices exemplify the very types of reading, writing, and analytical abilities for which critical literacy theorists call. Peter McLaren defines critical literacy as the "examination of the political and cultural assumptions underlying texts" (1992, 319). As illustrated throughout this work, community members not only understood the underlying assumptions in applications, letters, contracts, and forms, but they also shaped and assessed their own linguistic skills required to strategically respond to these texts.

Interestingly, these critical literacy competencies emerge with texts that many believe require only functional literate skills. To be considered functionally literate, one must "demonstrate the ability to read, write, or compute in social and economic situations that require these skills; for example ... fill[ing] out job applications and income tax forms, or read[ing] and comprehend[ing] instructional manuals" (Ogbu 1995, 227). As we've seen, the process of completing and critiquing applications and other forms required analytical abilities beyond those necessary to merely fill in the blank. Residents uncovered the implicit assumptions present in such texts, and, in doing so, contributed to the development of antihegemonic cultural logic. In essence, their literate practices collapse literacy scholars' dichotomies between instrumental and critical literacies.

Quayville's inner city residents' critical awareness and strategic linguistic activities, while a good check on our discussions of politics, seldom got them full-time employment, educational, and housing possibilities, or, for that matter, better treatment from public servants. In the end, being aware of one's oppression does not necessarily remove it, or even remove the burden of at least appearing to comply with it. This point alone undermines the best intentions of critical theorists. Supposedly, individuals can throw off the burdens of hegemonic forces—can, once and for all, mobilize together in a concerted effort to withdrawal their consent—if only we could teach them to be more attentive to their own complicity in cultural reproduction. Yet, as we've seen, even though politically astute, inner city residents must make do with their limited and hard-won resources and opportunities. The onus to be critically aware of and to change oppressive behaviors, then, rests, in no small measure, on society's public institutional representatives.

Perhaps one way to ameliorate the struggles would be for gatekeepers to consider their language use in day-to-day interactions, using means similar to those residents employ. In stating this, my goal isn't to lay blame or point the finger, but rather to understand how gatekeepers come to be inscribed by others. If we're to advance social change at micro-levels of interaction, we need to determine what our roles entail as society's institutional representatives. We need to comprehend how our roles can be constructed as burdensome, troubling, and demeaning by the people we hope our work serves. From previous chapters, we've seen the ways in which daily interactions with institutional agents built upon each other to shape the what community members call "the struggle." When minimally filling their roles, gatekeepers:

- responded curtly to questions;

- looked down or away from community members without obvious reason instead of maintaining eye contact;

- asked individuals to hand-carry documents between offices, as opposed to faxing these documents for them;

- asked individuals questions without telling them how their answers would affect their cases;

- used the individual's first name without permission;

- acted inconsistently with offers of help;

- refused to acknowledge that documents already existed on file;

- acted in quasi-policing roles by keeping surveillance on the activities of community members and reporting these activities to landlords or DSS representatives;

- refused to move residents up waiting lists for available housing;

- unduly and inappropriately asserted authority;

- inundated applicants with amounts and types of forms;

- assumed applicants lack literate abilities;

- insulted community members.

With this abbreviated list in mind, we can begin to fathom the depth and breadth of what these inner city residents termed, "the struggle." We need to be aware of how we contribute to the struggle with our speech, literacy demands, and gestures that may discourage and disrespect the individuals we want to teach, research, and serve.[21] Yet the struggle of the inner city residents has other ways to instruct us. The few gatekeeping encounters that went well exemplify the linguistic means gatekeepers can use to facilitate individuals' goals. In these encounters, the institutional representatives:

- addressed community members with respect;

- modeled discursive norms expected for that particular context;

- provided literacy resources needed to negotiate the institution;

- invited the use of community vernacular language tools;

- encouraged the individuals when they tried on the discursive tools of a particular institution;

- explained requirements for admission to the institution;

- made themselves accessible beyond what one would routinely expect (the EOP counselor spent 48 minutes with Sasha and Raejone, and the judge told Lucy to call him directly if she had any questions);

- established a personal connection by asking after the family (EOP counselor);

- invited questions from community members.

These findings help us complicate Erickson and Shultz's definition of gatekeepers as both judges and advocates. Clearly, in all situations the gatekeepers were at the very least maintenance people of the institutional standards who sometimes facilitated community members' attempts to better themselves. However, in some rare cases, particularly with the EOP counselor, the gatekeeper went beyond the judge and advocate dualism and fleshed out the role. The EOP counselor became a translator of the institutional discourse and standards, a host who invited community members to share resources, and a liaison who met community members linguistically halfway in their border crossings. As representatives of the educational system, teachers, scholars and administrators can, and do, practice civically minded gatekeeping activities.[22]

With the cyclic process of language development in this inner city as a model, perhaps we can (a) consciously build upon the institutional language tools we have; (b) deploy them carefully, paying special attention to the politics of our interactions and maintaining respect for the history and culture of our students, research participants and colleagues; and (c) assess and revamp our language tools especially when our exchanges don't go as planned. If gatekeepers want to avoid becoming part of the struggle, we need to internalize and practice the tacit belief community residents held about institutional literacy: Nothing taken for granted. Nothing easy.

My hope remains that this book gives pause to the numerous critical scholars who adopt the notion of false consciousness. At the local level, the workings of hegemony are incomplete, pushed at daily, far from taken-for-granted; they're named, questioned, and slowly, carefully scrutinized; they are resisted, not quickly internalized, rarely given over to easily. Every day, the language of domination is turned in upon itself by active agents who defy its categorizations, who subvert its influence, and who seek opportunity in its inconsistencies. The ideology of domination is objectified—brought up from the insidious level and moved into the conscious level—by those who feel its impact at the point of application. While the persistence of classist and racists beliefs discouraged, made for continuous struggles, and sometimes lead to despair, individuals also defined themselves and their counterhegemonic ideologies against it.

Admittedly, the notion of false consciousness seems to have some validity when one chooses to view public interactions between institutional representatives and community members. In public transcripts, individuals can appear to meekly acquiesce to gatekeepers, to wholeheartedly adopt gatekeeper's belief systems, to blindly accept treatment that may least serve their interests. One reason for this appearance is that individuals can, and do, don the White mask of obedience—even when their own antihegemonic perspectives and self-identifications remain intact and present behind the guise. However, when we rely solely on public interactions, for example, we limit the scope of what we can understand about hegemony. That is, we need to ask ourselves what leads up to and happens after these public encounters and, then, find ways to research the belief systems hidden therein. If we hope to cultivate a theory of hegemony that respectfully serves, we must gain access to and appreciate oppositional belief systems.

To do this, we need to practice and refine activist methodologies. Because activist research demands reciprocity and a focus on political issues salient for those with whom we study, we are much more likely to foster mutually beneficial relations through our research methods. Scholarship on oppression can potentially avoid making knowledge on the backs of those with whom we study, if we honor the knowledge, lived experiences, and linguistic sophistication of participants.

When we immerse ourselves in hidden symbolic systems, we begin to comprehend the limitations of our notions of politics at local levels and the analytical awareness present there. We see how individuals construct power relations, conceive positionality, develop and critique plans to circumvent unwanted influence, defy categorizations, read between the lines, delimit and safeguard boundaries of authority, "read" a situation, assign proxies, and metadiscursively analyze situations. The idea of false consciousness would downplay, or simply overlook, these linguistic means of surviving and the cultural logic that permeates them. The notion of ideological domination damages the people we hope to liberate with our critical theories of hegemony; with such a notion, we underestimate their critical awareness, obfuscate the political complexities of their everyday lives, and undermine the (potential) potency of their reflection, language, and agency.

The concept of false consciousness harms in another way. When it informs our discussion of politics, we end up with flat, one-dimensional depictions of power relations. We dichotomize power relations: on the one side, we characterize people as subjugated, their opportunities as predetermined, their hopes as naive; and, on the other side, we illustrate domination as an relentless force, its influence as ever inscribing subjects, its exercise as insidiously monolithic. Yet, between these polarities, a wide expanse of political and linguistic maneuvering exists that illustrates the dialogic ways power relations get negotiated at the local level. Although some have posited the dialogic nature of power relations, few have exemplified it in the particulars of daily existence.

Granted, the dialogic power relations presented here are by no means egalitarian, but that isn't the point. The point is that inner city residents perceive the mechanisms that sustain these asymmetrical relations. Their hidden social symbolic systems as well as their strategic language use should be appreciated as a foundational form of politics, foundational in the sense that more overt challenges to inequality could be supported there.

Overall, I hope this work provides a means for us to reconceptualize critical theory in order to link our assertions about hegemony and language to the everyday practices that bear them out. Rather than seeking grand historical transformations, large-scale social movements, or massive changes in consciousness, critical theory can collapse political binaries by depicting the complex everyday particulars in the middle place where most people live their lives. When we assume individuals have critical awareness, we are less likely to mistake silence for subjugation, appeasement for compliance, and concealment for consent. In the end, I hope this work has offered ways to respect the particulars of daily politics, the commonplace victories and defeats, the subtle and overt challenges. The struggle and the tools.

Notes

1. Because people in this study call themselves Black and African American, I will use both of these interchangeably to designate identity with their permission. They also use "Black" and "White" to categorize ways of talking and writing. Talking Black in this neighborhood was valued because most residents linked this discourse to their identity, while talking White meant using the code of the wider society in order to get ahead. Finally, all the pseudonyms for people in this study were chosen by the individuals about whom I write. I note those cases where the names are the actual street names of the people appearing in these pages.

2. Community residents and I identified with each other along many axes: gender, generation, family, class, and race. Many woman and I were close in age—early to mid twenties. Many came from large families; I am the youngest of seven. Even though I was a graduate student in a prestigious private university, my class standing went from working class, when my folks were married, to White trash, when they divorced and we were evicted. I was nine at the time, and I lived with my mother, who remained un(der)employed until I was seventeen. At seventeen, I found work at a Jack in the Box, and she found work on an Air Force base. Finally, a number of residents identified themselves as mixed-bloods—Black Cherokee in particular, while I'm a White Cherokee. Because of our common ways of identifying with each other, we shared perspectives on many points.

3. The amount of cash welfare recipients are granted depends on what DSS and policymakers perceive to be their "basic needs." They calculate this need based on outdated and overly optimistic indexes for what average families pay for heat, rent, and personal needs. Because these costs are underestimated, welfare recipients typically end up with little cash after rent and bills are paid. Lucy Cadens describes the situation this way: "I don't know what they're calling my basic needs because the money they give you don't cover

the things most people take for granted. Soap. Washing powder. Towels. Sheets. Shampoo. Deodorant. Toilet paper. Dish soap. Brooms. Garbage bags. You can't walk around nasty, and you want your house clean, but they don't consider any of these things as part of your basic need. What they take for granted, we can't, because we don't have it. I wanna tell them, 'You wash your ass every morning, I'd like to wash mine's too.' But they don't think about that. So you try to get as much money as possible, without lying, because the system isn't helping you the way it supposed to. We're not trying to steal. We're trying to make the system work for us." In essence, community members massaged institutional structures in an attempt to maintain what *the residents* defined as their "basic needs."

4. Because I sat close to the door, I saw Sue touch Marquis and also saw Sue staring hard at him as he loud-talked her. Of course, this vantage caught me in the rub between the public and hidden transcript, a privileged, yet awkward, position. At that point, I was still considered a volunteer at the center, therefore part of the establishment to some extent. On the one hand, I had to appear to Sue to support her discipline of Marquis, especially since I sat in her line of sight. At the same time, my immersion in the community meant I had to also show support for Marquis's position, especially since I sat in all three youths' line of sight as well. I kept a poker face throughout the exchange and waited until Marquis closed the office door again before I tipped my hand. The closed door signified that the four of us had returned to the hidden transcript where I could safely show my support of his loud-talking without risking the loss of my position in the center.

5. About this interaction, one insightful reviewer said: "Cushman treats the production of this document as evidence of strategic literacy rather than as an event that arises from the ethnographic relationship itself." Actually, we're both right, though I'd frame this issue differently. The prompts I used in this exchange (and the one before it) offer examples of the types of dialogue present in activist research. Afriganzia used my questions as a springboard for expressing her tacitly held beliefs and knowledge about power and language. I may have stimulated the event, but I surely didn't provide the knowledge to execute it. Afriganzia and the youths held these latent constructions by dint of living in a culture where so much critical consciousness manifested itself daily. The dialogic relations of activist research begin with a firm belief that individuals have extensive knowledge and many linguistic devices for keeping in check what they deem to be society's harmful influences. Dialogue calls forward these hidden ideologies.

6. On June 6, 1997, I called Afriganzia to get her insights on this chapter. This opening quote stems from our conversation.

7. In chapter 3, I discussed the structuring ideology of institutions in light of research by historians and social scientists. When compared to the ways

residents' understood institutions, the sociohistorical research cited in chapter 3 has noteworthy validity. See especially, Michael Katz's works *In the Shadow of the Poorhouse, The Undeserving Poor,* and *Improving Poor People,* for particularly apt discussions of poverty.

8. Lucy's interpretation hit the mark. When Raejone and I went to pick up the applications necessary for her to enter into the Higher Education Opportunity Program [HEOP] at a nearby Catholic college, the HEOP representative handed her a large stack of papers and explained: "It's a big stack, but if a person is willing to put the time and effort into filing these applications, then we know they're the type of person we want to let into college. They won't be daunted by the course work." I joked with the agent, "Ah, scare tactics." Failing to see my sarcasm, she enthusiastically replied, "That's right."

9. Raejone went through many drafts of her essay before coming to this one, which she termed her final one. As she wrote, she would become frustrated with the wording of a phrase and mumble "That just don't sound like me," or "No, this ain't working." She gave up on her second draft of this essay altogether because, as she told me, "It just ain't sounding like something I would say or someone I want to be. Let me take it home and figure out how I can get it to where I want it." She printed a copy of the paragraphs and took it home. After a number of tries, she wrote out by hand a draft of the above essay that she typed into the computer. Her sometimes stymied writing process indicates her frustrated attempts to balance her community perspective with the perspective she believed her readers would use to judge her essay.

Along the way, she would ask me questions in order to facilitate her writing. Given the activist nature of my ethnographic research, and given that she asked me to tutor her with her writing, I helped her in a variety of ways over the five-month-long process of applying. With this final draft in particular, she used a handout from my university's Writing Center describing how to compose an application essay, which helps account for her essay's organization. If she stumbled though a wording of a sentence, she would ask me to "say it a few ways for [her]," which I did. From these models she would cut and paste together her sentences that read to her, finally, as a combination of words that signify both her own values and the university's.

10. In his classic description of the Black family, sociologist Andrew Billingsley describes the family ethic of struggle to achieve despite tremendous social oppression: "Negro families have shown an amazing ability to survive in the face of impossible conditions. They have also shown remarkable ability to take the barest shreds of opportunity and turn them into the social capital of stability and achievement" (1968, 98). Raejone, despite being on social assistance, having two children, dropping out of high school, and living in the inner city, safeguards her goal to get a higher education, a goal representing the barest shred of opportunity for her.

11. In this section of the text, I will analyze the semantics, prosody, and proxemic distance these two young women and Mr. Villups used to socially construct their constellation of meaning in this context. Specifically, I'll chart the tonal configurations of his utterances to "locate the most salient stressed phrase(s) . . . and determine their melodic configuration" (Gumperz 1982a, 108). I chose this notational device, along with the others listed in on page xxv because they allowed me to focus on the most important signaling features of the rise and fall in the tone of Mr. Villups's utterances using a convenient and easily understood shorthand.

12. Labov showed how African-American children will defend themselves with silence and one-word answers when they felt threatened in interviews with White education researchers. The same seems to be going on here. Keith Basso offers another explanation for silence that seems appropriate here, even though it stems from his immersion in the Western Apache culture: "keeping silent among the Western Apache is a response to uncertainty and unpredictability in social relations" (1979, 83).

13. Both Mr. Villups and the women believed in the power of school language, a belief Heath also found in Trackton residents: "Intuitively they . . . feel language is power, and though they may not articulate precisely their reasons for needing to learn to read and write, and speak in the ways the school teaches, they believe that such learning has something to do with moving them up and out of Trackton and Roadville" (1983, 265). Mr. Villups recognized the intimidation of asking Sasha to try on a different social dialect, but asked her to do so anyway. Also, implicit in this interaction was the political assumption that knowledge of and practice with certain codes helps you move up the social ladder.

14. In the entire course of this study, I saw college application materials like these only twice. Since, at the request of Raejone and her sister, I helped introduce these literacy artifacts into this community, let me briefly reflect on the effects of the introduction of such atypical reading and writing materials. Heath describes the potential effects of introducing literacy artifacts into a community in her article "Bedtime Stories in the Piedmont," which she co-authored with Charlene Thomas. In this article, Heath describes how the introduction of a tape recorder and books into the home of a teenager helped the teen teach her youngster to achieve preschool literacy. Although I haven't evidence to show precisely how Raejone, her sister, and others used these artifacts in their house, these texts had been explored when I wasn't there because they were dog-eared and marked up when I came that Sunday. Perhaps, the presence of literacy artifacts from schools and universities around the house helps inner city residents become more versed in these literacy forms.

15. While I agree with his motivations for presenting vernacular theory, I disagree with McLaughlin's depiction of individuals and the "rigor" of their language use. He says, "individual subjects, in spite of the culture industry's efforts, can see through the game. And then in a second forget what they know and fall for the next game" (14). Perhaps the middle-class individuals in McLaughlin's research could forget what they knew, because it is in their favor to forget—the ideology they critique privileges them, and so it behooves them to forget. However, participants in this study never had the luxury to forget what they knew. If it appears inner city residents did indeed forget their critique, as it does in the example where Jolinda polices her daughter's language, then this appearance can be attributed to the political demands that separate the hidden from the public transcript.

McLaughlin also devalues the language use of participants in his study by comparing it to academic theory. "Vernacular theory does not differ in kind from academic theory," however, academic theory should be considered "a rigorous and scholarly version of a widely practiced analytical strategy" (1996, 6). The metacommunication presented in this chapter, indeed the language skills presented throughout this book, have revealed individuals' rigor, and have also revealed the capacity of Black English to sustain symbolic interpretations of nuanced linguistic practices. The social problems individuals faced weren't due to their lack of abilities, awareness, or rigor; the problems were due in large part to wider society's continual dismissing and devaluing of their language and knowledge. Said another way, the difference between academic and vernacular theory does not rest in rigor, but rests in larger societal beliefs that value and commodify "scholarly" language more than "Black English."

16. Street names used at the request of participants.

17. Although most of the analysis of this chapter centers on discourse, literacy plays into this interaction in subtle ways. The judge read the charges from the sheet in front of him. He also referred to Disco's record and information regarding legal services. The exchange that follows, then, centered on gatekeeping literacy that Disco never got to see, and that Lucy saw only at the end of the interaction with the judge. Heath describes a similar phenomenon between a Trackton resident and a credit union loan servicing agent: "The interaction took place around a loan servicing sheet that the client [had] not been able to see . . . or frame questions which would clarify their contents. This pattern occurred frequently for Trackton residents, who argued that the neighborhood center programs and other adult education programs should be aimed . . . at ways of getting through such interviews or other situations, when someone else held the information which they needed to know in order to ask questions about the contents of that written material in ways which would be acceptable to institution officials" (Heath 1988, 364). In the

upcoming interaction, the judge held the written information that Disco needed to know, but did not have access to.

18. In fact, Labov showed that similar defensive behaviors (silence and monosyllabic answers) were used by young African-American boys with educational researchers. Unfortunately, the researchers misinterpreted such defense mechanisms as indications of the intelligence of the adolescents they studied. Labov showed that these boy's reactions resulted more from the foreign and threatening nature of the situation.

19. Some may point to Lucy's behavior with the judge as a masterful performance of the dominant script, or little more than up-to-date Uncle Tom behavior. However, Scott reminds us that "rituals of subordination may be deployed both for the purposes of manipulation and concealment" (1990, 35). As we'll see later in the chapter, Lucy had many reasons for flattering the authority of the judge in the ways she did.

20. Since I claim to do activist research (Chapter 2), one might expect that I should have justification enough to intervene. During this entire interaction, I sat on the edge of my seat, jotting notes, thinking, "Ellen, say something. The judge doesn't understand. Disco's just scared." Just after Chaos blurted out "You," he shook his head and looked to me. I shrugged. I wanted very much to intervene and get the judge to rethink his position, which, from where Chaos and I sat, indeed seemed odious. But I didn't intervene, even though I considered it. The situation raises further and important issues about intervention. Part of my uncertainty came from the fact that I wasn't invited by Lucy or Disco to intervene. Without an invitation from the people in the gatekeeping encounter, scholarly intervention smacks sour as an imposition of our own values and beliefs onto other people. An axiom for activist research sums up my point: intervention only through invitation.

21. In *Language and Discrimination*, Roberts, Davies, and Jupp list numerous activities that the gatekeepers they studied still need to do in order to become fairer and more humane to the people with whom they work. For ten years, they studied ethnic minorities, first-generation immigrants to the United Kingdom, as they interacted with gatekeepers in their workplaces and public service institutions. Their results led them to three proposals, among others:

1. Action is required to expose to those concerned the ways in which individuals and institutions make judgments and control access through interactions which are based on unshared assumptions and expectations.

2. Actions are required to demonstrate the link between individual interaction and institutional decision-making and discrimination.

3. Changes in procedures and systems are potentially very helpful but cannot in themselves guarantee "fairness" because they do not neces-

sarily affect the quality of face-to-face interaction which is the point at which decisions are made. So there have to be changes in interactive behavior as well. (1992, 368–69).

22. For numerous examples of positive gatekeeping behaviors, see Mike Rose's latest work, *Possible Lives*, in which he examines schools from places including, but not limited to, the Los Angeles area, the Deep South, New York, and Chicago. In combinations of vignette and scenario, Rose articulates the day-to-day gatekeeping interactions of teachers and administrators who encompass the characteristics of the best kinds of gatekeeping activities. For example, the teachers showed many forms of respect for their students including, "fair treatment, decency, a respect for history, the language and culture of the peoples represented in the classroom. . . . [And, finally,] respect [with] an intellectual dimension. As New York principal Louis Delgado put it, 'It's not just about being polite—even the curriculum has to convey respect. [It] has to be challenging enough that it's respectful' " (1996, 414). As gatekeepers, these teachers had their share of authority and used their authority in socially generous ways: "a teacher's authority came from many sources—knowledge, care, the construction of safe and respectful space, solidarity with students' background—rather than solely from age or role" (414). And as evident throughout the book, teachers and principals found ways to distribute their authority so that individuals could participate in knowledge construction and decision-making. We see a benchmark for our performance in the language use of the EOP counselor as well as the teachers in Rose's study.

Works Cited

Abrahams, Roger. 1974. "Black Talking on the Streets." *Explorations in the Ethnography of Speaking.* Eds. Richard Bauman and Joal Sherzer. Cambridge: Cambridge UP. 115–34.

Akinnaso, F. N. and C. S. Ajirotutu. 1982. "Performance and Ethnic Style in Job Interviews." *Language and Social Identity.* Ed J. Gumperz. London: Cambridge UP. 119–44.

Apple, Michael and Lois Weis, eds. 1983. *Ideology and Practice in Schooling.* Philadelphia: Temple UP.

Austin, J. 1962. *How to Do Things with Words.* Oxford: Oxford UP.

Bartholomae, David. 1988. "Inventing the University." *Perspectives on Literacy.* Eds. E. Kingten, B. Kroll, and M. Rose. Carbondale: Southern Illinois UP. 324–67.

Basso, Keith. 1979. *Portraits of "the Whiteman."* Cambridge: Cambridge UP.

Baugh, John. 1983. *Black Street Speech: Its History, Structure, and Survival.* Austin: U of Texas P.

Baynham, Mike. 1993. "Code Switching and Mode Switching: Community Interpreters and Mediators of Literacy." *Cross Cultural.* Ed. B. Street. Cambridge: Cambridge UP. 294–310.

Berger, Peter and Thomas Luckmann. 1966. *The Social Construction of Reality.* Garden City, New York: Doubleday.

Billingsley, Andrew. 1968. *Black Families in White America.* New York: Simon & Schuster.

Bleich, David. 1993. "Ethnography and the Study of Literacy: Prospects for Socially Generous Research." *Into the Field: Sites of Composition Studies.* Ed. Anne Ruggles Gere. New York: MLA.

Bourdieu, Pierre. 1990. *The Logic of Practice.* Stanford, Calif.: Stanford UP.

Briggs, Charles. 1986. *Learning How to Ask*. Cambridge: Cambridge UP.

Clifford, James and G. Marcus. 1986. *Writing Culture*. Berkeley: U of California P.

Collins, James. 1993. "Determination and Contradiction." *Bourdieu: Critical Perspectives*. Eds. C. Calhoun, E. LiPuma, and M. Postone. Chicago: Chicago UP. 116–39.

Cook-Gumperz, Jenny. 1986. "Introduction." *The Social Construction of Literacy*. Ed. J. Cook-Gumperz. London: Cambridge UP. 1–15.

———. 1993. "Dilemmas of Identity: Oral and Written Literacies in the Making of a Basic Writing Student." *Anthropology and Education Quarterly*, 24.4: 336–56.

Cushman, Ellen. 1996. "Rhetorician as Agent of Social Change." *College Composition and Communication* 47.1: 29–41.

Cushman, Ellen and Terese Guinsatao Monberg. 1998. "Building Bridges: Reflexivity in Composition Research." *Under Construction: Working at the Intersections of Composition Theory, Research, and Practice*. Eds. Christine Farris and Chris Anson. Provost, UT: Utah State UP.

Davies, E., C. Roberts, and T. Jupp. 1992. *Language and Discrimination*. London: Longman.

de Certeau, Michel. 1984. *The Practice of Everyday Life*. Berkeley: U of California P.

Dirks, Nicholas. 1994. "Ritual and Resistance." *Culture/Power/History*. Eds. N. Dirks, G. Eley, and S. Ortner. Princeton, N.J.: Princeton UP. 483–503.

Dodd, Donald. 1993. *Historical Statistics of the States: 2 Centuries of Census 1790–1990*. Westport, CO: Greenwood Press.

Du Bois, W.E.B. 1990. *The Souls of Black Folks*. New York: Vintage.

Duranti, Allesandro and Charles Goodwin, eds. 1992. *Rethinking Context*. Cambridge: Cambridge UP.

Erickson, Frederick and Jeffrey Shultz. 1982. *The Counselor as Gatekeeper*. New York: Academic Press.

Fairclough, Norman. 1989. *Language and Power*. New York: Longman.

Fay, Brian. 1987. *Critical Social Science*. Ithaca, NY: Cornell UP.

Foucault, Michel. 1983. "The Subject and Power." Afterword. *Beyond Structuralism and Hermeneutics*. Eds. Hubert Dreyfus and Paul Rainbow. New Haven, Conn.: Yale UP. 208–26.

Freire, Paulo. 1970. *Pedagogy of the Oppressed*. New York: Continuum.

Freire, Paulo and Donaldo Macedo. 1987. *Literacy: Reading the Word and the World*. South Hadley, Mass.: Bergin and Garvey.

Gates, Henry L. 1988. *The Signifying Monkey: A Theory of Afro-American Literary Criticism*. New York: Vintage.

Gee, James. 1990. *Sociolinguisitcs and Literacies: Ideology in Discourses*. London: Fulmer Press.

Geertz, Clifford. *Interpretation of Cultures*. New York: Basic Books.

Geisler, Cheryl. 1994. *Academic Literacy and the Nature of Expertise*. Hillsdale, N.J.: Lawrence and Erlbaum.

Gere, Anne Ruggles. 1994. "The Extracurriculum of Composition." *College Composition and Communication*. 45.1: 75–93.

Giddens, Anthony. 1979. *Central Problems in Social Theory*. Berkeley: U of California P.

———. 1984. *The Constitution of Society*. Berkeley: U of California P.

Giroux, Henry. 1981. *Ideology, Culture, and the Process of Schooling*. Philadelphia: Temple UP.

Goffman, Erving. 1963. *Stigma*. New York, Simon & Schuster.

———. 1969. *Interaction Ritual: Essays on Face to Face Behavior*. Garden City, N.Y.: Doubleday.

———. 1981. *Forms of Talk*. Harper & Row.

Goody, Jack and Ian Watt. "The Consequences of Literacy." *Perspectives on Literacy*. Eds. Kingten et al. 3–27.

Gumperz, John. 1982a. *Discourse Strategies*. Cambridge: Cambridge UP.

———. 1982b. *Language and Social Identity*. London: Cambridge UP.

Habermas, Jurgen. 1984. *The Theory of Communicative Action*. Boston: Beacon.

Hannerz, Ulf. 1970. "The Notion of Ghetto Culture." *Black America*. Ed. J. Szwed. New York: Basic Books. 99–109.

Heath, Shirley B. 1983. *Ways with Words*. Cambridge: Cambridge UP.

———. 1988. "Protean Shapes in Literacy." *Perspectives on Literacy*. Eds. Kingten, et al. 348–71.

Heath, S. B. and C. Thomas. 1992. "Bedtime Stories in the Piedmont." *Reading Empirical Research Studies*. Eds. J. Hayes et al. Hillsdale, N.J.: Lawrence Erlbaum. 177–211.

Heller, Monica. 1983. "Negotiations of Language Choice in Montreal." *Language and Social Identity.* Ed. J. Gumperz. 108–18.

Herzberg, Bruce. 1994. "Community Service and Critical Teaching." *College Composition and Communication* 45.3: 307–19.

hooks, bell. 1995. *Killing Rage.* New York, Henry Holt.

———. 1995. *Outlaw Culture.* New York: Random House.

Huspek, Michael. 1993. "Dueling Structures: The Theory of Resistance in Discourse." *Communication Theory* 3.1: 1–25.

Hymes, Dell. 1974. *Foundations in Sociolinguistics.* Philadelphia: U of Pennsylvania P.

Johannsen, Agneta. 1992. "Applied Anthropology and Postmodernist Ethnography." *Human Organization* 50.1: 71–81.

Jones, Jacqueline. 1993. "Southern Diaspora: Origins of the Northern ' 'Underclass'." *The "Underclass" Debate.* Ed. M. Katz. 27–55.

Katz, Michael. 1993. "The Urban 'Underclass' as a Metaphor of Social Transformation." *The "Underclass" Debate: Views from History.* Princeton, N.J.: Princeton UP. 3–27.

———, Ed. 1993b. *The "Underclass" Debate: Views from History.* Princeton, N.J.: Princeton UP.

———. 1993c. *The Undeserving Poor.* Princeton, N.J.: Princeton UP.

———. 1994. *Improving Poor People.* New York: Random House.

Kernan, Claudia Mitchell. 1971. *Language Behavior in a Black Urban Community.* Berkeley: Language Behavior Research Laboratory.

Kernan, C. M. 1972. "Signifying and Marking: Two Afro-American Speech Acts." *Directions in Sociolinguistics: The Ethnography of Communication.* Eds. J. Gumperz and D. Hymes. New York: Holt. 161–79.

Kintgen, Eugene, Bob Kroll, and Mike Rose, Eds. 1988. *Perspectives on Literacy.* Carbondale: Southern Illinois UP.

Kochman, Thomas. 1970. "Toward an Ethnography of Black American Speech Behavior." *Afro-American Anthropology: Contemporary Perspectives.* Eds. N. Whitten and J. Szwed.

Kress, Gunther and Robert Hodge. 1979. *Language as Ideology.* Boston: Routledge.

Labov, William. 1969. "The Logic of Nonstandard English." *Georgetown U. Monographs in Language and Linguistics* 72: 1–31.

————. 1972. *Language in the Inner City: Studies in the Black English Vernacular.* Philadelphia: U of Pennsylvania P.

Lankshear, Colin and Peter McLaren, eds. 1993. *Critical Literacy: Politics, Praxis, and the Postmodern.* Albany: SUNY.

Lather, Patti. 1992. "Research as Praxis." *Harvard Education Review* 56: 257–77.

Lewis, Oscar. *Five Families.* 1959. New York: Basic Books.

————. 1961. Introduction. *The Children of Sanchez.* New York: Random House.

Luke, Carmen and Jennifer Gore. 1992. *Feminisms and Critical Pedagogy.* New York: Routledge.

Luria, A. R. 1976. *Cognitive Development: Its Cultural and Social Foundations.* Cambridge: Harvard UP.

Macedo, Donaldo. 1994. *Literacies of Power: What Americans Are Not Allowed to Know.* Boulder, Colo.: Westview Press.

McLaren, Peter. 1992. "Literacy Research and the Postmodern Turn: Cautions from the Margins." *Multidisciplinary Perspectives on Literacy Research.* Eds. R., Beach, J. Green, M. Kamil, and T. Shanahan. Urbana: National Council of Teachers of English. 319–339.

McLaughlin, Thomas. 1996. *Street Smarts and Critical Theory.* Madison: U. of Wisconsin P.

Moll, Luis and Estephan Diaz. 1987a. "Change as the Goal of Educational Research." *Anthropology and Education Quarterly* 18.4: 300–311.

————. 1987. "Teaching Writing as Communication: The Use of Ethnographic Findings in Classroom Practice." *Literacy and Schooling.* Ed. D. Bloome. Ablex. 193–221.

Oakley, Anne. 1981. "Interviewing Women: A Contradiction in Terms." *Doing Feminist Research.* London: Routledge. 30–62.

Ogbu, John. 1988. "Literacy and Schooling in Subordinate Cultures." *Perspectives on Literacy.* Eds. Kintgen et al. 227–43.

————. 1995. "Literacy and Black Americans: Comparative Perspectives." *Literacy among African-American Youth.* Eds. Vivian Gadsen and D. Wagner. Cresskill, N.J.: Hampton. 83–101.

Philips, Susan. 1994. "From Practice to Structure in Tongan Language Ideology: How Crimes of Bad Language Harm the Sister-Brother Relationship." Paper presented at Language Ideologies, School of American Research. Sante Fe, New Mexico.

Porter, James and Pat Sullivan. 1997. *Opening Spaces: Writing Technologies and Critical Research Practices*. Greenwich, CT: Ablex.

Porter, James. 1995, March 22. "Ethical Literacy." Conference on College Composition and Communication, Hyatt Regency, Washington, D.C.

Roberts, C., E. Davies, and T. Jupp, eds. 1992. *Language and Discrimination*. London: Longman.

Rose, Mike. 1988. "Narrowing the Mind and Page: Remedial Writers and Cognitive Reductionism." *College Composition and Communication* 39.3: 267–302.

———. 1996. *Possible Lives*. Boston: Houghton Mifflin.

Searle, John. 1979. *Expression and Meaning*. Cambridge: Oxford UP.

Scott, James. 1990. *Domination and the Arts of Resistance*. New Haven, Conn.: Yale UP.

———. 1985. *Weapons of the Weak*. New Haven, Conn.: Yale UP.

Scribner, Silvia and Mike Cole. 1981. *The Psychology of Literacy*. Cambridge, Mass.: Harvard UP.

Shoemaker, Pamela. 1991. *Gatekeeping*. Newbury Park: Sage.

Sinclair, April. 1994. *Coffee Will Make You Black*. New York, N.Y.: Avon Books.

Smitherman, G. 1977. *Talkin and Testifyin*. Detroit: Wayne State UP.

Spivak, Gayatri. 1988. "Can the Subaltern Speak?" *Marxism and the Interpretation of Culture*. Eds. Cary Nelson and Lawrence Grossberg. Urbana: UIP. 271–313.

Stack, Carol. 1977. *All Our Kin*. New York: Vintage.

Street, Brian. 1984. *Literacy in Theory and Practice*. London: Cambridge UP.

———, ed. 1993. *Cross Cultural Approaches to Literacy*. Cambridge: Cambridge UP.

Stubbs, Michael. 1983. *Discourse Analysis*. U of Chicago: Chicago P.

Sullivan, Patricia. 1996. "Ethnography and the Problem of the 'Other.' " *Ethics and Representation*. Eds. Peter Mortensen and Gesa Kirsch. Urbana, Ill.: National Council of Teachers of English (NCTE). 97–115.

Taylor, Denny. 1988. *Growing up Literate: Learning from Inner City Families*. Portsmouth: Heinemann.

Thompson, J., ed. 1991. "Introduction." *Language and Symbolic Power*. Cambridge, Mass.: Harvard UP. 1–42.

Trotter, Joe W. Jr. "The Structures of Urban Poverty: The Reorganization of Space and Work in Three Periods of American History." Ed. M. Katz. *The "Underclass" Debate*. 89–112.

Tyler, Stephen. 1986. "Post-Modern Ethnography: From Document of the Occult to Occult Document." *Writing Culture: The Poetics and Politics of Ethnography*. Eds. James Clifford and George Marcus. Berkeley, CA: University of California Press. 122–140.

U.S. Department of Commerce, Bureau of Census. 1963. *1960 Census of United States*. Washingon, D.C.: Dept. of Commerce. Table 201, 736.

———. 1953. *1950 Census of United States*. Washington, D.C.: Dept. of Commerce. Table 33, 135.

———. 1943. *1940 Census of United States*. Washington, D.C.: Dept. of Commerce. Tables 18a & 18b, 127.

———. 1933. *1930 Census of United States*. Washington, D.C.: Dept. of Commerce. 273.

———. 1923. *1920 Census of United States*. Washington, D.C.: Dept. of Commerce. 692.

U.S. Department of Labor Bureau of Statistics. 1989. *Employment, Hours, and Earnings: States and Areas, 1972–87*. Vol. 3. Washington D.C.: Labor Bureau. 2320.

Valentine, Charles and Betty Valentine. 1970. "Making the Scene, Digging the Action, and Telling It Like It Is: Anthropologists at Work in a Dark Ghetto." *Afro-American Anthropology*. Eds. Whitten and Szwed. 403–15.

Villanueva, Victor. 1992. "Hegemony: From and Organically Grown Intellectual." *Pre/Text* 13.1–2: 18–34.

———. 1993. *Bootstraps*. Urbana, Ill.: National Council of Teachers of English, (NCTE).

Warry, Wayne. 1992. "The Eleventh Thesis: Applied Anthropology as Praxis." *Human Organization* 51.2: 155–63.

Weaver, Robert. 1965. *Dilemmas of Urban America*. Cambridge, Mass.: Harvard UP.

Whitten, N. and J. Szwed. eds. 1970. *Afro-American Anthropology: Contemporary Perspectives*. New York: Free Press.

Index

Strategic maneuvering. *See*
   Linguistic strategies
Street, Brian, 233
Structures
   constraints of, 69, 92–93, 107–
      110, 194
   democracy and. *See* Institutions
   duality of. *See* Duality of
      structures
   hierarchical, 176–177
   institutions and, 142, 243
   opportunities in, 110, 202
   reproduction of, 220–221
   See also Habitus
Stubbs, Michael, 35, 289, 210
Struggles
   ideological, 3, 53, 203
   material, 53, 57, 73
Surveillance, 70–71
Sullivan, Patricia, 21
Systematic oppression. *See*
   Oppression

Talk, see Orality
Taylor, Denny, 98–99
Technology. *See* Computers
Time
   luxury of, 151
   small change over, 96–96, 166–167
Transfer

of language. *See* Linguistic
   transfer
of status. *See* Empowerment
Trotter, Joe, 41–42
Tyler, Stephen, 163

United States, census of
   Department of Labor Bureau of
      Statistics, 41–43
University. *See* Colleges and
   Universities
Urban renewal, 43–45
Utility companies, 110–111, 144

Validity. *See* Methodology
Value systems. *See* Ideology
Villanueva, Victor, 95–96, 123–124
Vernacular theory, 201–202, 245
Violence, 73–74

War on Poverty. *See* Poverty
Warry, Wayne, 28
Weaver, Robert, 43–44
Welfare. *See* Department of Social
   Services
Woman Infants Children (WIC),
   11–12
Work. *See* Employment
Writing. *See* Literacy, types of